Survival in the Corporate Fishbowl

Survival in the Corporate Fishbowl

Making It into Upper and Middle Management

by
John P. Fernandez

Lexington Books

D.C. Heath and Company/Lexington, Massachusetts/Toronto

Library of Congress Cataloging-in-Publication Data

Fernandez, John P., 1941–
Survival in the corporate fishbowl.

Includes index.
1. Industrial sociology—United States.
2. Discrimination in employment—United States.
3. Executives—United States. 4. Office politics—
United States. 5. Quality of work life—United
States. I. Title.
HD6957.U6F47   1987   302.3′5   85-40021
ISBN 0-669-10336-5 (alk. paper)

Published simultaneously in Canada
Printed in the United States of America
International Standard Book Number: 0-669-10336-5
Library of Congress Catalog Card Number: 85-40021

The paper used in this publication meets the minimum requirements of
American National Standard for Information Sciences—Permanence
of Paper for Printed Library Materials, ANSI Z39.48-1984.

ISBN 0-669-10336-5

87 88 89 90   8 7 6 5 4 3 2 1

Contents

Preface and **Acknowledgments**   xi

1. Introduction   1
   The Issues   1
   Purposes of the Book   7
   Overview of Chapters   10

2. The True Character of Bureaucracies and Human Nature   15
   Employees' Perceptions of Corporate Life   15
   The Ideal versus the Real Bureaucracy   18
   Some Basic Concepts about Human Nature   24
   Conclusions   29

3. Career Problems in Corporate America   31
   Motivational Theories   32
   Six Case Studies of Corporate Careers   37
   Specific Career Problems of Study Participants   44
   Perceptions of Being Rewarded and Valued   51
   Conclusions   54

4. The Real Criteria for Advancement   57
   Advancement Theories   57
   Who Gets Ahead and Why   59

Impact of Objective Evaluation Criteria   69

Impact of Race, Gender, and Age   71

Impact of Business Growth and Competition   73

Impact of Bosses, Mentors, and Politics   75

Conclusions   79

5. How to Sort through the Corporate Games and Make Them Work for You   83

   Reviewing the Issues   84

   Understanding People   84

   Dealing with Bosses, Peers, and Subordinates   89

   Knowing Yourself   91

   The Game   95

   Corporate Politics   96

   Manipulation   97

   Power   99

   Loyalty   102

   Honesty   103

   Trust   104

   Building Your Team   105

   Managing with Equity   106

   Your Attitude toward Work   106

   Managing Your Career   108

   Conclusions   113

6. Socialization: Racism and Sexism   115

   Employees' Views of Women and Minorities   115

   Racism and Sexism Defined   120

   History of Racism   121

   History of Sexism   126

   Forms of Racism and Sexism in the 1980s   130

Development of Racist and Sexist Attitudes and Behaviors   131
Impact of Racism and Sexism on Society   137
Racist and Sexist Stereotypes   140
Specific Stereotypes about Women   140
Specific Stereotypes about Minorities   150
Racism and Sexism in Society   161
Conclusions   163

7. Special Career Problems of White Males and Their
   Solutions   167

White Males' Perceptions of Reverse Discrimination   167
A Change in White Males' Advancement Opportunities   169
Reality No. 1: Corporate America Is Unfair to All   173
Reality No. 2: Image Is Vital to Success   174
Reality No. 3: Competition Is Keen   175
Reality No. 4: White Males Are Still Advantaged   175
Reality No. 5: "Reverse Discrimination" Is Based on Lies   177
Reality No. 6: Nothing Excuses Poor Performance   181
Reality No. 7: Adjust for Success   182
Conclusions   183

8. Extraordinary Problems of Women Employees and Their
   Solutions   185

The Situation of Women in Corporations   185
Overview of Gender Discrimination in Corporations   187
A Serious Contradiction Women Face   196
Should Women Conform?   197
Social-Interaction Problems Caused by Sexism   200
Strategies to Deal with Social-Interaction Problems   208
Power and Authority Problems   210
Strategies to Gain Power and Authority   213

Dual Performance Standards   214
Solutions to Dual Performance Standards   217
Impact of Dual Roles on Women's Careers   219
Solutions to Women's Dual-Role Problems   223
Conclusions   224

9. Extraordinary Problems of Minority Employees and Their
   Solutions   227

   Discrimination against Different Minorities   227
   Participants' Perceptions of Racial Discrimination   228
   A Recent History of Race Discrimination in Corporate
   America   234
   Race Discrimination in Corporate America Today   235
   The Problem of Racist Stereotypes   238
   Strategies to Counteract Racist Stereotypes   245
   Dual Performance Standards   247
   Solutions to Dual Performance Standards   251
   Power and Authority Problems   252
   Strategies to Increase Power and Authority   254
   Exclusion from Informal Work Groups   255
   Strategies for Inclusion in Informal Work Groups   256
   Other Survival Tactics for Minorities   259
   Conclusions   263

10. Bringing It All Together   267

    Surviving and Making It   269
    What Corporations Must Do   272
    Equal Opportunity Emphasis   275

Appendix   279

Notes   287

Contents

Bibliography 297
Index 303
Dedication 313
About the Author 315

Preface and Acknowledgments

As I wrote my previous books, *Black Managers in White Corporations* (1975), *Racism and Sexism in Corporate Life* (1981), and *Child Care and Corporate Productivity* (1985), I became acutely aware of the sometimes overt but most times covert dissatisfaction that many employees have with corporate careers and corporate work environments.

I have sensed an increase in employee dissatisfaction and an intensification of career concerns as the United States has begun losing its economic world dominance. Management has responded to economic hardships by terminating many jobs in the United States and moving operations to foreign countries.

I believe that several crucial factors are leading to increased job dissatisfaction and career concerns. One is that the good opportunities existing in corporate America overall have decreased, while the number of people entering the work force has increased. At the same time, those entering the work force are more educated than previous generations. Educated people have higher aspirations and goals; thus, while there has always been an imbalance between employee aspirations and corporate opportunities, this imbalance is greater today than in the past.

Another factor contributing to the overall low morale of corporate employees is the failure of corporate America to equitably introduce women and minorities into areas once perceived as the domains of white males.

The third factor contributing to the overall dissatisfaction of most employees is the inability of corporate leaders to recognize the inherent inequities and shortcomings of bureaucracies. In addition, they have not understood some basic fundamentals about human nature.

I sincerely believe that until corporate leaders and employees deal with the realities of bureaucracies and human nature, corporations will not operate as efficiently as they can, and many employees will be in a constant state of dissatisfaction.

This book gives readers a realistic understanding of bureaucracies and how the human element affects the effective and efficient operations of a bureaucracy. It also documents the continued existence of racism and sexism which, in most companies, does not allow the full use of more than half of the work force. Only through understanding these factors can employees develop realistic strategies to survive and make it into middle and upper management.

I hope that the readers of this book will walk away with some new insights and a confirmation of some old ones, which will allow them to better achieve their career goals. Corporate executives who read this book to run their companies better should be able to come up with more realistic strategies for their future successes.

Acknowledgments

I would like to express my great appreciation to the employees of the thirteen companies whose total cooperation made this book possible. To protect the anonymity of their companies, I cannot name the managers who were my coordinators and advisers. However, I would be remiss if I did not mention that they all went well beyond their normal duties to make my surveys and this book a success.

Peggy Albert, Ann Zinn, Emily Bassman, Wendy Johnson, Mary Ella Brady, Geri Fudge, Jane Balin, Penny Morey, Eileen Hammer, Ann Nelson, Roy Stewart, Miriam Fleming, and Ellen Ball greatly influenced the analyses of all the data and the basic direction of the book, provided very helpful editorial suggestions, and made substantial changes throughout the stages of manuscript preparation. In addition, Eileen and Jane were valued assistants in researching new concepts and ideas.

David Nasatir, Ashima Basu, and Mary Ella Brady assisted me in the use of statistical analyses.

I would also like to thank my students at CIGNA for their help in the editing process: Elizabeth Crosson, Donna Dennis, Catherine D'Imperio, Nanci Goodstein, Christina Grau, Minel Isaminger, Robert Krupak, Carol Kusner, Barbara Niles, Lynn Oliver, Mary-ann Santitoro, and Catherine Whalen.

Pat Buerkle, Lori Green, Maria Hartman, and Joey White took their valued personal time to assist me in the typing and distribution of the manuscript.

Maureen T. McGinley served as a typist, editor, researcher, and proofreader and did many other chores, but most of all, she provided moral support at crucial times.

My daughters, Michele, Eleni, and Sevgi, have decided that their lot in life is to have a father who likes to write. I greatly appreciate them not only for their understanding but for being good human beings.

1
Introduction

The Issues

The comments presented in the following chapters represent responses of more than 12,000 management and nonmanagement employees in thirteen companies.* For this book, since 1984, I have surveyed employees' perceptions of their careers with a particular focus on the social aspects of their work lives: social interaction, cross-cultural/cross-racial experiences, race/gender effects, and pluralism issues. By pluralism I mean the reflection within the corporate hierarchy of the heterogeneous mixture of people that make up U.S. society in the 1980s. These surveys reveal grave concerns that employees have about corporate America: that it is unimaginative and authoritarian, and has untrustworthy leadership, a debilitating environment not conducive to risk taking, a plethora of politicking, insufficient opportunities, lack of proper recognition and reward, and discrimination based on race, gender, and age.

These comments come from both genders and from all races and levels of the corporate hierarchy—a sure sign that something is wrong with corporate America.

The comments were made in response to open-ended statements such as: "Please make any additional comments you wish to make about yourself and your career." In other words, the statements were neutral in tone and unbiased toward eliciting either negative or positive responses.

Throughout this book I discuss three race groups: blacks, other minorities, and whites. Other than blacks, Hispanics were by far the largest minority group in these studies. Since the responses of Hispanics, Asians, and Native Americans were very similar in most cases, I combined all minorities except for blacks under the name of other minorities.

The following responses primarily concern corporate leadership:

> There is very little feedback concerning what is considered when promoting, giving raises or bonuses. Our department head and his high level staff do not fight for the staff, and the staff is aware of this.
>
> —black, male, upper-level manager

> I feel stranded without support, goals, paths or challenges. I feel underemployed as compared to my positions in the past. I want a chance to succeed but cannot find a way. I want to use the knowledge and skills I've obtained.
>
> —white, female, lower-level manager

> As a new employee with a college degree, I feel my contributions will be better recognized in another company where creativity, risk, ambition and marketing are recognized as key components for success.
>
> —black, female, lower-level manager

> I really like the challenge of my job, but things would go much smoother if I had a middle-level manager who appreciated my knowledge and job expertise. Instead, decisions are always second-guessed because he manages by the "shut up and do it because I am the boss" style of management.
>
> —white, male, craftsworker

> Biggest obstacle to my advancement and satisfaction lies in the amount of *exposure* I receive and a lack of commitment on the part of my management (not immediate supervisor) to help me and let me perform functions that I do best.
>
> —white, female, lower-level manager

> I was told that I was "acting" so long (over two years) because I was being punished for referring a job issue to the Equal Employment Opportunity Commission.
>
> —white, female, lower-level manager

> It's pretty difficult when your middle-level supervisor lies to you and afterwards admits that he lied in order to advance his own objectives. It would be a lot less aggravating if he were honest in his approach; after all, he is middle management and has final

word. Being pluralistic, I believe, is necessary in order to compete; however, being honest in one's approach is most important.

—Hispanic, female, craftsworker

We still profess a positive atmosphere of "risk taking," yet the result is squelching creativity through non-acceptance and reprimand.

—white, male, lower-level manager

Lip service and hot air! Are there other jobs out there that could use my talents? If there are, then how do I find them? Managerial job openings are hidden and will never be advertised because our V.P. of Personnel doesn't want managerial job openings advertised. By the time an opening is heard about, the job is filled. Can't even compete! Blah! . . . you have people with tunnel vision running this company . . .

—Hispanic, male, lower-level manager

I have had good, challenging assignments although my abilities and skills have been underutilized. Organizational politics seem dishonest and insincere to me so I have not succeeded well in that arena.

—white, male, upper-level manager

The next series of responses demonstrate the pervasiveness of politics as perceived by employees in the corporate bureaucracy:

Generally, I believe promotions are too often given to those who have "showcased" or otherwise exercised political means to get recognition. Often the results are not evaluated but the window dressing is rewarded. In our efforts to encourage a pluralistic mix, I hope we will not continue this propensity toward promoting the "flashers." Among all groups of employees there are those who deserve promotion and don't necessarily "grab the microphone" at every opportunity.

—white, female, upper-level manager

I truly feel that most women who advanced got there for favors rendered or for knowing the right person. Management is a buddy system that promotes friends and partners. Rarely does someone who really deserves it get promoted to management.

—black, female, craftsworker

We fear internal repercussions from filing an Equal Employment Opportunity complaint. No support from superiors, or their bosses. Internal merit pay raises were outright discrimination—popularity contests, the "good old boy" network at its finest. Utterly discouraging . . .

> —Asian, female, lower-level manager

I wish playing good-old-boy politics were not a prerequisite for any type of promotion—it makes me feel bad.

> —American Indian, female, craftsworker

I feel that the sponsorship program to get into management should be eliminated because the majority of management people are whites. A lot of people of color that are qualified are overlooked because whites sponsor other whites regardless of qualifications. I have facts to back this statement.

> —black, female, lower-level manager

I have found in my 13.5 years with the company that most of the people that get ahead aren't necessarily the best qualified. They were picked a lot by whom they knew and who they are. I don't see that it will ever change—it has gone on too long and it will continue. Prejudices still exist at the company that will never change.

> —Hispanic, female, lower-level manager

Although there is much rhetoric about "excellence," we seem to be managing the same old way. The company still seems to place more weight on political (good old boy/girl) acceptability than on honest, dedicated performance. My last appraisal was based 100 percent on perceptions of personality, not on performance.

> —white, male, lower-level manager

Surrounded by a climate of poor leadership and politics, it is not surprising that employees sense a system that is not organically responsive to them as individuals:

Even though I am an over 40 white male with over 20 years' experience, I feel I still have something to give to this company. If I am told one more time I ought to be glad I still have a job, I'll scream.

> —white, male, middle-level manager

I feel the "surplus" conditions are handled unfairly—those with a few years of service are working twice as hard as those who have 20 years of service and are out the door first, even though the ones who have less seniority may be better qualified for a particular job.

—white, female, craftsworker

I have finally come to grips with what is possible in this company and what isn't—that is, unless you're willing to sell your soul and give up who you are, you won't advance. I now work for quality in my life and what I have control of and I have quit worrying about what I don't.

—white, female, lower-level manager

It used to be fun working for this company; now you don't know whether you have a job or not.

—white, male, craftsworker

Considering the previous comments, it is not surprising that employees doubt that they are valued and rewarded:

I am a hard-working, conscientious, devoted employee. I should be treated as a valued employee who earns his money and then some—instead of the same or not as good as the flunky who doesn't earn his pay and gets promoted.

—Hispanic, male, craftsworker

My experience has been that informal rewards are seldom received. "No news is good news" holds true here. You are told only about the mistakes, and no one says "That was a good job." This is a shame because often a lack of informal rewards leads to frustration.

—white, female, lower-level manager

I feel that many employees with talent and ability are routinely overlooked and unappreciated *regardless* of race, sex, or cultural background. The company does not discriminate against any particular group nearly as much as it discriminates against individuals who show signs of intelligent, independent thought.

—white, female, craftsworker

As employees believe that management has poor leadership

skills and has created an unpleasant work environment engulfed by politics instead of rewarding and valuing people fairly, it is understandable that they perceive a great deal of discrimination based on subjective factors such as race and gender:

> Women are not taken seriously enough. They are bypassed in promotion opportunities, always losing to a man who may not be equally qualified.
>
> —Hispanic, female, lower-level manager

> The only time a minority is hired or promoted in this company (even if he or she is ten times more qualified than a white) is when it's quota time. (Thank God for the Federal Government Civil Rights Commission!) Otherwise, no qualified minorities would get jobs or promotions, especially in this company.
>
> —white, female, craftsworker

> I strongly feel that many minorities have not been given the same opportunities for exposure (or "showcased") as have white males/ females.
>
> —white, female, upper-level manager

> Cultural diversity related to values and aspirations is generally misunderstood and compared against too narrow an ideal. In other words, if you talk like a white, walk like a white and act like a white, then you are ready for advancement.
>
> —Hispanic, male, lower-level manager

> After eight years at lower-level management, when I spent two years developing myself into an excellent supervisor and six years grooming myself for a second level position in my job, I not only didn't advance when the vacancy came, I didn't even get an interview.
>
> —black, female, lower-level manager

What causes these negative perceptions? Are they reality for a few or for many employees? What role does the nature of bureaucracies play? What roles do society's expectations, human nature, and the employees themselves play? What role do all of these factors play in one's survival and ability to move up the corporate ladder?

Purposes of the Book

This book answers the above questions and suggests ways employees can survive and make it in the corporate fishbowl. It also suggests some concrete solutions to employee dissatisfaction that corporations can implement. The book is based on observations accumulated during thirteen years of working in eight corporate departments (human resources, engineering, telecommunications-equipment installation and repair, construction, central office switching, labor relations and—last but not least—personnel). These first-hand observations are buttressed by the consulting work and research I have done over the past sixteen years. My cumulative data are derived from surveys conducted in 1972, 1976–1978, and 1984–1986, among 17,000 employees at twenty-three companies. These are presented in large part, in my first three books: *Black Managers in White Corporations* (1975), *Racism and Sexism in Corporate Life* (1981), and *Child Care and Corporate Productivity* (1985).

I am not another academic who has stood outside the corporate fishbowl and looked in through the glass. I have lived inside it, swimming eventually into upper-middle level management "waters." This book presents no easy, comfortable analyses or solutions, nor does it reiterate what society, schools, and companies themselves insist that corporate America is like. This book sets forth the reality of corporate survival and advancement in straightforward, honest terms. Some readers will be surprised and annoyed by my analyses. Confronting the truth, stripped of our comforting ideologies, can be brutal. But for those who take heed it will be a useful tool.

Employees who recognize the realities of advancement and survival in the corporate fishbowl will find themselves better able to improve their chances for advancement, adapt their career goals, or accept their fate. Corporations can become better able to deal with their employees' competitive desires. The general leadership may be encouraged to be more honest in socializing America's children—the work force of the future.

We must begin by recognizing, despite what we have been taught, that although bureaucracies have brought about some efficiencies in the production of goods and services, they are insensitive structures. Bureaucracies use people in service of their own needs. They are inherently unfair. Despite their claim to equitably reward all of those who are deserving, bureaucracies have too few advancement opportunities and resources to keep this promise to all employees.

Despite the conviction that we are on the whole objective, rational, healthy people, we must acknowledge that we humans as a species are neither objective, rational, nor wholly healthy. On the contrary, the operative question is not *whether* we are mentally healthy, but the degree to which, as individuals and groups, we are unhealthy. Contrary to the myth of mental health, people who recognize their neuroses and work with them are healthier than the vast majority who have never taken a hard look at themselves. In short, corporate America is in large part an inherently unfair organization made up of many unhealthy people.

Despite these facts, we teach our children that if they work hard, get an education, and don't rock the boat, the world will be their oyster. This is the myth that our so-called meritocracy feeds us from our first breaths. The reality is that even if bureaucracies were fair and just organizations and even if we were a totally healthy species, bureaucracies are hierarchical by nature and structure. At each successive step up the corporate ladder, increasing numbers of people slip into failure.

Tied into these facts are important demographic issues. The post-World-War-II "baby boomers" are now seeking middle and upper management positions—at the very time when opportunities are shrinking. The educational level of the work force is rising and, with it, aspirations to move up the corporate ladder are increasing. More women and minorities are completing college and entering the work force on a permanent, full-time basis, creating a much larger pool of talent seeking fewer positions. As corporate America tries to adjust to world competition through reorganizing, selling off or closing unprofitable operations, and generally cutting its work force, the level of frustration among American workers is ever increasing.

In sum, growing numbers of educated people are competing for fewer and fewer managerial jobs, especially at the middle and upper levels of management. Most of these employees, taught to believe in the "meritocracy" of American society, are shocked when their careers seem to end prematurely. The problem of who advances has become more complex because many of these educated employees are first-generation corporate managers who come from race and/ or gender backgrounds different from those of the people who have traditionally run corporate America. This creates a problem for the new entrants and a serious threat to the opportunities of white males, who represent only one-third of the population, yet control virtually all top-level corporate positions.

In *Racism and Sexism in Corporate Life: Changing Values in American Business*, I wrote:

> Not only has the clashing of different backgrounds created tensions but also the new competition from women and minorities. In the past, white men dominated 95 percent of the corporate-management ranks, while representing only 33 percent of the population. Now, they must compete with 67 percent of the population with whom they have never had to compete. Thus, many of these white males now believe that they are treated unfairly and that reverse discrimination is a common occurrence. However, large numbers of minorities and women believe that even after 16 years of equal-employment-opportunity progress, white men are still the preferred race/gender group by far. This phenomenon of perception can be attributed largely to the differences between the people who have been accustomed to having almost all of the power in the corporate hierarchy and the people who have had almost none. Any loss from exclusivity is viewed as great, while small gains from exclusion are not viewed as being important.[1]

The inherent nature of bureaucracies with limited resources, compounded by the neurotic nature of humans who have been brought up in a society professing but not having unlimited opportunities, has led to many of the problems and conflicts detailed by the 12,000 people who participated in my 1984–1986 surveys.

Social scientist Kathryn Welds wisely cites the ultimately destructive effects we can expect if such conflict is not dealt with honestly and effectively. She notes that overt displacements are only part of the story when conflict is ignored. Besides decreased organizational effectiveness, subtle, self-destructive issues are often masked by absenteeism, high turnover, and decreased levels of productivity. Serious stress-related symptoms such as headaches, asthma, uncontrolled use of drugs, and depression stem from unresolved conflicts in the workplace. They all contribute to occupational burnout.[2]

The question is no longer one of the moral responsibility to use and develop employees in the most fair and equitable fashion possible. Facing problems such as those articulated by the employees in our sampling is, purely and simply, a matter of corporate survival. To be competitive in the new world economy corporations must begin to use and develop *fully* all of their human resources, particularly in light of the fact that personnel costs are the largest expense item in most corporate budgets, often amounting to as much as 42 percent. Corporate leaders and employees must arrive at a clear understanding of the limitations of bureaucracies and of human nature. Corporations must present a more realistic view of corporate opportunities to present and future employees.

Overview of Chapters

The nine chapters in this book expand upon these ideas and present recommendations for change. Chapter 2 critically assesses Max Weber's concept of bureaucracy, pointing out, as have many sociologists after Weber, that many of the characteristics of bureaucracies that are supposed to lead toward efficiency create inefficiencies when implemented by most people. The natural structure of bureaucratic organization condemns it to be unfair and inequitable. The chapter also briefly discusses human psychological limitations. Because of our early socialization, family structure, and societal values, Americans have a certain degree of neurosis which, unless we understand it, affects our ability to advance, survive, and make realistic life decisions. I review a number of Machiavelli's enlightening concepts about human nature as they relate to behavior in the corporate world.

Chapter 3 reviews career problems identified by some of the 12,000 employees surveyed—problems that for the most part are common to all employees regardless of race and/or gender. This chapter clearly shows that a great deal of dissatisfaction exists in corporate America about career opportunities, work atmosphere, and fair, equitable treatment. Extreme contradictions exist between the way employees believe people *should* interact and their perceptions of how people actually *do* interact in corporate America. As a white, female, craftsworker wrote: "In too many instances, I've seen both management and non-management profess to believe in one thing but do another."

Chapter 4 discusses theories of advancement and examines data on employees' beliefs about advancement opportunities. It reveals that the vast majority of the employees surveyed do not believe that corporate America is a meritocracy with unlimited opportunities. However, many of their comments about the "old days when people got promoted on ability," as well as their complaints that "qualifications should be the only factor for promotions," suggest that the societal concept of a meritocracy with unlimited resources still lives within their hearts.

Chapter 5 offers realistic, concrete advice and strategies for how employees can make the best of their current situations and also advance within bureaucracies. Some of the advice may be unsettling to some employees because it deals with the corporate American reality and not with "the American dream." It explicates the true nature of people and of bureaucracies. This chapter does *not* focus on the tactics and advice given in other books on management. Rather, it emphasizes the realities of the corporate "game," how to be aware of it, and how to play to win. Being *aware* and not denying reality is the crucial element in surviving in the corporate fishbowl and making it into middle and upper management.

Chapter 6 uncovers issues of racism and sexism, two of the most important factors hampering corporate efficiency and productivity. This chapter takes a fresh look at these concepts and discusses how socialization processes negatively affect *everyone* in society. Current, stubborn, sexist and racist stereotypes about women and minorities are also exposed and explored.

Chapter 7 focuses on the concerns of white males. It drives home the implications of the fact that white males no longer have exclusive opportunities for middle and upper management positions, because they must now compete with a much larger group of talented people, as certain doors open to minorities and women. It also points out that according to social theory and statistics white males remain the advantaged group. Suggestions to help white males advance their careers focus on correcting some distorted impressions and developing strategies to enhance their *individual* opportunities.

Chapters 8 and 9 analyze additional problems facing women and minorities in their careers. These two chapters rely a great deal on the statistical and anecdotal data I have collected in the past three years from the thirteen companies and 12,000 employees I surveyed. Specific solutions are presented to help women and minorities engage in more successful and rewarding careers. The main purpose is to encourage them as individuals to understand the corporate "games," by quantitative and qualitative measures. The rules are significantly different for women and minorities. I argue that only *collectively* can these employees develop a reasonable chance to overcome corporate racism and sexism. Specific strategies for doing this are presented.

The concluding chapter recapitulates the overall thrust of the book and makes concrete recommendations to corporations for better using and developing their work forces in order to compete more effectively in the worldwide market.

One set of problems that employers face is a function of the bureaucratic social structures. A second set is a function of the human neurosis. A third set is related to our American value system as imparted through our socialization processes. A fourth set stems directly from differences in race and gender. Recognition of the problems inherent in bureaucracies, human nature, and our value system will help companies to relieve some of the conflict and stress by implementing more objective, systematic employment policies and practices in place of current policies that are idiosyncratic, subjective, and nonsystematic, policies that were developed for a mythical rational meritocracy with unlimited opportunities. Current policies allow employers to blame their employment-related problems on others and on race and gender differences rather than on their own shortcomings, the deficiencies of bureaucratic organizations, and economic and psychological realities.

By writing a book that deals with what is rather than what should be, I seek to assist individual employees and corporations to compete effectively in the new world economy. Competitive corporations depend on a well-balanced, diverse work force whose members are realistic about bureaucracies and human nature and who believe that generally they are being treated equitably and fairly. That corporations should try to make the odds equal for all to advance may be an ideal that will never be reached, but it is certainly worth striving for.

In the words of Francis Bacon:

> We must be grateful to Machiavelli and to authors like him, who write about what men do and not about what they should do. It is not possible to join the wisdom of the serpent to the innocence of the dove, if we do not know all the characteristics of the serpent—his meanness, his dragging belly, his slipperiness, his inconstancy, his malice, his poison: and all the rest—that is, all the forms and aspects of evil. Because without this knowledge, virtue is vulnerable and defenseless. On the contrary, honest people could not even redeem evil ones without the help of the knowledge of evil. Men of corrupt minds believe that honesty is characteristic of a simple soul.[3]

2
The True Character of
Bureaucracies and
Human Nature

This chapter details the problems that the study participants see in the bureaucratic structure of their corporations, in the context of Max Weber's theory of bureaucracies and some important concepts about human psychology. A mistake most sociologists make is separating discussions of personality from discussions of social structure. In fact, the two are inseparable. To survive in the corporate fishbowl, the reader must have a clear, unclouded view of the true climate of bureaucracies and an accurate understanding of personality.

Employees' Perceptions of Corporate Life

The employees in our surveys see a host of problems in their corporations. Many express concern about the highly political, militaristic, intimidating, and less-than-open atmosphere within their corporations.

> I have often thought about quitting because of a certain person I work with who knows it all (so she thinks) and is very intimidating.
>
> —black, female, craftsworker

This company established a committee to look at the future of management in the '80s. It identified middle level as the largest barrier to upward and downward communications in the company. . . . I also find it extremely significant that within the past few years the middle level position has begun to use some of the restrictions to communications first used by upper levels.

—white, female, lower-level manager

The company is very militarily regimented and politically oriented in its working system on most levels. Since this is the way it works, there's no sense in changing it on any level to be pluralistic, even if it does help the company function better.

—black, male, craftsworker

We do not reward or accept creativity, non-conformism, or excellence in performance. Anyone who excels is a target and bosses are intimidated. Only WASPs need to apply—preferably male WASPs.

—white, female, lower-level manager

Other employees in our survey refer to the unfair and insensitive treatment they experience at their companies:

I feel the management personnel, due to restructure, is really uptight. They don't treat people like people and are more concerned about keeping their jobs. This makes our jobs more stressful, unbearable.

—Hispanic, female, craftsworker

As a term employee, I am bound by all rules and regulations of craft and I do the same job, but I'm treated as an expendable commodity. I work hard for this company and I want some recognition for the job I've done.

—white, female, craftsworker

Our leadership is totally insensitive to what they are doing to their employees. Just cut, cut, cut.

—black, male, middle-level manager

The atmosphere is awful—nothing but backbiting, immature, bitchy women and ineffective supervisors. If I had any other viable option, I'd quit in a second. We are generally treated like cattle or machines, with no consideration for our needs or feelings.

—white, female, craftsworker

This company and its managers and the employees act as if we are all in grade school! They need to allow more growth for the growth-oriented person.

—black, female, craftsworker

Everyone has opinions on what is right and wrong—how can you expect them to make impartial decisions when most decisions are based on personal knowledge and opinions?

—white, female, craftsworker

Finally, many of our survey employees mention poor supervision and lack of cooperation as major problems within their corporations:

I believe that efforts by upper level management are being sabotaged by middle and upper level managers who have the most power on promotions to those levels.

—white, female, lower-level manager

Managers are closed, uptight, scared and turf builders.

—white, male, craftsworker

Something drastic needs to be done in this workforce. The attitudes are terrible. There is no trust of management and total dissatisfaction.

—white, female, craftsworker

Too much emphasis on turf issues and office politics; supervisors fail to recognize talents and allow projects and duties to develop me towards career advancements.

—white, male, craftsworker

The comments of the study participants reflect some of the tension and problems that exist in the corporation, the most efficient bureaucracy in America. If Max Weber, one of the founders of sociology, read or heard the comments of modern-day employees and saw the failure of many major corporate entities, would he question some of his theories on bureaucracies?

The Ideal versus the Real Bureaucracy

Weber believed that bureaucracies, primarily because of their technical efficiency, are indispensable in meeting the production needs of modern society. According to Weber, bureaucracies ideally are first and foremost rationally organized structures bound by specific rules. They are characterized by a hierarchical division of labor among bureaucratic members, each with sufficient competency and authority to carry out designated tasks. The authority is inherent in the office and not in the person. Individual officials should be appointed on the basis of technical qualifications, rather than chosen by an electorate, because only knowledge gives power and control. The bureaucratic structure as Weber envisioned it pays a fixed salary according to level and/or responsibilities. Promotions follow from achievement and/or seniority, based on the superior's judgment, which is, of course, objective. In addition, Weber described bureaucracies as ensuring the right to employment security. Only under certain (fair) circumstances should employment be terminated. On a personal level, individuals are free to be and to act. On an organizational level, they are under the authority of the bureaucracy only with respect "to the impersonal official obligations." Despite the formal hierarchical nature of bureaucracies, Weber felt that employees should have the right to appeal decisions and enter grievances from lower to higher levels. In addition, relationships, according to Weber, are clearly defined and formal, based on social rituals reserved for various office levels.

Weber wrote that bureaucracies tend to "level" interest, to develop a rational, unemotional, unfeeling set of interactions. In his own words:

> The following are the principal more general social consequences of bureaucratic control:
>
> 1. The tendency to "levelling" in the interest of the broadest possible basis of recruitment in terms of technical competence . . .
> 2. The dominance of a spirit of formalistic impersonality . . . without hatred or passion, and hence without affection or enthusiasm.

3. The dominant norms are concepts of straightforward duty
without regard to personal considerations. Everyone is subject
to formal equality of treatment. . . . This is the spirit in which
the ideal official conducts his office.[1]

Many of Weber's views as put forth in the previous paragraphs
are still held on a "gut" or intellectual level by many corporate executives, professors, consultants, and parents, who maintain that
the corporate world is basically an objective, rational, efficient, and
fair meritocracy. Others, however, have taken Weber's observations
to task. It is obvious from some of their comments that our study
participants do not perceive bureaucracies as operating as efficiently, harmoniously, and fairly as Weber described. Let's look at
some of Weber's major points and analyze them within the context
of what really happens in bureaucracies rather than what, on an
ideal level, should happen.

Weber's glaring flaw in describing bureaucracies is his omission
of the human element. It seems that Weber attempts to separate the
human being from the social process. If organizations are made up
of individuals, can bureaucracy function separately from the human
mind, nature, and neurosis? Bureaucracies as they are perceived by
my survey sample do *not* operate rationally, smoothly, or according
to logical rules. I agree with Karl Mannheim and others who have
recognized that bureaucracies are arenas in which individuals compete and struggle for limited commodities such as authority, power,
status, money, promotion, and recognition. K. Mannheim wrote
that a fundamental characteristic of bureaucratic thought is that it
treats problems as administrative rather than as political. He argued, however, that behind all the rational "laws and rules" of bureaucracies are "socially fashioned" interests of specific social
groups. Order, therefore, is based not on reason but on socially conflicting, irrational forces that become reconciled in the "rational"
order—in short, a very political process.[2]

Ferguson supports Mannheim's views of the true political nature of bureaucracies. "A bureaucracy," she writes, "is not just a
structure but also a *process* that orders human interactions. In order
to remain viable, the bureaucracy has developed an on-going process of domination that constantly searches for and suppresses op-

position. Because it is both structure and process, a bureaucracy can be understood only in its social context . . . a context in which social relations between classes, races, and sexes are fundamentally unequal." Bureaucracies as rational, scientific, efficient, fair organizations are used as a filter for control, suppression, and domination in "an institutional arena that both rationalizes and maintains them."[3]

As noted earlier, Weber believed that formal sets of rules help bureaucracies secure specific behaviors and performances and eliminate "friction," thus increasing efficiencies. R. Kanter echoed Weber in stressing the importance of corporations establishing immediately for people "the ground rules and boundary conditions under which they are working, the issues, and the extent to which they can decide issues." She argued that the time spent by employees on unproductive matters increased as constraints upon their freedom decreased.[4]

Notwithstanding the assumptions of Weber, Kanter, and the modern corporation that rules are necessary to ensure the predictable, rational, efficient functioning of bureaucracies, such rules—as R. Merton warned—do not always prevail. Rules and regulations can be transformed "into absolutes" and become ends in themselves. When this occurs, bureaucracies have great difficulty in adapting to special conditions and new situations not envisaged by the rule makers. Merton thus concluded that "the very elements that are supposed to produce efficiency, instead 'produce inefficiency in specific instances.'" Moreover, it is difficult for many of the initial rule makers to divorce themselves from the symbolic "meanings" that the rules have for them.[5]

In support of Merton, M. H. McCormack wrote in *What They Don't Teach You at Harvard Business School:*

> If structures create a drag on business momentum, then outdated, outmoded policies create a drag on the business itself. . . . Yet on countless occasions I have run into corporations in which some ridiculously restrictive policy prevented them from doing something they actually wanted to do. I have seen chairmen of boards, when pressed for the reasons behind some of these policies, shrug their shoulders and confess they didn't remember, or wonder out loud why such a policy ever existed in the first place.[6]

Because of their bureaucratic structures and rules, the steel industry, the auto industry, and the heavy manufacturing industry
have failed, and others have almost lost their organizations to bank-
ruptcy. To be effective in this new, competitively changing production environment, corporations need flexibility, *not* rigidity. They
must understand that there are not sufficient rules and regulations
to cover all possible contingencies. This is especially true in indus-
tries where high levels of skill adaptability are necessary and technology is changing so rapidly that product life cycles are no longer
five years but six months.

Another widely accepted Weberian notion, used as a double-
edged sword in today's business world, is that of technical competence. No one can argue that technical skills aren't necessary. However, as Merton warns, too-specific training can precipitate a failure
to recognize new and different conditions that will require new procedures and strategies. In other words, overtraining and exagger-
ated experience in an area could become incapacitating.[7] A white,
male craftsworker put it this way:

> . . . but why not get to what the real problem is! Old management
> people, namely middle and upper levels, who should retire but
> won't because they don't think this company can run without
> them. They won't let the people with ideas come in and try some-
> thing new because all they know is how it used to be and can't get
> used to the way it is now; they are unable to change and this
> creates friction between all departments. They fight with each
> other and it is passed down through the ranks. This is where most
> of the attitude problems are coming from.

A very good example of a company struggling to break its "past
training" in order to be more efficient and competitive in a new
environment is AT&T. The fact that the unregulated, competitive
side of the business has been losing more than a billion dollars a
year suggests a serious problem of adaptation to new conditions, a
problem exacerbated by past training and experience. Many managers of all ages and at all levels still have operating styles and logic
that are suitable only in a regulated, monopolized environment.
AT&T (like other conservative companies) has followed to its own

detriment Weber's concept of formal, impersonal relationships. A rigid perception of what relationships *should* be makes it more difficult for bureaucracies to recognize the need to deal with external clients in a personal and informal manner. In this highly competitive environment, informal, personal relationships give companies the edge in helping clients differentiate products and services that are quite similar.

Additional problems are created in bureaucracies by their hierarchical nature, which dictates that few people reach the top, while most believe that they *should* reach the top. This phenomenon, together with the fact that the higher one goes in the corporation the more likely he or she is to be "elected" rather than "selected," creates a stressful, hostile, uncooperative, competitive environment (more about this in chapter 4). Furthermore, this hierarchical structure emphasizes differences, such as special privileges for higher-level managers relative to lower-level managers and craftsworkers. Such differences and special privileges do not encourage cooperation, teamwork, and open communications; they foster divisiveness, selfishness, and poor communications.

The division of labor, which is supposed to enhance efficiency, also leads to inefficiencies. The hierarchical nature of bureaucracies, coupled with individual competitiveness, creates divisiveness and in some cases alienation among people in various functions and departments as they compete for scarce resources.

One of the most critical statements about bureaucracies is put forth by Ferguson. She argues that the main purpose of the rules, regulations, and cultural values of bureaucracies is to eliminate uncertainty and to assure control. She believes that political situations depersonalize social relationships, mystify communications, and disguise dominance, and that the claims of efficiency and effectiveness are secondary and frequently irrelevant. In her words, "They are justifications, rather than explanations, of bureaucracy." She believes that fragmented work; worker isolation; strict adherence to rules, regulations, and procedures; formal relationships; and the "illusion of upward mobility" that promises opportunities for the masses of employees are all strategies to control employees and make them dependent on the higher levels of management. All of these factors create anger, frustration, alienation, and cause physical and emotional problems, which ultimately result in lower productivity. These, in turn, affect the economic health of the corporation.[8]

Considering the nature of the bureaucracy, it is not surprising that an unpublished survey of over 10,000 employees in several high tech firms found that only a small percentage of the employees believed that their company was not too bureaucratic. Many of the employees, especially managers (64 percent), and to a lesser extent craft (47 percent), rated their companies as *poor* or *very poor* on having successfully minimized bureaucracy. Less than 18 percent, regardless of occupational levels, rated their organization *good* or *very good*.

The same study revealed that few employees believed that their corporation permitted employees to participate in the decision-making process. Few believed that they had good teamwork, although very high percentages of these employees believed these issues to be important. Let's look at some of the figures.

Ninety percent of the employees in this survey said teamwork was "important" or "very important," and 68 percent of the managers and 85 percent of the craftsworkers rated participation in decision making similarly. Most of the employees at all levels, however, found their companies lacking in both respects. Only 14 percent of the managers and 20 percent of the craftsworkers said the opportunities for participating in decision making were "good" or "very good." On teamwork, 18 percent of managers and 30 percent of craftsworkers rated their companies "good" or "very good."

The end goal of bureaucracies, according to Weber, is to attain excellence. More than 80 percent of the surveyed employees of high tech firms, regardless of level, agreed that excellence is "very important." However, less than half said their companies were doing a "very good" or "good" job of attaining excellence.

One should not rush to assume that Weber's conceptualizations of bureaucracies are totally invalid; many still hold. The problem is that Weber perceived and described an "ideal" bureaucracy. As we see in the next section, Weber's inaccuracies are in many respects the result of his failure to take into consideration the impact of human nature on bureaucracies. The vagaries of human psychology play a crucial role in determining the bureaucratic process.

Some Basic Concepts about Human Nature

Most corporate executives and consultants argue that a manager cannot be a psychologist. Nonetheless, to survive, a manager must understand some basic concepts about human nature and how people interact in bureaucratic social systems. Harry Levinson writes:

> Managers must know and understand ... psychology [and] ... motivation with the same degree of proficiency as ... marketing, manufacturing, economics, sales, engineering, and so on. Not every manager must be a master of all of these, but each must have a basic knowledge and understanding of people or he will be unable to meet the demands inside and outside of the organization that are inevitably to come.[9]

There will always be conflict between an organization's goals, regardless of structural definition, and the employees' aspirations, needs, and wants. P. Selznick accurately notes that although bureaucracies attempt to mobilize human and technical resources as means of producing goods and/or services,

> the individuals within the system tend to resist being treated as means. They interact as wholes, bring to bear their own special problems and purposes; moreover, the organization is imbedded in an institutional matrix and is, therefore, subject to pressures upon it from its environment, to which some general adjustment must be made. As a result, the organization may be significantly viewed as an adaptive social structure, facing problems that arise simply because it exists.[10]

Levinson expands on Selznick's concepts by stating that bureaucracies are social instruments that people use to meet their own basic needs. Because people influence bureaucracies and vice versa, it is of crucial importance to understand both.[11]

The basic observations about people introduced here will be expanded and reiterated throughout this book. The concepts about individual subjectivity and neurosis may be unpopular; however, survival in the corporate world requires understanding and acknowledgment of these points.

G. Prezzolini makes some astute observations about human nature:

> People seldom believe what seems reasonable, nor do they always willingly accept what is expressed clearly, because logic and clarity have a weaker hold than imagination and mystery. Propositions that run counter to common morality do not create a desire for discussion or even contradiction but rather an urge to sidestep, ignore, or misinterpret. Life, which is full of such blindness to the most clearly expressed ideas, is ruled not by intellect but by desire and pride. Men want to live, not to understand; and they want to live in their own way. If an idea seems to contradict what they want to believe, they refuse to accept it. If they really understand it, they either suppress it or avert their gaze in order not to see it.[12]

R. W. White in describing the value of psychoanalytic theory supports Prezzolini. White notes that "the constant play of impulse beneath and through the rational, conscious, goal-directed activities of everyday life" discussed by Freud shows that "beneath the surface of awareness lies a zone of teeming emotion, urge, fantasy, from which spring the effective driving forces, as well as various disrupting agents in our behaviors."[13]

Let's review some of the comments by our study participants that support Prezzolini's and White's comments. Overall, employees describe a work environment that includes a great deal of politics, unfair treatment, and rigidity—quite the opposite of the ideal of a cooperative, efficient environment:

> I enjoy the work very much, but there are too many petty turf issues within the company. People have an antiquated tendency to build their own kingdoms and not work as a *"company."*
>
> —white, female, lower-level manager

> I find that, no matter how hard you work, the company expects more and when you reach your potential or limit, the company chastises you for not being able to give more.
>
> —white, male, lower-level manager

> I feel a sense of dedication to the company; however, I feel that

we have too many old-age thinkers/traditionalists at the top that are too concerned about their own empire and turf. I would like to contribute more.

—Hispanic, male, lower-level manager

The company wants paper pushers and smiling people who always agree with their bosses, and who can stab their co-workers in the back without blinking an eye.

—Hispanic, male, lower-level manager

Management is paranoid. Innovation and entrepreneurism are scary and dangerous as they could result in the loss of the manager's "empire" if successful. "Technology" is going to replace me before I retire if I don't drag my feet to slow it down.

—white, male, craftsworker

To what extent do these responses reflect reality and to what extent do they reflect the neurotic views of these employees? In Prezzolini's terms, to what extent are these employees sidestepping, ignoring, or misinterpreting their situation?

As I noted earlier, the question is not whether we are mentally healthy but the extent to which we are unhealthy. Levinson, who has written numerous books on managerial psychology, would agree, but his definition of mental illness allows for ups and downs in human nature. All of us, for example, have days when we are on an even keel and other days when we are not. When we are in emotional distress, we can be considered to be temporarily mentally ill. Given the inherent inequality, stress, conflicts, and contradiction of bureaucracies, it is clear that some employees in corporate America are in a constant state of stress and are therefore mentally ill.

T. Pettigrew, in attempting to describe "positive mental health," came up with a definition that could exclude most of the human race:

Six categories of human functioning have been suggested to define the concept of a positive mental health: (1) the mentally healthy individual is self-aware, self-accepting, and enjoys a stable identity; (2) an individual's degree of development and actualization of his or her potential is also indicative of positive mental health;

(3) so, too, is an individual's integration of the many *psychic functions*; (4) an individual's autonomy, relative independence from social pressures, and ability to act independently under internal controls are also important indicators; (5) the adequacy of an individual's perception of reality has also been advanced as a criterion by a number of writers; and, finally, (6) positive mental health requires the ability to master one's environment at a reasonable level of competency.[14]

The degree of mental illness or mental healthiness we experience has a great deal to do with our natural temperament. One can look at children at birth and recognize that some are quiet and some are not, that some are easygoing and others are not. "Each person from birth differs both in his particular combination of natural endowments and in the degree to which these permit him to contend with various aspects of life."[15] However, these tendencies are either encouraged or discouraged by cultural conditioning, by the parents, teachers, and other agents of socialization.

Far more critical for the understanding of personality are those aspects of mental health that have to do with socialization. As Ruth Benedict, Margaret Mead, and others have shown, some societies instruct children, both explicitly and implicitly, to forsake individual success and prominence in favor of pleasant group interaction. Cooperation, generosity, and avoidance of greed or selfishness are emphasized. As adults, children trained in these traditions avoid public distinction. In contrast, we "train [our] children instead to climb to the top" through what Mead's and Benedict's informants might consider "sharp practice, theft and the use of magic."[16]

Kenneth Keniston notes that as adults we lose touch with our spontaneity; growing up means leaving "a world of directness, immediacy, diversity, wholeness, integral fantasy," in favor of "abstractions, distance, specialization, dissociated fantasy and conformity."[17]

White maintains that studies of culture and psychoanalysis have a great deal in common; namely, the belief that personality is more than the sum total of conscious, rational self-direction and also includes irrational urges, anxieties, and overworked protective devices. Similarly, our customs, beliefs, and cultures exercise a tyranny of unconsciousness through socialization.[18]

I contend that our psychological problems are compounded because these socialization processes do not always send either clear or objectively healthy signals about our worth, who we are, and what we are. Many of us have not taken the time to understand ourselves, and so share no real understanding of our own neuroses. Rather, we employ a repertoire of defense mechanisms that allows us to survive but not flourish in a neurotic world, in an environment of conflicting signals and cross-purposes.

We use such coping strategies as sublimation, repression, rationalization, projection, displacement, substitution, and denial. Levinson delineates four basic ways that people cope: (1) channeling their energies into problem-solving or environment-mastering activity; (2) displacing energies onto substitute targets; (3) containing or holding on to energies by repression; and (4) turning energies against themselves, which leads to self-defeating behavior and accidents. We all use all of these modes to varying degrees much of the time.[19]

Corporate America, because of its "objective rational" purpose of providing goods and services in a capitalistic, market-driven economy, has, I believe, attracted a certain personality type. A disproportionate number of people who use the last three methods described above more frequently than the first one have found their way into corporations, and the bureaucracy acts as a convenient shield. Behind its hierarchy, its rules, regulations, and procedures, its division of labor, and its concept of an "objective rational" purpose, such people are free to act out their neuroses. Moreover, the corporate hierarchy and bureaucracy has rewarded the last three methods more often than the first one, thereby increasing the frequency of these behaviors among employees. In other words, even those people who would ordinarily choose the first method of coping will not find themselves rewarded for it in an American corporation. Since people tend to adopt those behaviors for which they are rewarded, even those who know how to cope in a healthy way and actually prefer to do so will begin to stop using those methods that aren't rewarded and adopt the unhealthy ones that are.

Conclusions

Weber described bureaucracies as efficient, effective, fair, and equitable organizations. He elaborated:

> Bureaucratization offers above all the optimum possibility for carrying through the principle of specializing administrative functions according to purely objective considerations. Individual performances are allocated to functionaries who have specialized training and who by constant practice learn more and more. The "objective" discharge of business primarily means a discharge of business according to calculable rules and "without regard for persons."

> "Without regard for persons" is also the watchword of the "market" and, in general, of all pursuits of naked economic interests. A consistent execution of bureaucratic domination means the leveling of status "honor."[20]

As the comments of many of our study participants indicate, however, their corporate bureaucracies are inflexible, ineffective, unfair, inequitable, and officious. Since the species of mentally healthy human beings is extinct if not mythical, corporate bureaucracies are able to attract a good share of neurotic people. This perpetuates the bureaucratic structure, whose "rational mission" allows the ill to believe that they are "rational" healthy human beings.

I propose that the popular misconceptions of the true natures of bureaucracies and humans create the constant conflicts to which corporate employees have alluded. The denial of these problems creates an atmosphere that has led to the underuse and underdevelopment of large numbers of employees and therefore to the inefficient functioning of the corporation, with a resulting negative impact on the corporate bottom line. John DeLorean made some comments that serve as a fitting conclusion for this chapter. He described GM's infamous fourteenth floor as abounding in "rumors, gossip, pettiness and role playing despite the aura and mystique of precise and calculated management." GM, to DeLorean, was *not* a "grand coordinated machine." He concluded that the pattern of

American business "often produces wrong, immoral and irresponsible business decisions." He distinguished group morality from individual ethics, arguing that the corporation's group identity insulates it from individual moral critique, allowing it to "produce ineffective or dangerous products, deal dictatorially and often unfairly with suppliers, pay bribes for business, abrogate the rights of employees by demanding blind loyalty to management or tamper with the democratic process of government through illegal political contributions." These devious "deviations" have become normal because business is impersonal, especially when conducted by large, multinational corporations. These are faceless entities, without individual personality or accountability. Their ultimate measure of success is derived from their earnings per share of stock.[21] A white, female, lower-level manager put it this way:

> It's a farce, like most big projects this company begins. Admit it! Big business is in business of making $$ and it cares about its employees only to the extent that they can make more $$$. That's *all*.

3
Career Problems in Corporate America

Obviously, bureaucracy in the modern American corporation falls far short of the ideal envisioned by some social theorists. The observations from 12,000 corporate employees at all levels reflect a high degree of stress, conflict, disappointment, discouragement, and hostility. These employees find their companies' operations inefficient, wasteful, and unfair. From their comments emerges a theme of disillusionment—and justifiably so, given how most of us are brought up.

At birth we inherit the myth that America is the land of opportunity, and that success will be ours if we really want it, if we work hard, and if we stay out of trouble. In fact, opportunities in corporate America are severely limited and shrinking. The factors that determine success are far more complex and subjective than sheer determination and hard work. But because, as Machiavelli tells us, human beings always want more than we can get and think we deserve it, we are lured by the myth of infinite opportunity—much as gamblers are lured by the jackpot or the million-dollar sweepstakes. We ignore the odds, pin our hopes on winning, and walk away in anger and resentment when we lose. Machiavelli put it this way:

> And certainly anybody wise enough to understand the times and the types of affairs and adapt himself to them would always have good fortune, or he would protect himself always from bad, and it would come to be true that the wise man would rule the stars

and the Fates. But because there never are such wise men, since men in the first place are short-sighted, and in the second cannot command their natures, it follows that Fortune varies and commands men, and holds them under her yoke.[1]

This chapter focuses on problems that are in a sense generic—problems that cross over race and gender lines. In all likelihood you will be confronted with some if not many of these problems in your corporate lives. We begin by reviewing several basic motivational and managerial theories put forth over the past twenty-five years to deal with employees' attitudes, desires, and motivations.

Motivational Theories

Over the past quarter of a century social scientists have come up with motivational theories to spur people on to more productive and satisfying jobs. Our data suggest that either the particular corporations where our survey participants work are not using these theories, or the theories themselves are less than valid. My contention is the latter. Most of these theories ignore the realities of bureaucracies and the mental unhealthiness of the people who make them up. The fact is that corporations cannot hope to eliminate totally conflicts and employee problems, but they can certainly improve their treatment of people by dealing with reality rather than with a vision of an ideal world. Employees, for their part, must recognize that even in a perfect bureaucracy, their own imperfections and neuroses would cause some dissatisfaction. They must learn to sort out the reality from the neurosis. Let's look now at some of the prominent motivational theories.

A. H. Maslow has suggested that human beings continuously experience complex fluctuations of motivation. Only for short periods are we able to satisfy all of our needs. From this concept Maslow developed his theory of a hierarchy of needs. According to this hierarchy, our basic needs are physiological (for water and food). Once these are satisfied, we seek to satisfy "safety" needs (for protection from danger, threat, and deprivation). Next come the social needs of belongingness, love, acceptance and friendship. After social needs come the ego needs, which are seldom fully satisfied, such as self-esteem, achievement, competence, knowledge, status, recognition, appreciation, and respect. At the top of the pyramid is the need for self-fulfillment, for realization of our own potential.[2]

M. Maccoby has taken issue with Maslow's theory. He argues that there is no evidence to support the concept of a need hierarchy in which satisfaction of lower needs triggers drives toward the satisfaction of higher needs. Maccoby maintains that no one fully satisfies any of these needs once and for all. He adds the astute observation that needs can vary across races, genders, cultures, and societies.[3]

M. Fair has reported that women are much more likely than men to seek out and maintain "intimate, confiding relationships." She noted that women are more likely to seek out relationships that provide emotional support, guidance, and advice.[4] Thus one might say that women are more likely than men to place social needs above ego needs.

With respect to differentials among races, it stands to reason given American social, economic, political, and demographic realities that many blacks and Hispanics are stuck at the ego-needs stage, where they are constantly striving for respect and status in a racist society. Since racism in many subtle forms blocks them from satisfying their ego needs, many never move on to the self-fulfillment stage.

Furthermore, as Maccoby has demonstrated, need satisfaction does not necessarily provide motivation to work in a positive manner. He cites the example of the "power-grabbing jungle fighter" who will never be satisfied by success because each success whets the appetite for still more.[5] I would add the example of employees who want more freedom to "manage" their jobs, only to complain, when given that opportunity, that they are not given enough direction from management. Rather than moving on to the higher level of self-actualization, they engage in an endless spiral of complaining. Machiavelli made numerous comments about the human inability to be satisfied:

> Nature has made men able to crave everything but unable to attain everything.[6]

Men are never contented but, having got one thing, they are not satisfied with it and want a second.[7]

Men [are] wont to get annoyed with adversity and fed up with prosperity.[8]

It has long been recognized that work plays an essential role for human beings. The nature of work is crucial and at the center of most adults' lives. It gives us a sense of identity, self-esteem, and order. If an individual's job is unsatisfying and frustrating, all aspects of his or her life can be seriously and negatively affected. In Maslow's terms, both ego and social needs depend heavily on the work situation for fulfillment. Some of our survey participants described the personal satisfaction they get from their jobs:

I feel very fortunate to have had opportunities and bosses who, through their personal behavior and actions, demonstrated they care about me and my development.

—white, female, upper-level manager

I enjoy my job. This company is a great place to work and I have been fortunate to work for some very good supervisors. They all let me manage.

—white, male, lower-level manager

Money cannot buy job satisfaction, only hard work and self-confidence can bring about job satisfaction.

—white, female, lower-level manager

Like most careers, mine had its ups and downs. Currently it's up because I have a challenging, interesting job. Naturally I'd like to move up, but since I do enjoy my current position, my current level within the corporation is OK.

—Hispanic, male, craftsworker

Since the early 1960s psychologists and sociologists have stressed the importance of good working relationships, characterized by high degrees of trust, supportiveness, and interest among subordinates, peers, and superiors, in maintaining efficient corporations.

Good work-group relationships are enhanced by a getting-along-together attitude and by clear role responsibilities. Ambiguity occurs when an employee is deprived of necessary information because the immediate work group of subordinates, peers, and/or superiors withholds understanding, trust, and support. If employees are already in an ambiguous position because of inadequate information about role responsibilities and/or access to information, they will have poor working relationships and conflicts. In addition, any ambiguity about whether they will have jobs the next day creates tremendous stress. This increasingly occurs in the era of corporate consolidation and downsizing. These conflicts often lead to both physical and mental health problems among employees that affect their job performance.

> Since I returned to work eight years ago I have known no job security at all. The threat of being forced surplus for eight years has damaged both my mental and physical health. Nothing is stable, solid.
>
> —white, female, craftsworker

Getting along refers to the critical ability to influence others, particularly in terms of acquiring the resources and information necessary for successful job performance. Since more and more people demand to be treated as contributing human beings, the tangible and intangible resources are seldom accessible through formal position or authority alone.

One of the most important egotistic needs is *fulfillment in terms of accomplishment*—that is, the individual's sense of the importance of his or her own work and evidence of productivity. People like to measure their progress and productivity; they need to know whether they are progressing at a satisfactory rate and they need to see their assignments completed.

When jobs do not offer these satisfactions, workers become alienated. R. Blauner has theorized that job alienation results from a lack of certain crucial elements. Jobs that do not allow employees to control their immediate work environment result in a sense of powerlessness. Jobs that do not establish a relationship between the actions of the individual worker and the broader corporate objectives fail to give the employee a sense of belonging and contribution to the overall goals of the organization. In such a situation, the worker develops a feeling of meaninglessness.[9]

Boring, monotonous jobs that stifle opportunities for self-growth provoke feelings of self-estrangement. Such jobs are seen as means rather than fulfilling ends. All these negative aspects can and too often do lead to alienation and at times even to aggressive, antisocial behavior.

Some researchers have also noted that a sense of active participation is extremely important in the employee's life. R. Caplan and J. French found that a lack of participation in decision-making processes can lead to strain among employees and can adversely affect productivity.[10]

Yankelovich has noted that the failure of the old incentive system to catch with "new-breed values" has resulted in such deterioration in the work place that our position as the foremost industrial nation is threatened. He pointed to the lack of appeal that present-day incentive systems hold for workers and a growing trend on the part of employees to give less and demand more. He also noted, however, that workers often embark on a new job with great willingness to work hard and be productive. However, when jobs fail to meet expectations, the lack of incentives leads to a loss of interest. New-breed managers share a preoccupation with self that "places the burden of providing incentives for hard work more squarely on the employer than under the old value system."[11]

This causes problems for employers. No longer does the threat of lost income and joblessness completely cow employees into corporate conformity; rather, quality-of-life considerations are becoming more paramount for increasing numbers of employees. These considerations, being less tangible, are not well understood by large organizations, which in any case are unschooled in balancing these motivations with their needs for efficiency and productivity.

It is evident from our survey and corroborated by other reviews of literature that the task of improving work performance—and at the same time contributing to employees' feelings of satisfaction—is very difficult. No single approach will provide the key to motivating all employees toward the ultimate of increased and improved production. Since each employee is unique and what motivates one will not motivate all, a combination of motivational techniques must be directed toward the needs and desires of the individual.

Let's look at what participants in my surveys conducted during the past ten years say are the most important motivating factors in their selecting a new job. Since the data collected in 1976 and 1986 are quite similar, we will discuss the 1986 results. The most frequent motivating factors identified by employees were: (1) more interesting, challenging work (25 percent), (2) better advancement opportunities (19 percent), (3) more freedom for individual thought and initiative (14 percent), (4) better salary (11 percent), and (5) more job security (11 percent). A Gallup survey done in the same ten-year period found that nearly two-thirds of employees want more of the following factors in their jobs: good pay (77 percent); recognition for good work (70 percent); good fringe benefits (68 percent); chance for advancement (65 percent); job security (65 percent); interesting work (62 percent); pay tied to performance (61 percent); and the opportunity to learn new skills (61 percent).

These data and what we know about personality, bureaucracy, and the false expectations our society inculcates in us suggest that corporate America has a lot of disappointed people, stress, and conflict. Let's look at some of the career problems and concerns that affect corporate employees.

Six Case Studies of Corporate Careers

To clarify the career problems facing employees, we can examine six case studies of managers who are considered very successful— two white males, one black male, one Hispanic female, one black female, and one white female. The cases of these successful managers demonstrate what corporate America is like even for the very successful, and show that success is not simply (as a woman said during the Statue of Liberty celebration) wanting it, but wanting it badly enough and working for it. The case studies are not analytical but simply a descriptive series of facts about six individuals' corporate lives.

Case Study One: White Male[12]

Had a supportive good boss early in career.

Demoted after a few very successful years working for the company because of a recession.

Promoted because he developed an innovative financial system that made him stand out. Considered a success in ten years.

Deliberately humiliated in public by his immediate supervisor.

Phone records reviewed by immediate boss.

Desk ruffled through when he reached the top.

Boss tried to keep him feeling anxious and off-balance.

Travel expenses audited.

Full-scale investigation by private eye.

Offices and phones were tapped.

Hoped things would get better.

Started writing down everything to protect self.

Reorganized out of position—power diluted.

Individual and his family had great pressures and stresses.

Felt like he was killing himself, going crazy.

Fired from job.

Lost all but two "friends" after being fired; lost one friend whom he protected for twenty-five years.

Case Study Two: White Male[13]

Moved rapidly up the hierarchy.

Took over failing organization—had tremendous success.

Hated job, bored by endless meetings, inundated with paperwork.

Accused of not being a team player when questioned bosses' decisions.

Boss dedicated to getting person fired because of life-style: enjoyed living and had wide circle of diverse friends.

Questioned about expenses and high living. Company refused to pay expense voucher; paid it himself.

Hairstyle and dress style were criticized and created conflict with boss.

Divorced and remarried, a fact seen as a hindrance to career by upper management.

Boss unable to fire him because of extreme success in sales and financial contributions to organization.

Peers had personal vendettas—were out to get him with grapevine gossip; accused of building a special company product for own personal use with company money.

Suddenly support from a mentor ended.

Peers, who smiled in each other's faces including his, were going for "each other's jugular" in private and behind one another's backs.

Personal life informally investigated by company officials on an ongoing basis.

Lost weight, doubted self; wondered why he could not become what they wanted him to become.

Quit the company before being fired.

Case Study Three: Black Male[14]

Got rapid promotions.

Had best results for the entire company.

Investigated by security because of unfounded charges of conflict of interest.

Boss C supported person during security investigation.

Finance department scrutinized all vouchers, no matter how simple.

Boss A had employees drive by his house to see "who is there."

Bosses A and B refused to pay legitimate company expenses.

Several peers started rumors about his cheating because he was number one in results; division constantly audited.

Boss A had phone tapped.

Boss B had his own office put under sound and videotape surveillance to catch person giving information to the union; the assumption was totally incorrect.

Questioned by bosses A and B about living area and life-style.

Boss C gave him tremendous freedom to do the job.

Boss C told him he deserved merit increase and a place on the high-potential list but age, race, and work background got in the way.

Accused of sleeping with all the white women.

Boss B gave one performance appraisal to person; wrote a different one for secret file shared with officers.

Officer attempted to make moves on "woman friend"; officer rebuffed; turns against person.

New style of more liberal human management and creative ideas attacked as being "not like we do it here."

Accused of being arrogant because of education, background, and Ivy League schools attended.

Announcement for promotion to be made. Rescinded at last moment because not considered to be a team player and too critical of immediate boss A.

Case Study Four: Hispanic Woman[15]

> College degree in math.
>
> Rapidly advanced in operations to lower-middle management.
>
> Boss A believed women should be married and at home.
>
> Boss A sent her to a number of development assignments.
>
> Boss A left. Boss B promoted her six months later to middle management in operations.
>
> Transferred to EEO minority-recruiting job for a two-year term.
>
> Began to run into a lot of criticism because of minority-recruitment efforts.
>
> Boss C not committed to supporting her efforts. Believed there was no problem.
>
> Boss C took away some responsibilities.
>
> Boss C tried to reorganize her out of the company.
>
> Boss C transferred. Boss D more supportive.
>
> Boss D tried to transfer her to another department for career reasons.
>
> Has become labeled an EEO specialist—career ended!

Case Study Five: Black Woman[16]

> Brought in on fast-track, high-potential program.
>
> Moved rapidly from one assignment to another in marketing.
>
> Made middle management in three years.
>
> Males did not listen to her opinions until V.P. said, "Let's hear her out."
>
> Mentor left the company.

Moved from one staff position to another in public relations and personnel.

Never given any negative feedback on performance, only positive feedback during first six years.

Suddenly told she is lowest rated person out of five people.

Told not salable because does not have a technical background. Not given a chance to get technical background.

Eight years later told *only* reason she got promoted rapidly is that they needed a black woman.

Last boss who rated her low withheld needed information to get job done.

Last boss bypassed her and went to her subordinates.

Told was too active in black management organization.

Declared surplus; did not have a job for six months.

Job saved because of pressure on company by black employee organization.

Case Study Six: White Woman[17]

Brought in on the high-potential, fast-track program.

Did extremely well in marketing.

Promoted rapidly to lower-middle management.

Believed her career was on its way, that there was no sexism in the company.

Believed women were their own worst enemy.

Was acting middle-level manager for four months.

Was promised permanent middle-level manager job.

White male with only two years in the company promoted to the job. (She had four years with the company.)

Told by her boss that white male got the job because of politics; not because he was better than she or because she did not do an outstanding job.

Five months later promoted to new job.

Some members of her work group tried to sabotage her because she had new, creative ideas and they wanted to do things the old way.

Did an outstanding job. Her clients were extremely satisfied.

Began to have personal problems at home, but they did not affect job.

Spoke to too many people about personal problems. Began to develop reputation of having problems.

Still rated number one two years in a row by boss and his peers; however, their boss did not agree. He rated her number two.

Taken off the high-potential list because she was not "polished" enough.

Several high-level men wanted to take her under their wing to help her. She found out their main interest was to get her in bed.

She refused their advances. They begin to spread rumors about her not being able to get along.

Difficult to find a new job because of character assassination.

She is still doing an outstanding job; however, she is thinking about leaving the company because she feels the company only appreciates conformity and not talent.

These histories are not isolated cases; they are the norm. The two white males were Lee Iaccoca and John DeLorean. To substantiate the problems and inequities described above, let's look at some statistics from the recently completed study of high-tech firms and some quotations from my 1984–86 surveys.

Specific Career Problems of Study Participants

The unpublished study performed in several high tech firms that I cited earlier found the following:

Slightly more than 50 percent of the managers and 70 percent of the craftsworkers believe that their supervisors evaluated their performances unfairly.

Only 40 percent of the managers but 63 percent of the craftsworkers say their supervisors give them feedback to help improve their performances.

More than 90 percent believe that it is important to provide opportunities for individual development, but only 25 percent say that their companies do so.

Only 25 percent of the managers and 33 percent of the craftsworkers say that their supervisors assisted with career planning. Over 90 percent believe this is very important, but less than 20 percent believe it happens in practice.

Slightly over 50 percent of the employees believe that their working conditions allow them to be productive.

About 65 percent of the employees say that they are at least satisfied with their jobs.

Approximately 56 percent are at least satisfied with their companies. Interestingly, upper-level employees are less satisfied than those at lower levels.

Less than 30 percent of the employees believe rewards for risks outweigh consequences of failures.

Less than 50 percent of the employees regardless of level believe management treats them with dignity and respect.

Ninety percent rate open and honest communication as important; however, only 25 percent believe it happens in practice.

Finally, over 90 percent of the employees believe mutual trust among company employees is at least important, but only 24 percent say it happens in practice.

These data clearly demonstrate the conflict between theory and practice in corporate America. One must wonder, for example, when 90 percent of the employees rate open, honest communication as important and only 25 percent believe that it exists, whether the other 65 percent recognize that they could be part of the problem.

Gross statistical data do not give the essence of the specific career concerns and problems that employees face. Let's look at some selected comments from the individual participants. Notice that these employees' comments contradict many of Weber's theories on bureaucracies and bring into serious question the adequacies of motivational theories.

Many employees commented on their treatment as human beings and on their lack of job security despite years of service:

> I realize it takes a long time to complete a turnaround, but as long as some of the bad managers stand around and collect their paychecks and bad-mouth their employees, then there will never be any respect gained on either side. Most of the phones were removed from our office because some employees abused the usage. Now a first level's main job is to time all employees on lunch, breaks and phone calls. Managers come to the rest rooms to see how long you have been away from your desk. Obviously these managers have nothing better to do. They certainly couldn't perform well on a job that really requires some decision making. Why aren't they being reeducated to become better managers? It seems like they are being hard. Some people will go to their graves thinking they really performed a service to the company.
>
> —white, female, craftsworker

> Emphasis everywhere seems to be pad/justify your own job. The company does not seem to be concerned with employees in the least. Individual survival is the attitude.
>
> —white, male, lower-level manager

> I enjoy working in my position and would appreciate an opportunity to advance. However, due to apathy, no movement, surplus

conditions, pessimistic projections, etc., I have no hope. I am thankful I just have my job. P.S. I have just been notified that I am now surplus. I have 15 years of service.

—Hispanic, female, lower-level manager

Once upon a time I loved my job. Not any more . . . because of poor management and being treated like shit day in and day out and being lied to. Craft has done a great job all along. It is management that has overstaffed, overspent and screwed up all in all. Thank God for the union. I am not a union man, but you have to be one in this company because of the way we are treated and handled. We need a more progressive management than we have right now. This company's head is in the ground with time sharing, sick days and just handling people.

—white, male, craftsworker

The only commitment the company has made to the future concerning its employees is that it will do what it takes to make lots of money and the workforce be damned.

—white, female, lower-level manager

Tied into these views of insensitive treatment of employees are the issues of fair and equitable evaluation and promotion. Many employees perceive unfair treatment, some citing racism, some sexism, and some incompetent and self-serving superiors:

All managers have problems, regardless of sex. All managers deal with the problem of being selected by personal contacts, attractiveness, or age (for opportunities), rather than on a basis of performance or ability.

—white, male, upper-level manager

Many [women] managers have proven their competency with this company. Why, then, are there so few in middle and upper management? If they can do the job, let them run the department-section-level-or company.

—white, female, middle-level manager

I feel that this company has more women in higher positions than men (and I'm not being prejudiced either). I feel men don't have a chance to move from craft positions to first level. Above that second level and up, men do! That's also interesting to note.

—white, male, craftsworker

This is a damn good company! I just want my share! It just won't let me play the game! Blacks don't get promoted.

—black, male, lower-level manager

My boss doesn't even know how to administer the appraisal process correctly. How can he identify a good candidate of any race or sex? It's still all done by who you know!

—black, female, lower-level manager

Many other employees leveled criticism at management:

I found the "old" ways at the company to be extremely frustrating and an obstacle to the growth of the company as well as the individual.

—white, female, lower-level manager

My boss treats her employees very badly. She is rude, she interrupts us when we are on a phone call and she treats us as if she is far better than we are. And, of course, *she* never makes a mistake. We are always to blame. She never would even think of standing up for us if a problem arose.

—white, female, craftsworker

In the company it is who you know that counts—not what you know. In many cases, candidate requests are specifically written for pre-selected individuals; there are no real "open" opportunities for most employees. Employees are also penalized for doing a good job. If your job performance is good, your boss won't promote you as a candidate because the boss doesn't want to train a replacement.

—white, female, lower-level manager

People in positions of authority who are threatened by the changing environment are the biggest obstacle to getting the job done in today's environment.

—black, female, middle-level manager

We still have too many "mid" and "high" level managers who are only paying "lip" service. When the chips are down, their behavior and decision-making are not acceptable. Too much "politics" is still around.

—Asian, male, lower-level manager

In this department, the middle-level manager will have things go his way or not at all. I don't care how much common sense you think you use; it will go HIS way; he will do as he damn well pleases because *he* is *boss*. He was put in this position to be a hatchet man, and believe me, he hasn't failed his mission. He has lower-level females under him, but they can't make any decisions because they are incompetent. His wife, who also is a second level and used to work up here, may disagree. So, if it doesn't go HIS way then it will go HER way or it won't go *any* way!

—white, female, lower-level manager

Bosses know nothing about my job and can only say "NO" because they don't know how to take risks and say "YES!" We have confusion (due to alcoholism in management, no direction for production, unfair treatment, no recognition). BOSS sees us only on payday and there are no mentors.

—white, female, craftsworker

Many of these criticisms stem from the failure of management to use employees' talents properly:

This company has never fully utilized its workforce. Many people have talents that go totally unused in their present jobs. Their talents aren't recognized and go unused and unrecognized.

—Hispanic, male, craftsworker

I have a severe case of job burnout on my present position. I feel my intelligence is being wasted and yet I'm simply stuck there.

—black, female, craftsworker

There are many talents throughout the company that are being wasted as the people are working in positions that aren't using their talents to their fullest potential.

—Native American, female, craftsworker

All of these conflicts and concerns will cause employees to become so dissatisfied that they will ultimately leave, as these three employees' words indicate:

Make life miserable for others. Too bad the few have to ruin it for the rest. I think this company is suffering in a big way because of it. And it's going to get worse before it gets better if . . . has anything to say about it. I feel I am a good loyal employee with lots to contribute. But I don't know how much longer I can take this petty, back-biting, selfish BS. There is too much greed in this place . . . too many power-hungry, power-conscious people who are guilty of character assassination. Part of the assassination is based on those who haven't volunteered to be "born again." I'll leave first.

—white, male, middle-level manager

There are a lot of good people working for this company who are overlooked, ignored and underemployed. I think a serious effort to change this is in order. Present management is bridled with incompetence and craft is in need of direction and support. Our middle-level manager is considered a joke by his subordinates and peers, and one wonders why everyone can see it except his boss. I'm just a clerk and it makes my heart ache to observe this circus every day. I'm seriously seeking other employment in search of some kind of self-actualization and I feel sorry for those I will leave behind. I also regret that this company will suffer a great loss in not utilizing my skills or contributions and those who are like me.

—white, female, craftsworker

I predict I will get discouraged enough with my job that I will seek and obtain employment elsewhere within the year. This company has made it clear that if the employees don't like the job situation, they can leave. No one is important enough to listen to and work with to resolve conflicts.

—white, female, lower-level manager

Many of the underlying conflicts in careers occur because we believe that we are not valued and rewarded appropriately by our companies. In other words, there is a high "perception gap" between what we believe we deserve and what our companies believe we deserve or consider themselves able to give us. I strongly disagree with Kanter when she wrote,

> In the companies with a great deal of entrepreneurial activity, managers frequently could see no relation between eventual rewards like promotions and salary increases and their most significant accomplishments—but, unlike managers in less innovative companies, they also did not seem bothered by this.[18]

The companies in my studies are "innovative," "entrepreneurial" companies in terms of personnel policies and practices and managerial approach; however, they are still bureaucracies made up of individuals who, regardless of age, have aspirations to move up the corporate ladder, to receive big bonuses, and to be rewarded generally. These people feel frustrated that they will never reach their goals and get their just reward. While some of Kanter's participants might have expressed the feelings that she describes, they are likely the annointed ones who can afford to be magnanimous about their rewards because they know that they are part of the "in-group" who will eventually be taken care of. It seems to me that Kanter's view is an ideal one, which has no place as a formula for a society that stresses individualism and competition, with great emphasis on winning, especially individual winning.

In addition, Kanter is ignoring some extremely valid information put forth by Levinson, who argues that one of corporate employees' greatest needs is for approval from superiors. The most important way that supervisors demonstrate their approval is through promotions and salary increases. Approval from superiors enhances self-image and sanctions certain behaviors. Levinson sees our vulnerability to the opinions of our bosses as based on a failure to overcome the child/parent relationship. Despite widespread denial, this child-parent dyad forms the fundamental model of chain-of-command relationships in the bureaucratic hierarchy.[19]

Perceptions of Being Rewarded and Valued

Considering the comments of my study participants, it is not surprising that few of them feel that they are valued and fairly rewarded.

I made an index* of the 1986 responses to the following questions to gain a sense of how strongly the participants felt about the rewards and value they received from their employers:

> To what extent have the informal rewards (praise, recognition) you have received in your company been what you deserve, considering your performance and contributions?

> To what extent have the formal rewards (money, promotions) you have received been what you deserve, considering your performance and contributions?

> To what extent do you believe your company values you as an employee?

I found that 26 percent of all employees believe that the company does not value or reward them at all; 33 percent believe that the company values and rewards them to a small extent; 22 percent believe that they are valued to some extent; and 20 percent believe they are valued to a great extent. Table 1 in the appendix shows the detailed responses by race, gender, and occupational level.

The data show that, with the notable exception of black males, craft employees are less likely than management employees to believe that the company rewards and values them.

Managerial level has a significant impact on the responses of all

---

*Throughout the book, I use indexes to help determine the strengths of participants' views about certain issues. I formed the indexes by taking employees' responses to a specific question and giving them a value of one or zero, depending on how the question was phrased. For example, for the index on values and rewards, if the employees responded, "to a great extent" or "some extent" to the question, "To what extent do you believe your company values you as an employee?" they would receive a one. If they responded, "to a small extent" or "to no extent at all," they would receive a zero. All of their responses are added and they receive a score.

groups except for blacks. The higher the managerial level, the lower the percentage of employees who feel they are not being rewarded and valued by the company. For example, 20 percent of the white males at lower levels compared to 43 percent at the upper levels feel greatly valued and rewarded.

It is not surprising that in every race and gender group a strong correlation exists between the prospect of quitting and how the respondents perceive they are being treated by the company. For example, 32 percent of the black women who believe that the company is not treating them at all fairly are seriously considering quitting, while none of those who believe the company is treating them very fairly are seriously considering quitting. The figures for white women are 49 percent and 8 percent, respectively.

We can conclude that a significant majority of the employees at both craft and managerial levels believe that their companies do not adequately reward or value them and that those who feel undervalued are most inclined to quit or seek other jobs. We can also conclude that such feelings can lead to lower productivity. Indeed, two out of five employees believe that their performances have been negatively affected at least to some extent by their perceptions that their companies do not appreciate them. Such a disparity between performance and reward can lead to lower profits through the loss of talented people to competitors.

Our data are not unique. In the major high-tech companies study cited earlier, only 25 percent of craftsworkers, 29 percent of lower managers, and 35 percent of middle- and upper-level managers say that individual contributions are recognized and rewarded frequently. In addition, only 39 percent regardless of level say that they are satisfied with the recognition they get for doing a good job, and only 25 percent believe that their company is better than "just fair" on giving rewards for performance.

Let's look at some employees' comments about recognition and rewards.

> This company's efforts should not be limited to timetables; within our workforce we have highly trained minorities in both craft and management positions who are underutilized. Our politics does not permit equal recognition, support and encouragement.
>
> —black, female, craftsworker

Sometimes you wonder if it's worth it. What's the tangible reward for the nights and weekends? Associates who don't give a darn have the same rewards—why should a few carry the load for many with minimal recognition?

—white, female, middle-level manager

Quite frankly, I'm so sick of filling out these things and finding myself writing the same responses year after year. Here so far I've been candid about my comments, but I'm fed up with all of this lip service and this time you are getting my true gut reaction because I don't care any more. This company has a wealth of talent that is just wasting away because the white society (mostly the white male) is keeping its foot on our throat. Don't ask me to work three times as hard and receive no compensation or praise. Do you ask that of your white sisters or mother? Get with the program, middle management: it's "sink or survive" time.

—black, female, craftsworker

I had a lower-level boss who refused to give me praise, recognition, or positive reinforcement on my appraisal for the first 17 months I worked for her. She was promoted from office manager to acting supervisor. My only hope is that when her acting position is eliminated, she will be, too.

—white, female, craftsworker

It seems as if management in general wants to keep you on the edge of your seat (as far as your job is concerned). They are always saying "I think you're lucky to have a job." The truth is the company is lucky to have such dedicated employees.

—white, male, craftsworker

How can the company pay so much attention to race and gender when it cannot treat its employees with respect? No thanks for a job well done, no Christmas dinners, can't get vacation with family, etc.

—white, male, craftsworker

Office pets. Favoritism. No recognition for good work but plenty for bad.

—white, female, middle-level manager

I am a single person (single income, mid-career). Only the fear of a lower income and standard of living prevents me from leaving. There is no other reason to stay. None of the higher management in my department have ever indicated in any way that I am valuable to the company.

—white, female, middle-level manager

The problems described above are not unusual; they are the norm in corporate America. They are inherent in hierarchical bureaucracy because of the limited opportunities in a society that tells everyone they need only to work hard, keep their noses clean, and the world is theirs—a society that prides itself on being a meritocracy but is a far cry from it.

As Levinson writes, while much is said about organizations as instruments for individual achievement, and about motivational practices as being rewarding rather than punishing, the fact is that bureaucratic organizations are essentially geared for defeat. For every person who is promoted, a vast number are left behind.[20]

My review of motivational theory, along with my research and personal observations, leads me to concur with Machiavelli's view that people are by nature unappreciative, especially when they achieve or approximate the objects of their desire. He explained:

> For it may be said of men in general that they are ungrateful, voluble, dissembling, anxious to avoid danger, and covetous of gain. As long as you benefit them, they are entirely yours; they offer you their blood, their goods, their life, and their children, as I have said before, when the necessity is remote; but when it approaches, they revolt. In prosperity men are insolent, and in adversity abject and humble. How blind men are to things in which they sin, and what sharp persecutors they are of the vices they do not have.[21]

Conclusions

Weber defined the ideal bureaucracy as a hierarchical structure with a rational division of labor or activities, all governed or ruled by a set of general policies and procedures, administered by objectively evaluated, recruited, and promoted (not elected) people who are loyal to the organization and who have a clear understanding of their limited and specific role, its values, and culture. He believed that bureaucratic authority resides in the office, not the person, and that a strict separation should exist between professional and personal life. This supposedly leads to the smooth functioning of the organization.

This chapter presents data that vividly contradict many aspects of Weber's theory. What we have in corporate America is a structure that pits people against one another competitively and eventually condemns all but a few to failure. This structure discourages cooperation and risk taking and nurtures empire building, self-centeredness, inertia, conformity, and employer control. It breeds fear, distrust, dishonesty, and intolerance of diversity.

Ferguson suggests additional reasons for the negative views in corporate America about work, careers, and rewards. The depersonalization inherent in bureaucratic relations requires that individuals be isolated from one another. Formal association takes the place of rewarding social interaction. As bureaucratization spreads, so does alienation; once-overlapping activities become atomized; formerly complementary roles are fragmented.

M. Fair agrees that determination and effort do not yield the greatest reward: "Noses to the grindstone, hearts filled with commitment, and faces beaming with good intentions come face-to-face with the parade of power seekers, power brokers, and political maneuverers, who pass by in a rush of wind that drowns out the career plans of persons who have dedicated all of their energies to only getting the job done."[22]

DeLorean also sheds light on the groundswell of resentment at personal treatment in corporations. He explains that these organizations leave no room for humanistic considerations in rigid, cost-benefit decision making, except when a measurable "effect on the workers will hurt or enhance earnings per share." Our worship of the bottom line in American enterprise has been unswerving. Dishonesty has become not only excusable but routine. For example, "when one is forced into early retirement in a management power-play or a supplier is cheated out of a sale by under-the-table dealings, the public reaction is generally, 'Oh, well. That's business.'"[23]

In the words of Iacocca: "Our struggle also had its dark side. To cut expenses, we had to fire a lot of people. It's like a war; we won, but my son didn't come back. There was a lot of agony. People were getting destroyed, taking their kids out of college, drinking, getting divorced. Overall we preserved the company, but only at enormous personal expense for a great many human beings."[24]

If you believe that you will never be one of those casualties, you may be sadly mistaken. As Nicholas von Hoffman said when Lee Iacocca was fired from Ford, "If a guy like Iacocca's job isn't safe, is yours?"

The frustration inherent in bureaucratic structures is further clarified by Machiavelli's comments about human nature: "Nature has made men able to crave everything but unable to attain everything. Hence, since men's craving is always greater than their power to attain they are discontented with their acquirements and get slight satisfaction from them. Men's fortunes, therefore, vary because, since some strive to get more and others fear to lose what they have gained, they indulge in enmity and war."[25]

Making it to the top in corporate America is like passing through the eye of a needle. Society's myths feed the massive desires for "success," yet the reality of bureaucratic structure bars entry to the top to all but a very few. The potential for frustration, anger, and dog-eat-dog competition is enormous. Overcoming these barriers and surviving in the corporate fishbowl is possible. We will now turn to the realities of swimming against the tide into middle and upper management.

4
The Real Criteria
for Advancement

This chapter focuses on the realities of advancing up the corporate hierarchy. Despite the vast amount of defensive denial that goes on in corporate America, most employees express the conviction that they should be at least two levels above where they are now. This has a special poignancy in our society, where bureaucracies, schools, and parents tell us to be competitive, to "go for the top."

Advancement Theories

In American culture, self-esteem, dignity, and worth are measured as direct functions of our successes at work. As Maccoby has said, we are heirs to a culture placing maximal value and emphasis on winning. From an early age children are told, "The only thing that will hold you back is yourself." R. Turner makes some very relevant comments about our society and our unlimited optimism. He writes: "Individuals in the United States grow up believing that everyone has the opportunity to advance and that, as "the land of opportunity," the United States has no policies or practices which cut off anyone's possibility for advancement."[1]

Turner calls this the *contest mobility norm*. In a selection system that follows the contest mobility norm, he says, "individuals are allowed complete freedom for mobility throughout most of their careers. It instills an insecurity of elite position." Sadly, there is no final arrival under contest mobility; every person may be displaced by newcomers at any time throughout his or her life. Nor are there any final losses, since everyone is kept in the running and offered another chance to qualify for advancement.[2]

The vast majority of those who stay in the running come to be viewed as failures some day, because of the stringent limitations on opportunities at middle and upper management.

Our economic ideology promotes the idea that the job market is a perfect market, offering opportunities and rewards for those who get the proper training and education, work hard, and have innate abilities and talent. Ability and work, then, constitute resources, or "human capital," which can be increased by education and training. This fits very neatly into the popular versions of the American Dream, which is not and never has been true. Of the thousands who set out, many of them with the same ability, personality characteristics, and behaviors, only one can and does make it all the way to the top.

Recognizing that, as Machiavelli said, we always desire more than we can get, that one of the most widely held values in America is to advance in the corporate structure, and that corporate America reinforces employees' illusions that they are always in the running for a promotion, it is surprising that advancement is not a constant obsession of *all* corporate employees. During the research for my book, *Racism and Sexism in Corporate Life,* I found that, regardless of age and race, high percentages of male college graduates want to become upper-level managers (see table 2 in the appendix). More than 900 college graduates aspired to top positions in top U.S. corporations. Hundreds more without college degrees also aspired to those positions. Since only about 400 such positions existed, one can readily conclude that there were a great number of disappointed people.

The bureaucratic structure not only condemns practically everyone to failure; it also does something to those who succeed. Merton accurately cites the constant pressure on corporate managers to be "methodical, prudent, disciplined" as a means of ensuring that they will be predictable and conforming.[3] Employees who want to be promoted will behave as the corporations want them to. These arms of the corporate leviathan reach out to control the lives, actions, and thoughts of employees who are upwardly oriented, influencing them in direct proportion to the extent of their ambition.

Given the odds against reaching the top and the price extracted from those who try, why do people strive so persistently? Our society has brought us up to weigh our self-esteem and self-worth on an external scale calibrated with career advancement. The whole world, it seems, is swimming in spirals, struggling to succeed.

Promotions not only bring financial and material rewards and high status in our society; they gratify the individual ego and sense of self-esteem; they validate one's feeling of personal worth. These factors underscore the unbridgeable hiatus between available socio-economic opportunity and psychological needs. As Levinson says, "Needs for status and esteem are essentially needs for love and affection." Citing studies on infants, concentration camp survivors, and elderly people, he notes that many of those who did not give or receive love became ill and even died. He argues that we desire and work hard for status, in the form of promotions, to win the esteem, admiration, and love of others. We need that affection and gratification because status alone cannot satisfy our needs.[4] Thus, when we base our self-esteem on status, our need becomes insatiable.

Just as the incentive of promotions is a mixed bag, so is personal ambition. The desire to advance can make an employee work harder, and the competition can be healthy. Untempered, however, it can be destructive to both the person and the corporation. When goals become too important, or unrealistic, the disappointment of failure—which is virtually inevitable—is devastating. By the same token, the employee who is committed to achieving certain goals, (for example, vice president by age forty) often loses sight of human concerns for family and other workers, as well as of broader corporate goals. To such a person only advancement is important, and anyone or anything is ruthlessly sacrificed to attain it. This is one type of mental imbalance that the corporate world fosters.

Who Gets Ahead and Why

While promotions can be beneficial incentives, the promotional process itself can have disastrous effects on the organization at large. Consider the Peter Principle, which says that in a hierarchy employees tend to rise to their level of incompetence. Since most promotions are based on present performance, conformity, likabil-

ity, and the approval of key people rather than on potential to perform the proposed job, many employees are promoted until they
reach positions in which they can no longer perform competently.
To the corporations' detriment, these employees are likely to stay
in those positions. A white, male, lower-level manager put it this
way:"I think the company does a poor job of recruiting and/or developing individuals for any type of position whether they be white,
black, female, etc. I guess mediocrity begets mediocrity."

The truth of the Peter Principle is clear when corporate managers, especially senior executives, are asked the following question:
"As you look around the room, do you see people who are your
peers and superiors and wonder 'How the hell did such incompetent
people get into these jobs?'" The response is always acknowledging
laughter. What is more, the laughter is the heartiest at the higher-
level meetings! A white, male, craftsworker wrote: "Middle management seems inundated with incompetence. Since like promotes
like, I see little chance of change until this situation is re-evaluated.
Present management, at least middle level and down, is not qualified to even recognize intelligence or leadership potential."

One reason for the Peter Principle is the extreme difficulty of
defining and quantifying the qualifications for managerial jobs. For
entry-level management positions, companies often specify a degree
or training certification rather than attempt to define and enumer-
ate the capabilities they are seeking. They rely on the ability of educational institutions to provide the skills needed to fulfill the requirements of a specific job such as writer, marketing manager,
financial analyst, or engineer.

A second method that companies use to hire without specifying
qualifications is to assume that the only qualification necessary is
to demonstrate success at a comparable job. This is often true for
positions in "soft" areas such as personnel, where the problem of
delineating explicit qualifications is more difficult than for technical
jobs.

This ambiguity makes even more awesome the attempt to
choose the truly most qualified person out of a number of personnel
specialists, electrical engineers, or financial analysts. As difficult as
technical and professional skills are to evaluate, they are more readily identified or quantified than the more intangible skills needed

for middle and upper managerial positions. Some of these are leadership, organizing and planning, reasoning, and communication skills. The needed abilities become increasingly important and abstract as one moves up the corporate ladder and therefore invites decision makers' subjectivity to play a greater role in determining who eventually will be promoted. The higher one advances in the corporate hierarchy, the more important image management becomes. That is, the higher one goes, the more one is forced to conform to non-ability-related criteria.

F. R. Presthus wrote:

> Facial expressions, verbal responses, subtle unspoken expectations provide the cues. . . . The upwardly-mobile reads the signals his behavior evokes in others. Although the skill will vary among individuals, the distinguishing mark of the upwardly-mobile is that he thinks in such strategic terms and is able to modify his behavior accordingly.[5]

The greater the similarity in outwardly identifiable characteristics (race, sex, dress, language, style, height, and weight), the more likely an aspirant is to be seen as the "right kind of person" and given access to positions of discretion and power. Thus the patterns of racial, sexual, and class stratification of the larger society are reproduced in the organization.[6] A white, female, lower-level manager wrote: "I have seen only "lip service" paid to pluralism in this company. The upper levels still replace people only with like kind. In other words, ineffective and unqualified men are still given positions of authority when women and people of color are clearly available and should be given the opportunity."

Chester Barnard, a former president of the old Bell System, in 1941 said that the smooth functioning of an organization depends on the homogeneity of employees. Studies I have done over the past sixteen years show that large percentages of employees still concur with Barnard. Kanter offered these explanations for the social homogeneity of managers: fear of uncertainty, the impulse toward control through conformity, exclusion of strangers through insistence on unbounded loyalty, and preference for comfortable communication with those who seem similar over the strains of dealing with people who appear "different."[7]

A. Downs made some additional relevant arguments about the mobility process:

> If recruiting is done only at the lowest levels, all top officials have to work themselves upward through the hierarchy, presumably by repeatedly pleasing their superiors. Superiors usually approve of continuous development of their policies, rather than sharp breaks with tradition. Therefore, the screening process of upward movement tends to reject radicals and create a relatively homogeneous group unless the bureaucracy operates in a very volatile environment.[8]

The demand for homogeneity requires "team players" to conform in terms of where they live and how they live: in the choice of housing, cars, food, entertainment, schools attended, rituals of greeting, behavior at business meetings, ways of socializing, and with whom they socialize. In short, the ambitious employee conforms internally and externally. This conformity serves as a kind of survival mechanism. The literature of social psychology tells us that we make stronger attributions about underlying personality characteristics when we see behavior that is clearly inconsistent with implicit role requirements, whereas we take for granted behaviors that are consistent with role requirements. To avoid exposing his or her "true self"—which may be inconsistent with what higher management is looking for—the ambitious employee conforms and in this way keeps everyone guessing. Behavior that is within role requirements allows managers to see what they want to see; at least the employee has given no cause for anyone to assume otherwise.

As soon as an employee steps into the work place, she or he is under pressure to blend in, to tone down her or his individuality, and become the "corporate person." The company has well-defined goals; it wants no interference; and anyone who doesn't think or act in the prescribed manner becomes a hazard.[9] All of this leads to a great deal of uniformity in corporate America, and the higher the level, the greater the conformity. This has not changed in the permissive 1960s, "the me-too" 1970s or the Reagan 1980s.

Indeed, today's corporate profile is more uniform than that in the supposedly "conforming" 1950s. In addition to being exclusively male and Caucasian, and predominantly Protestant, Republican, of eastern U.S. origin, from relatively affluent families, and educated at one of a handful of select universities or colleges (as has always been the case), today's executives are closer in age, and more of them have little or no work experience outside their companies.[10] A middle-level, white male recognized that even white males are discriminated against if they do not fit the proper image: "White males who do not fit the traditional mold are subjected to discrimination because they do not conform to "proper" image. Obviously, the effects of this type of discrimination are not as devastating as discrimination against women and people of color. Nonetheless it still hurts."

The overall picture that emerges is one of a business leadership lacking in diversity of background and, indeed, increasingly an indistinguishable mass. Does this profile reinforce the easy, stereotyped view of a gray-flannel mentality dominating the executive suite? Or does it simply support the notion that "success breeds success"?

F. D. Sturdivant's and R. D. Adler's study, among others, underscores the fact that, even for white men, the promotion system has never been based strictly on merit or ability.[11] Those white men who fit very rigid and subjective molds have comprised the vast majority of those promoted to the upper levels in corporate management. When social criteria serve as the measurement tool for surrogates, managers tend to reproduce themselves. This "managerial cloning" apparently serves as a risk-reduction mechanism in the face of the nonquantitative nature of potential measurement and the subjective judgment of qualifications. It reinforces the notion that those who are at the top deserve to be there.

Closely related to this compulsory conformity is the phenomenon of sycophantism, which is reaching epidemic proportions. Employees who seek to conform and to *please* their supervisors at all costs quickly become chameleons and "yes-people." They no longer think independently, question, or advance ideas that are very far from the status quo. They ape, mimic, and cater to their supervisors to such an extent that they lose sight of their own selves and become reflections of their supervisors. That this process happens so easily can be explained by two factors, one psychological, the other a sociological characteristic of bureaucracies. The psychological explanation is found in the literature of social psychology, specifically self-perception theory, which proposes that a person infers the meaning of his or her own behavior. According to the theory of "insufficient justification," when people are induced to engage in unpleasant or attitudinally inconsistent behavior for little external justification (for example, no reward or a very small one), they come to believe that their behavior was intrinsically motivated. In effect, the person says to himself or herself, "I did this for such a small (or nonexistent) reward, that I must have done it because I wanted to (or believed in it)."[12]

The second factor, which is endemic to bureaucracies, is that real rewards, in terms of advancement in corporate America, are very scarce. People engage in behavior that may be inconsistent with their beliefs and attitudes purely to please their superiors and increase their chances of promotion. When this fails (which it usually does), they justify their behavior by convincing themselves that they *wanted* to behave as they did, because they believed in what they were doing. In effect, they become what they were pretending to be and in this way conform more closely to their superiors.

The personal losses of uniqueness and independence are enormous. The corporation loses creativity and the opportunities that come with risk taking. Managers themselves lose, too. They trade, for the fawning agreement of subordinates, the very valuable suggestions and feedback (even in disagreement) that independent, secure employees contribute.

W. Moore made some relevant comments:

> In a "pure" market, success or failure in competition is the result of many actions by individuals largely unknown. The judgment is impersonal. A managerial employee of the corporation is somewhat affected by the impersonal labor market for administrators but usually much more affected by the personal judgments of colleagues and superiors. This situation places a maximum and often excessive strain on the rules of merit and performance. Particularly in the hazy areas of desirable "personal characteristics," dis-

passionate judgment may be difficult to achieve and difficult to maintain. Ingratiating manners may be substituted for outstanding performance, and the shadow of dedicated duty may conceal the substance of extreme self-interest or vindictive intentions toward unsuccessful rivals.[13]

In light of these issues, how do the employees in my 1984–86 surveys feel about what it takes to advance in their company? Do their perceptions coincide with my position that the most important factors influencing one's promotion are non-ability-related criteria?

Let's look at some of their responses to the following open-ended questions:

Please make any additional comments you may have on you and your career.

Please make any additional comments you may have on your company's pluralistic efforts.

Please indicate any further comments you may have about women as employees and/or problems they face because of gender discrimination in your company.

Please indicate any further comments you may have about people of color as employees and/or problems they face because of race/ethnic discrimination in your company.

Of the thousands of responses to these questions collected in the 1984–1986 surveys, very few disagreed with those quoted below. Almost no one believed that the advancement process was fair.

Efforts to place women and minorities in Director or Officer positions have been only nominal. We have a minority officer (the job was changed to officer when he took the job), one female officer (she is only a middle level but fulfills the quota) and one female at upper level (the first to make it there in an operations job—not personnel!). We have few women and minorities in upper level positions, and no efforts to develop middle levels to assume these positions in the future.

—white, female, upper-level manager

We have good pools at the lower management to move into middle management positions, but there is little support to move women/minorities into the "Old Boy Power Network."

—white, female, middle-level manager

Very political!! Dedication, truth, and effort mean nothing. Unless you have a mentor, no one really cares!

—white, male, lower-level manager

In many areas of this company, there are very few male employees. These male employees very quickly get promoted before their female fellow employees.

—black, female, middle-level manager

In this company, advancement is by four criteria—(1) Relative ability (i.e., a well placed relative), (2) Sponsorship, (3) Satisfaction of EEO requirements, (4) Competence, knowledge, experience—last and least.

—white, male, middle-level manager

The more you know, the worse off you are. Height is more important in this company than intelligence. It's not what you know, it's who you blow.

—white, male, lower-level manager

Favoritism and nepotism have always overridden diligent and consistently faithful workers.

—white, male, craftsworker

I'm a hard-working, dedicated employee, but I feel that I'll never advance in the company because I don't play the political arenas or go along with the so-called socialites.

—black, female, craftsworker

Because I'm fat, I've had to work harder to prove my abilities.

—Hispanic, female, craftsworker

If you are cute and sexy, you don't have to have a brain in your head.

—Hispanic, female, craftsworker

A great deal of emphasis is placed on racism, sexism and age. What about the prejudiced treatment I've received about my weight. Many jokes (which I heard about through other managers) had been made behind my back because of my weight.

—white, female, craftsworker

I feel the company has too many people who manipulate the system to get the people they want promoted.

—American Indian, male, lower-level manager

Rewards go to whites, friends, relatives—a totally unfair situation. Blacks usually have no sponsor, mentor or patron, due to racism.

—black, female, craftsworker

The promotion process tends to bury and forget people. If a person gets stuck at one level for a period of time, he/she is no longer considered for promotion regardless of the reason for the lack of movement. Too often it is because their boss was afraid to let them go when opportunities were available.

—white, male, middle-level manager

Hard-working highly motivated employees are discouraged when they have done a good job and are "bypassed" for promotions because they don't have the support of their immediate supervisor or they don't socialize with the "right" people.

—black, female, middle-level manager

Sometimes an employee is doing such a fine job that the boss won't let him/her go. Then a person's achievement can become an obstacle rather than an advantage to his/her career.

—Asian, female, lower-level manager

I think a lot of the management people were not picked on their qualifications but on who they knew, and they are the biggest abusers of taking advantage of the company. Until that changes, there is no chance of any career advancement for people who really deserve it.

—Hispanic, female, craftsworker

I was hired by this company by default. I was promoted to management by default. I am staying at the same level by design—someone else's design.

—black, male, lower-level manager

Qualifications should be based on ability and experience, not race or gender. The most capable person should get the job. I don't feel the company's policies are currently based on this idea. Nor is it headed in that direction.

—Asian, female, craftsworker

It's one thing to promote women and people of color but putting them in positions they are not qualified for sets them up for failure and reinforces the traditionalists who "knew" that the woman or minority person couldn't handle the task. Qualifications should be adhered to.

—white, female, middle-level manager

Male bosses seem to favor the young pretty ladies, but female bosses do not have favorites.

—white, male, craftsworker

Very few people at this company are demoted or fired as needed regardless of the level of competence shown. Too many "yes men" and "smilers" are kept and promoted.

—black, male, upper-level manager

Our middle level managers are the biggest stumbling blocks to pluralism. They have the most to lose and no incentive to promote employees who will become their competitors for the available upper level jobs.

—white, female, middle-level manager

Regardless of qualifications, experience, job performance, or education, there is always some excuse for not interviewing candidates that are not shown to the owner of a job. Now the excuse is I'm only interviewing people on the high potential list. If they do not get you one way, they will another.

—black, male, middle-level manager

Company should actively seek out and promote gay men/lesbians—even though supposedly non-discriminatory in regard to affectional preference. I feel there is still strong undercurrent of prejudice.

—white, male, craftsworker

I feel strongly that unless he had someone pulling the right strings for him, Jesus Christ would be lost in the shuffle.

—white, male, lower-level manager

These comments reflect a wide variety of issues that employees confront in their desire to advance. They range from factors that employees absolutely can't change, such as race, gender, age, and height, to factors that are difficult to change, such as visibility, weight, sexiness, and cuteness. Other factors mentioned such as lack of mentors and company politics are also not easy to change.

It is clear from these comments that anyone who believes that advancement totally or primarily depends on one's abilities and merit is living in a world of illusion. A review of the findings from other studies supports this proposition.

In 1980 T. A. Beehr et al. found in a study of 957 employees at all levels in a manufacturing plant that employees perceived three factors as influential in obtaining a better job in the plant: performance, race/sex, and luck/favoritism.[14]

Several years earlier G. Gemmill and D. DeSalvia, in their study of 209 managers in two companies, discovered that managers believe they got ahead by being proficient, by presenting the right public image, and by being good "politicians."[15]

In a related study of 250 managers (1979), P. Pedigo and H. Meyer found that managers believed both objective criteria such as technical skills and performance and subjective criteria such as whom you know influenced promotion decisions.[16]

Impact of Objective Evaluation Criteria

Over the years I have asked employees to rate the impact of a series of objective and subjective factors on achievement of career goals. Employees were asked if certain criteria would be helpful, harmful, or irrelevant. Let us analyze data for 1986 from the four objective criteria, which were formed into an index. The objective criteria were:

Accomplishments/achievements on the job.

Technical, professional, or scientific knowledge.

Work experience.

Educational level.

We found that 19 percent of the employees believe that none of the four factors will be an advantage in their achieving their desired position. Only 17 percent of the employees believe all four criteria will be an advantage.

There are many legitimate reasons why more employees did not select all four criteria as advantages. One reason is that the educational level of many of these employees is below a college degree. Of people with college backgrounds, a much higher percentage believe that their education will be an advantage. As we shall see later, a college degree gives some employees an advantage; however, education does not have the same strong favorable influence on the careers of women and minorities as it does on the careers of white males.

Table 3 in the appendix shows the details of the employees' responses to the value of the objective criteria, by employees' race, gender, and occupational level. The impact of occupational level is significant. Craft employees are less likely than managers to believe that objective criteria will be an advantage, the result perhaps of their lesser education and nonmanagement status. Another explanation could be that managers believe objective criteria will be an advantage because they like to believe they got promoted on merit. As a young, upper-level woman who is the highest ranking woman in her company said, "The cream always rises to the top." Table 3 also shows that a smaller percentage of black male craftsworkers than the other race, gender, or occupation groups are likely to believe that these objective evaluation criteria will be an advantage in their achieving their desired position. Black male managers are most likely to believe that all these criteria will be advantages in their achieving their desired position. This is an interesting finding, since black male managers are the most critical group about race discrimination. Their positive responses here could be a reflection of their confidence in their ability. Also, they are the most educated group in this study.

There is a significant relationship between managerial level and responses on this index for white employees but not for minority employees. The white men who believe that all four factors will be advantages to their achieving their desired position are 14 percent at lower management, 24 percent at middle management, and 61 percent at upper management. The white women's responses follow the same pattern. Obviously having "made it" in this system makes one perceive it to be more objective. To believe otherwise would be tantamount to admitting that one got to the top through illegitimate means.

It is clear from the previous data that so-called "objective" evaluation criteria do not seem to be universally advantageous to all employees. Clearly, while the vast majority of readers no doubt agree in principle that these four factors should be advantageous, the human, subjective, decision-making faculty interprets these factors in different ways for different categories of people. The truth of this proposition has been demonstrated by a group exercise conducted repeatedly by my colleagues and myself over the past twelve years. The exercise asks participants in three or more groups to evaluate the job performance and potential of three people. The only difference in the information given to the groups is the race and/or gender of the people to be evaluated. Despite the fact that the cases are identical in all other respects, each group comes back with very different perceptions about the performance and potential of the person. White males are usually evaluated higher than other race and/or gender groups. In addition, subtle (and at times not so subtle) racist and sexist adjectives are frequently used in describing the behavior of minorities and women. The same behavior by white males is usually described with positive adjectives.

Impact of Race, Gender, and Age

When we take the responses to three subjective criteria—race, gender, and age—and form them into an index, 20 percent of men and 10 percent of women believe that these criteria will be relevant to their achieving their desired positions. On the other end of the scale, 37 percent of the women and 27 percent of the men believe that these three factors will be irrelevant. It is not surprising that almost double the percentage of whites (34 percent) than blacks (17 percent) feel that all three subjective criteria (race, gender and age) *will* be irrelevant to their achieving their desired positions. Twenty-five percent of the other minorities concur.

As detailed in table 4 in the appendix, factors that the study participants cannot change—their race, gender, and age—will be relevant (at least in their minds) to their achieving their desired position. Such a realization combined with high aspirations inevitably leads to large numbers of frustrated, marginally productive employees. Race and gender are discussed in detail in coming chapters. Let us now look more carefully at perceptions of the impact of age on employees' careers.

Age discrimination is becoming a more vital issue as U.S. society reaches middle age. The studies of Garda Bowman (1964) and Fernandez (1975) clearly showed that substantial majorities of managers believe that being under forty-five should be a helpful factor for promotions. For example, 76 percent of the managers in Bowman's study and 62 percent in Fernandez's said that being under forty-five should be helpful for promotion. Similarly, 54 percent of the managers in Bowman's study and 52 percent in Fernandez's believed that being over forty-five was harmful to advancement. These studies showed that age clearly was believed to be, and actually was, a factor in promotions.

In a 1976–78 study I found that the older the manager the more likely he or she was to believe that age was an obstacle—13 percent of the managers thirty and under compared to 72 percent of those over fifty believed age was an obstacle to their advancement.

Our 1986 data suggest that, as America ages, we are viewing age as less important. In 1976–78, 48 percent of employees thought their age was irrelevant; in 1986, 64 percent believed it was. A lower percentage in 1986 than in 1976–78 saw age as an advantage. However, age is still a factor in the minds of 36 percent of the employees.

To discriminate against a manager because of age is as nonproductive as discriminating against him or her because of race and/ or gender. People age at different rates mentally and physically— that is, some sixty-five-year-olds are younger in body and mind than some forty-year-olds are. To use age as a promotion factor robs corporations of a vast supply of competent, energetic, and creative managers, especially as our population ages.

The following comments are from those who still view age as a factor.

> The 50-year-old white male has no chance for promotion any more.
>
> —white, male, middle-level manager

> I've just about decided that, given my age, I may not even make promotion to senior clerk, least of all to something more challenging.
>
> —black, female, craftsworker

> I think the company is treating employees very badly by creating the atmosphere that 50 years old is old and experience is not required any more. They have a meeting and tell people to look for another job, inside or outside the company. They talk a good story about how employees are the number one resource, but they get rid of employees with little thought of how they will get along on a pension that is below poverty level. No loyalty to employees.
>
> —American Indian, male, middle-level manager

In my corporate experience, age becomes a factor primarily when a corporation is looking for an excuse not to promote an employee or to refuse him or her a lateral assignment, additional training, or so forth. If by direct or indirect statements a company uses age as a reason for a negative decision on a person's career, the employee should recognize the signals: this is probably a smoke screen covering up the real reason the company does not want to promote, train or move the person laterally.

Impact of Business Growth and Competition

Growth of business and economic conditions, and competition for the desired position, can influence anyone's career. Forty-two percent of the employees believe business conditions and 32 percent believe competition will be obstacles to their achieving their desired positions. Women (40 percent) are more likely than men (24 percent) to see competition for the desired positions as an obstacle. There are no significant differences of opinion among the races. These factors clearly suggest that, if one is upwardly mobile, selecting the correct firm is of crucial importance, especially considering that competition for desired positions is affected not only by the economy and business but also by the changing demographics of the work force. Numerous articles, television stories, and government reports have noted that the influx of foreign goods and "the new competitive world economy" have heightened job insecurity as U.S. companies shrink, close facilities, and move operations overseas. At the same time, the number of women entering the labor force on a full-time basis is increasing dramatically. Another factor is the large number of young, well-educated people who are competing for the same entry-level jobs. Still another complication is that the "baby boomers" and the post-World-War-II babies are approaching middle age and are anxious to improve their job status, while economic predictors forecast fewer opportunities for economic advancement. Add to these factors the increasing numbers of educated minorities entering the work force and one can readily see that the supply of and demand for good job opportunities are way out of kilter.

Several comments from our participants document this anxiety-ridden picture:

> Competition is an obstacle when the "baby boomer" effect doesn't allow for many opportunities due to too many in mid-age, mid-career life status.
>
> —white, female, lower-level manager

> Because of the company's downsizing, I feel that I am more or less locked into my present position, especially in the town I am now in.
>
> —black, female, craftsworker

> With our constant downsizing and the blockage at middle and upper management by old white males, there are few opportunities for minorities and women.
>
> —black, male, middle-level manager

Opportunities for advancement seem so bad that if I were not at upper management now, I would seriously consider leaving the company.

—white, male, upper-level manager

This last comment suggests good advice for the person who desires to advance up the corporate ladder. If you are in a no-growth company with few opportunities, get out and find greener pastures. A word of caution: most companies in a no-growth or slow-growth area will try to sell most of their average and all of their above-average employees a bill of goods by urging them to wait out the rough times and assuring them that the company will take care of them. Do not believe it—look out for yourself!

Impact of Bosses, Mentors, and Politics

This section discusses three factors that could have considerable impact on one's career: bosses, sponsors, and political skills. Let's look at bosses first.

Almost equal percentages of employees see their bosses as an asset (33 percent), as irrelevant (40 percent), and as an obstacle (27 percent) to their achieving their desired position.

Many employees do not really appreciate how influential bosses can be, in a negative sense. Very strong bosses with an excellent reputation who have reached their summit, as well as others who are still rising stars, can be very helpful to one advancing up the corporate ladder. However, most bosses are not powerful enough to single-handedly help a subordinate advance into middle and upper management. Many bosses, regardless of reputation, can hurt one's career simply by making some subtle negative comments. True or not, these comments become lethal weapons in the minds of those competing or hostile employees who oppose a person's advancement.

Another important fact about most bosses is that their primary concern is themselves and their own careers, and most do not have the time, inclination, or the energy to support a subordinate or assist in his or her development. Some employees make the mistake of believing that, because their bosses' careers have apparently "ended," these bosses no longer see subordinates as a competitive threat. This is a serious mistake. I have seen bosses who have been passed over numerous times, whose background, education, and age are all against them, turn on subordinates whom they believe are competition and hold up, if not end, their careers. As the next chapter will suggest, the most important lesson corporate employees can learn about their relationships with their bosses is how to manage them rather than being managed by them. If you can manage your boss, you enhance your chances of gaining his or her support or neutralizing any potential negative effect your boss can have.

While many bosses are not able to help their subordinates make it into middle and upper management, higher-level sponsors and mentors can. Let me state outright that if one has the right sponsor or mentor, in most situations one can be what one is, one can make mistakes, one can even violate company practices, and still one will survive and prosper. Most corporations do not want to admit this, but it is true. Many corporations do not even want to admit that their companies *have* sponsors and mentors. The great reluctance to grant formal recognition to this follows Freud's description of the dynamic of "resistance," largely because this is frequently a very subjective, emotionally-charged, irrational relationship.[17] Top management wants employees to believe that all is fair and equitable in promotions; it is difficult to admit that some employees have mentors or sponsors.

Let's look into the mentoring concept in more detail.

While 28 percent of all employees see a mentor or sponsor as an advantage to their achieving their desired position, 20 percent of the men and 13 percent of the women believe a mentor will be an obstacle. Fifty-nine percent of the women and 52 percent of the men believe a mentor will be irrelevant to their success. These people have bought into the myth that in the corporation everyone has an equal chance and that mentorship is nonexistent. As a white, female craftsworker wrote: "Why should anyone need a sponsor or mentor? Their work should speak for them." Blacks (24 percent) are most likely to see a mentor as an obstacle. Sixteen percent of the whites and 19 percent of the other minorities concur. Several comments from the study participants are useful.

> I said a mentor was an obstacle because I can't find one.
>> —black, female, lower-level manager

> Company politics and a sponsor/mentor are most important. Without both, you cannot move in this company.
>> —white, female, middle-level manager

> My mentor turned on me! Why? I don't know?
>> —Hispanic, male, middle-level manager

> The only people who have gotten anywhere in this company are those who have mentors.
>> —white, male, upper-level manager

> As a relative newcomer to this company, I enjoy and appreciate my job, peers and company. The boss I have is the best I've had in 16 years of professional life and my job is challenging. I feel grossly impaired for future promotion and development, though, due to my lack of "networking contacts," sponsorship and political positioning.
>> —white, male, upper-level manager

> In the company's new emphasis on pluralism, there appears to be no chance for a white male without a sponsor or mentor. My only regret is that I didn't leave when I had an opportunity to leave at a much greater salary level. I only stayed because I assumed that possibly an opportunity would open up here. How wrong I was.
>> —white, male, middle-level manager

Levinson wrote about the importance of mentors and suggested that women and minorities are at a disadvantage in this key area. He noted that many managerial skills are taught through the apprentice-master relationship. Because women and minorities are generally excluded from these informal relationships, their chances of advancement are limited.[18]

Expanding on the concept of mentorship, R. America and B. Anderson wrote that sponsors should display confidence in the judgment of their junior executive by showing willingness to share personal concerns, as well as to listen to the problems and doubts of others. "A real sponsor will tell you things he wouldn't tell others in the firm. If such trust is absent, the relationship probably is not really a sponsoring one." They observe that the sponsor's stakes should also be out on the table: "Strictly altruistic sponsorship can be dangerously close to paternalism and cannot long be an attractive arrangement." Real sponsorship is reciprocal, a fact that is largely ignored. Often, sponsors are seen as "doing a favor." In reality, sponsors themselves gain valuable support and information.[19]

M. London and S. Stumpf cite Kram in support of a number of notions on mentorship:

> Kram found that developmental relationships between junior and senior managers provide career functions and psychosocial functions that enhance the development of both managers. Career functions are those elements of the relationship that enhance career advancement. Examples are coaching, exposure to managers at higher levels, protection in the face of criticism from above, and challenging work assignments.
>
> Psychosocial functions are those elements of the relationship that enhance the feeling of self-competence and effectiveness as a manager. Examples are role modeling, counseling, and friendship.[20]

One important point that America, Anderson, and London do *not* make is that the mentors select their protégés and not vice versa. Another is that one can quickly become a political liability to the mentor and find oneself out in the cold.

In addition, many minorities and women, recognizing that they have a more difficult time finding sponsors, attempt to become the "image of a promotable." That is, they attempt to emulate the dominant race and gender group in thought and spirit in the hope that they will be more acceptable. This is a dysfunctional approach to the problem. The most important factor for minorities and women, as well as white males, to bear in mind is that in most cases a sponsor selects his or her protégé not only because they share some common reference point but because the protégé has some unique quality that distinguishes him or her from the masses of managers.

Dealing with one's boss, getting the job done, finding a mentor, and getting promoted are political processes. Yet my 1986 study found that 45 percent of the participants believe that their political skills are irrelevant to their achieving their desired position.

Those who believe their political skills are irrelevant have bought into the corporate "Hyppocratic oath" that politics do not exist or are minimal. On the contrary, politics are the essence of corporate life and thus corporate advancement. One of the most important qualities needed to make it into middle and upper management is political astuteness.

As DeLorean explained:

> This is because men rose in power who did not seem to have the capabilities or broad business outlook necessary. They had gotten into power because they were part of a management system which, for the most part, put personal loyalties from one executive to another and protection of the system above management skills; and put the use of corporate politics in the place of sound business leadership.[21]

The next chapter deals extensively with corporate politics.

Conclusions

Data and comments from the gamut of survey participants clearly demonstrate that we have all been fed a great deal of propaganda about advancement opportunities and who gets them. The inherent nature of the pyramid-shaped bureaucracy is that opportunities are very limited, at the middle and even more so at the upper levels. The vast majority of employees will fail to achieve their ambitions.

Those who get ahead in corporate America do so, in large part, not on merit and ability but on subjective criteria such as race, gender, age, schools attended, and so on. The more you are like the corporate leaders, both physically and mentally, the greater your chances are for advancement. Let's review the essentials of why bureaucracies promote at all. Merton and others accurately observed that the main purpose of promotions, pensions, incremental salaries, and various bonuses is "to provide incentives for disciplined action and conformity to the corporate way of doing things."[22] Since most corporate employees are upwardly mobile in mental attitude and since human beings, by culture, always desire more than we have, the promise of promotion for correct behaviors is a very strong motivating factor.

A. Wheelis put forth some additional interesting conceptions on how and why human beings conform:

> Nowadays the sense of self is deficient. The questions of adolescence—"Who am I?" "Where am I going?" "What is the meaning of life?" receive no final answers. Nor can they be laid aside. . . .
>
> Personal identity does not become fixed, does not, therefore, provide an unchanging vantage point from which to view experience. Man is still the measure of all things, but it is no longer the inner man that measures, it is the other man. Specifically, it is the plurality of men, the group. And what the group provides is shifting patterns, what it measures is conformity."[23]

As the next chapter demonstrates, making it in the corporate structure requires recognition that bureaucracies are social systems with a whole set of acceptable acts, behaviors, mannerisms, dress, life-styles, and other factors that are designed to control employees and thus maintain the "bureaucratic social system," which ultimately produces goods and services. Employees who assist in maintaining the "social system" are rewarded, valued, and encouraged to continue their conformity. M. J. Gannon simply makes explicit what other writers have implied: "In technical society, the rhetoric of merit provides a thinly veiled rationale for a process of organizational cloning."[24]

Most readers will say that they know of nonconformists who have made it. Many, in fact, consider themselves to be nonconformists. The only way a true nonconformist can make it is to be so good and so lucky that several higher-level managers support him or her. All nonconformists, or potential nonconformists, who are intent on making it in the corporate world should recognize that if the corporation has reason to "downsize" (that is, lay off people), they will be much more vulnerable than average-performing conformists.

Those who become members of the corporate culture must

make crucial decisions about their lives and how they will conform. R. Unger accurately describes this dilemma: "To the extent they sacrifice the private self to the public one, they surrender their individual identities. When they try to cast off convention and to follow their own course without definite roles, they undergo the disintegration of the unity of self. To suffer at the same time from resignation and disintegration has become the ordinary circumstance of moral life."[25]

Ferguson has stated, "as the cost of conformity is resignation, while the cost of resistance is disintegration; like other oppressed people, the victims of bureaucracy find that, whatever course of action they choose, the range of possible choices is determined by the organizational environment bureaucratic capitalism."[26]

G. Ritzer supports this viewpoint. He noted how stress can have a deleterious effect on managers' ambitions for advancement:

> The fact is that occupational stress, in whatever occupational category, is associated with a number of personal problems. Upwardly mobile managers, who typically have extraordinary workloads and great pressure and responsibility, have far greater incidence of heart disease, ulcers, arthritis, stroke, and various forms of mental illness. Then, too, job-related stress may manifest itself in a series of behaviors such as alcoholism, drug abuse, and even suicide. Even those who are successful in their efforts to move up in the organization are subjected to stress.[27]

In this chapter I suggest that in order to advance in corporate America one must be the "image of the promotable" manager. It helps to have a supportive boss; it is important to have a mentor, and it is essential to have political skills. However, there is much more to advancing and surviving in corporate America. The next chapters deal with additional issues.

5
How to Sort through the Corporate Games and Make Them Work for You

Most readers no doubt have begun to develop some strategies for making it into the middle and upper levels of management in corporate America. This chapter analyzes these survival tactics, with a focus on the practical.

In an effort to concentrate on realities, I inevitably propose some strategies that are not popular—strategies that are, in fact, forbidden discussion in the halls of corporate America and American business schools. The realities I cite and advice I give can apply to all corporations, despite the fact that some are fairer and/or less bureaucratic than others. The bibliography lists several excellent books on some basic tactics and strategies for survival in corporate America.

Theodore Caplow correctly notes that organizations are like machines with a multitude of specialized moving parts, which invariably break down and must be repaired. Unlike machines, functioning organizations are composed of human beings, who, as we have seen, are not totally predictable, and who in fact often have their own objectives and goals that conflict with the overall purposes of the organization.[1] All business organizations have their hierarchies, their breed of politics, their corporate cultures, their identities, organizational charts, rules and regulations, formal and informal networks, symbols, rituals, customs, and vocabularies. They have many people seeking a few promotions, and consequently a highly competitive environment. All corporations have their wide spectrum of "unhealthy" people.

Only by learning to "read" people and by understanding themselves can employees develop a clear understanding of the true nature of the corporate game. Then they can begin to develop strategies to enhance their chances of surviving and making it in the corporate fishbowl.

Reviewing the Issues

First of all, you must remember that corporate opportunities are limited, that we do not live in a meritocracy, and that your company is an irrational, political, social system that values conformity over risk taking and difference. Because of these facts and our ingrained tendency to ignore them, corporate employees will always have complaints about their jobs and careers.

How does one effectively deal with these issues? How does one enhance his or her chances of making it in corporate America? Let's now look at some tactics one can use to survive in the corporate fishbowl.

Understanding People

As mentioned earlier, a popular belief in corporate America is that managers should not try to be psychologists. Nonsense! Survival in the corporate fishbowl demands that one have a clear understanding of the psychological mind set of the people one is dealing with and those who can influence one's career. You need to know the other person's "real self." Because business situations always come down to "people" situations, the more you know about the person you are dealing with, the more you can enhance your career. It is crucial that you form your own opinion of people; do not naively accept the opinions of others.

Many of our motives arise not from external factors but from the inner workings of our own personalities. Thus we cannot predict how an individual will act in particular instances unless we have a fix on her or his personality as a whole. Gaining such understanding can be very difficult, especially in the corporate fishbowl where people try to hide their true selves as a survival tactic. It is considered inappropriate generally to discuss one's personal feelings, and especially in a corporate setting. This means that what we hear is in no way a realistic or reliable reflection of other people's personal thoughts. Indeed, some people, particularly those who are insecure or not pleased with what they see in themselves, will deliberately project a false image just as those with feelings of inferiority will often overcompensate by bragging or putting on an air of superiority. In addition, as corporate clones tend to avoid as anathema any self-examination it is often extremely difficult for them to explain honestly and accurately what they feel or why they believe in a certain way.

E. Goffman made these relevant comments about behavior: "[In] situations where a subordinate must take orders or suggestions and must go along with the situation as defined by subordinates . . . we often find that although the subordinate is careful not to threaten those who are . . . in charge of the situation, he may be just as careful to show . . . that he is not capitulating completely to the work situation in which he finds himself."[2]

Most of us are brought up to believe that people are basically good, kind, and honest, but from an early age we experience great conflict and pain, pain administered by parents, siblings, peers, adults, and society. Most parents *try* to be good parents; they try to protect us, teach us, nurture and mold us. They tell us to be honest and open; yet how many of us have really talked openly to our parents about sensitive problems? How many of us have felt that our parents did not tell us the truth about crucial issues like sex? How many of us have felt that our parents had their favorite child who could do no wrong, who got more than he or she deserved? The point is that if we have conflict and problems with our own blood relatives around issues of support, honesty, and fairness, why should we expect that most people in corporations, who are strangers, can be trusted, supportive, or fair?

As the philosopher Sissela Bok said, we *all* lie.

We sense differences among . . . choices; but whether to lie, equivocate, be silent or tell the truth in any given situation is often a hard decision. Hard because duplicity can take so many forms, be present to such different degrees, and have such purposes and result. Hard also because we know how questions of truth and lying inevitably pervade all that is said or left unspoken within our families, our communities.[3]

The ways that we are supposed to act within a role—and the ways that we would feel comfortable acting—can cause this confusion and sometimes neurotic behavior. Although I don't feel that people can be categorized into a few broad categories, numerous psychologists have attempted to define the various types of managers by categorizing them into a few distinct types. For example, Michael Maccoby has proposed five types of managers: the team builders, the facilitators, the experts, the administrators, and the innovators.[4] Although these classifications can be useful, I believe they are simplistic, encourage stereotyping, and ignore the complexities of human relationships. Most people have a combination of traits, and each individual is unique. A successful manager must understand this concept of uniqueness and individuality.

Categorization like Maccoby's does not allow for the fact that people behave differently in different situations. I have seen people act one way with the boss, another with their peers, and still another with their subordinates. An even different behavior pattern is evident when members of the various groups are together. If you are astute enough, however, you can get beyond the obvious behavior to the heart and mind of the person. Erik Erikson wrote that "from the point of view of psychological economy, 'bosses' and 'machines,' are a danger to the American identity, and thus to the mental health of the nation." Models of success are those who get by on "what [they] can appear to be." They make industrial "functioning" itself a value above all other values by use of "a machinery kept deliberately complicated in order that it may remain dependent on the hard-bitten professional and expert of the 'inside track.'" Erikson concluded, "That these men run themselves like machinery is a matter for their doctor, psychiatrist, or undertaker. That they view the world and run the people as machinery becomes a danger to man."[5]

What are some strategies for understanding people? There is no simple formula. If your company employs 300,000 people, you have 300,000 unique individuals to understand.

To understand a person, it is essential to interact with him or her not only in the work environment where the corporate faces are usually on but also at work-related and non-work-related social functions. In these casual situations people are most likely to reveal their true selves. You should go so far as to invite people to social functions for the sole purpose of finding out their true nature.

At these functions limit your own alcohol intake. Let the others do the drinking, and when they begin to let their guards down, you can begin probing, watching behaviors, and listening to conversations. It has always amazed me how one drink can get some of the seemingly most controlled people to open up and reveal their true selves.

Learn as much as you can about the personal lives of the people you are trying to influence: how they live and what they do outside of work. This will give you some key indications of who they really are. You may consider it inappropriate to probe into other people's personal lives, but the fact is that other people and the corporation itself do it all the time. Gain the confidence of key people. Get to know their family members, who often will readily share with you some very important information about the person. Discover several areas of common interest—like good wine, readings, the theatre, or gourmet foods. Use these as further entrée into their minds.

Be particularly attentive to how people handle others as you travel with them on business trips. How do they behave at different types of activities outside the office? How do they interact with waitresses, waiters, and bellhops? How do they accept and interact with different types of people? Are they at ease or are they uncomfortable?

Test people by acting in a manner you would not normally use to see how they respond. Demand things to which you know you have no right. Be exceptionally kind to people when it is not called for. Be exceptionally helpful to people when you do not have to be. And watch the responses.

Personally, I dislike the "rumor mill," or office gossip, but listening to it can provide information that might be helpful in understanding a coworker or in confirming or contradicting your own opinion. Use it not as a sole source but as one of many sources of information and insight. Another use of the rumor mill is as a test of people. Share a spicy tidbit (true or untrue) with one person, telling him or her that it is strictly confidential, and see whether it finds its way into the rumor mill.

The work environment is not the best setting in which to gain a true understanding of people, but it can be useful. Remember, however, that most people are playing a role at work and are not, therefore, revealing themselves fully. One key is to watch how people react nonverbally as well as verbally, where they sit in meetings, the expressions on their faces, whether they are attentive or in their own world, whether they move around in a meeting or in a conversation.

While some of these tactics might seem inappropriate and/or unethical, they are necessary to survive and to make it into middle and upper management because moving up is a strategic, difficult game.

Certain basic views about people are, in my opinion, essential to being a successful manager. Centuries ago Machiavelli had the insight to recognize that the nature of human beings is always to desire more than we can get. A related concept is that we all fool ourselves into believing that we are better than we are. The person with an inflated sense of his or her own ability sets himself or herself up for almost inevitable disappointment. Those who underestimate their capabilities, however—and some do, even in corporations—consign themselves to failure. Overconfidence can be hazardous, but some self-confidence is absolutely essential.

Something else that you must understand about people is that they come into the corporation to advance and gain power. Most people aren't working because they love the company or primarily because they love to work. Although no employee will publicly admit it, most of them spend considerable time in activities that are at least partially aimed at acquiring or maintaining power for themselves. The most insidious thing about this aspect of human behavior is that most employees are not even "aware of how much time they spend or the exact methods they use in acquiring power, because they do it so intuitively."[6]

This common drive to advance and gain power creates—in a

bureaucratic structure with limited opportunities and resources to "fully reward" all—conflicts and problems that make people act in a way that most would deny.

You must ascertain where people "are coming from" as quickly as possible. Then you must be prepared to change your mind if you find that you have made a judgment error or if the person really does change. Once you understand the person, however, do not necessarily try to change or challenge him or her. Try to use the knowledge you have about this person to your advantage.

Dealing with Bosses, Peers, and Subordinates

Those whom you must understand are your bosses, peers, and subordinates. Many good books listed in the bibliography have valid suggestions for dealing with these people; therefore, I shall focus on a few crucial concepts.

One is that you must learn how to manage all of these groups— your boss as well as your subordinates and peers.

Another is that one management style will not be sufficient to deal with the multitude of personalities you will encounter in accomplishing your job. Regardless of work group, some people will respond to kindness, others to threats, others to a combination of the two. Some people require a lot of direction and control; others do not. Again, I am referring not only to subordinates but to peers and bosses. No matter how reluctant we are to admit it, in most cases our bosses are the most important influences on our career. As M. A. Allison and E. Allison wrote: "A good working relationship with your superiors is the foundation of being a successful middle manager. Without that relationship, you will expend needless time and effort that could more productively be used in doing your job."[7]

The best advice I can give about bosses is that no matter how weak and ineffective they might be, don't take them on. If you do, you will lose because top management will assume that if you can successfully take on your boss, you can also successfully take on the corporate hierarchy, and they will never allow that to happen. Manage your boss and keep him or her out of trouble. Make him or her look good even if he or she is bad. Don't challenge; manage!

For example, one group had a boss who was fairly incompetent and not a risk taker; therefore, his subordinates never told him about any risky plans until they were well under way. He appreciated this because he knew his limitations and so did his subordinates. Another example of "boss management" was the case of the paranoid and distrusting manager, who wanted to know "everything" his subordinates were doing. Several new subordinates, recognizing his affinity for visiting people, decided they would manage his paranoia by keeping him so busy visiting various parts of their organization, meeting the "people," presenting awards, and attending retirements that he no longer had time to be paranoid about the crucial decisions his subordinates were making for him in order to run the business.

With regard to subordinates, let me say simply that some disgruntled, unhappy subordinates will always believe that they are treated unfairly. One way to keep employees from focusing their energies on criticizing higher-ups is to involve them in finding the solutions to their problems through committees and task forces. As the manager, your job is to keep these problem-solving groups together, active, and dealing with the problems they identify. When they come up with reasonable solutions, support them. Where appropriate, make subordinates responsible for implementing the plans. Finally, make them responsible for evaluating and refining the solutions. This method not only gives the subordinates a sense of ownership in the problems; it focuses on the problem and its true source, to which, in many cases, all the parties have contributed. You will find, in most instances, that once they are given the problems and discover how to resolve them, most employees will find many of the "problems" not important enough to spend time on; if, however, you let them off the hook, you will find that you once again become the focus of their attention. Your subordinates must recognize that you give top priority and support to their solving their problems.

With regard to peers, you must recognize that you can really trust very few of them because, regardless of age or lack of potential to advance, most of them are competing with you. On certain issues, however, you and your peers can be natural allies. What you must do is actively seek out opportunities where your interests are mutual and cultivate relationships while still remaining alert to those situations in which you have competing interests. You must actively manage these relationships as well.

Allison and Allison wrote that mutual support, problem-solving advice, and counseling activities are uniquely suited to peer relationships, since peers can learn from each other's experiences. Peer relations are nonhierarchical; neither party is responsible for evaluating the performance of the other. Although the competitiveness inherent in corporate bureaucracy can stifle cooperation among peers, it is possible to compete and collaborate simultaneously. It is important to be selective; for example, to discuss strategies for managing work and even family pressures with a peer, "but not discuss a particular job opportunity to which both aspire." The key is to identify shared and complementary needs, and steer clear of stirring up competitive areas.[8]

In conclusion, bosses, peers, and subordinates are clearly enmeshed in interdependent relationships. It is foolhardy for employees to believe that they can be successful in performing their jobs and/or advancing in the corporation without the support of all three groups. To survive and make it in the corporate structure you must actively manage these three groups; you can't let them manage you. You must be the initiator, the driver of ideas and plans. You must know who they are and what it takes to get them to do what you want them to do.

Knowing Yourself

To truly understand and manage other people, you must first and foremost know yourself. You must be honest with yourself; your primary loyalty must be to yourself, not to the corporation; and you must assume responsibility for your career.

In addition, you must clearly understand both formal and informal rules, structures, norms, and cultures of the corporation. You must recognize that many corporations do not act or think as they say they do.

The most important survival technique in the corporate fishbowl is to understand who *you* really are. Many of us think we know, but we really do not. A. N. Schoonmaker wrote: "You may feel that you are too honest to deceive yourself, that you can accept the truth about yourself, but you probably cannot. You are as human as everyone else, and everyone tries to preserve her/his self-image. That is why psychological counseling takes so long."[9]

As I noted earlier, we are all neurotic; the extent of our neurosis depends on our mental makeup at birth, how our parents or those who brought us up cared, nurtured, loved, and molded us; and how society has treated and valued us. Because our personalities developed in large part when we were babies and young children, it is difficult for us to understand what really makes us tick.

For this reason I strongly recommend psychoanalysis or some other type of professional help in understanding yourself. Such guided introspection will also help you to understand other people. It will improve your ability to read signals from people and to understand when you do and don't contribute to your successes, failures, challenges, and problems. It will help you to understand better when you are being manipulated and treated unfairly, and when you are manipulating and being unfair. It will help you to develop an inventory of your strengths and weaknesses.

Clearly understanding your strengths and weaknesses will allow you to develop strategies that will enhance your career and your ability to deal with the bureaucratic structure without much damage to your person. It will help you to recognize whether your failure to make it to the pinnacle of corporate America was due to your deficiencies, to the deficiencies of bureaucracies and the people who control them, or a combination thereof. A key point to remember is that in general strengths and weaknesses are not fixed. They depend on the situation and circumstances: a strength in one context can be a weakness in another. As noted earlier, a key survival tactic is to accurately determine when to be controlling, compromising, or fair, and when not to be.

Another way to understand your weaknesses and strengths and who you are is to have some trusted confidants, a few in your organization and a few outside it, against whom you can bounce your feelings and ideas. The ones inside your organization may have a better picture than you of the work issues you need to understand and deal with and those outside will be more objective because they are not caught up in your corporate environment.

Self-understanding will improve your chance of advancing because it will make you more aware of the image you are presenting and why. You will not be lying to yourself or denying yourself. You will be better able to create the image that is necessary to advance in your corporation.

Probably the most fundamental question all of us must ask ourselves is "To what extent do we want to try to be what the corporation says we *should* be in order to advance?" This is a moral question with no right answer, and each individual must decide what makes him or her feel comfortable. Let me suggest, however, that very few people can be happy if they are trying to be only what other people want them to be. Eventually many corporate executives look at themselves in the mirror and say, "Was it all worth it? Is this what life is all about?" I once heard an older V. P. say to a forty-four-year-old white male who "peaked" at the upper-middle level of management after a meteoric rise, "I see you are still your own unique self. You are still marching to your own drummer." The younger man responded, "Yes, I am! Isn't that what life and living are all about?" The V. P. turned pale and acknowledged that he was right.

While it feels healthiest to be ourselves, some degree of conformity is essential in order to make it in the corporate world. Depending on the situation, we all have to do things such as holding our tongues, being nice to people we despise, and occasionally putting aside a value that is not essential to us as persons. Some people even resist conforming to rules such as "proper" business attire. However, as Schoonmaker noted, such battles are not worth fighting unless you are content to stay where you are in the company:

> You may feel that doing these things is a cop-out, a sacrifice of part of your identity. Perhaps you are right, but there is another viewpoint. Your identity is not just what you wear or the language you use; it is what you believe in and the strength of your character and self-confidence. If your sense of identity depends only on your clothes, you are really in bad shape, and letting your hair grow will not solve your identity problems.[10]

Healthy managers are those who have a keen sense of who they are, like themselves, conform because they want to, and recognize that they are conforming. By knowing yourself you will be able to determine more accurately your goals in life and what you are willing and unwilling to do to reach those goals. Understanding this, you will be better able to select the corporate environment that will give you the best chances for advancement and fulfillment of your goals.

Let me caution you that if your self-concept is based solely on extrinsic factors, such as income and management level, you are placing your self-worth, your identity, and your person in the hands of others. In addition, you will eventually lose that sense of self when you stop advancing or when you no longer receive the salary increases you believe you deserve.

I believe that to survive in corporate America you must distance yourself from the corporate world and not place your identity in it. Allison and Allison wrote:

> When you are criticized for your work or your action, remind yourself that it is your work or, at most, your corporate image that is being criticized. The essential you is not being judged. . . . Although it may seem strange, when you are promoted or complimented, you must say to yourself: this is an evaluation of my efforts at work, not of me as a person. Certainly you should be pleased, but leave some distance, which will help you to retain your sanity and health in times of stress.[11]

While knowing yourself and others is crucial to your career success, letting people know only what you want them to know is also very crucial. One rule of thumb is to let people know only those things about you that are necessary. When it comes to your personal and family life, the less your colleagues know, the better—except for those matters that will present a picture that supports your company values. Inviting coworkers into your home under orchestrated conditions can sometimes be beneficial. However, you must make certain that you are clear about the purpose and in control of the situation.

In sum, unless you know and value yourself, you will find it very difficult to understand the true nature of the people you must work with in corporate America. Lack of such understanding will greatly decrease your chances of surviving in the corporate fish-bowl. In addition, it will create unnecessary stress and anxieties on your part because you will be unable to distinguish between your role and that of others in your successes and failures. You will not be equipped to understand and play the corporate game.

The Game

Survival in the corporate fishbowl must be regarded as a game, a political game, a power game, a manipulative game, and a vicious game. You must take it seriously but not too seriously. M. E. Di-mock notes that managers must shape their strategies according to the appropriate use of power, timing, and influence. Managers must be tacticians and philosophers: they must understand psychology and social forces. In other words, they must hone their skills as leaders. They do not operate in a fixed, self-contained vacuum but "must change their environment or adapt to it where necessary, and then try to influence the environment in any ways that seem indicated in order to accomplish the ultimate purposes of their program."[12]

Machiavelli noted that *how* one gets the job done is not relevant to most people. All that matters is whether one has achieved his or her end result: "Men in this respect are blind in judging good and bad actions from the results."[13]

On the other end of the spectrum, David McClelland argued that, while good managers have a strong motivation for power, that motivation is oriented toward institutional success, not toward personal aggrandizement.[14] If his hypothesis is true, then there are few good managers in corporate America.

All the talk about the "corporate good" and "teamwork" has little relevancy to most corporate types, except in the sense that these concepts satisfy their internal psychological needs and, to a much lesser extent, make it easier for the corporate bureaucracies to manipulate them. One principle of the game, therefore, is to understand that beyond the rhetoric of "the corporate good" lies very little substance. In corporate America, in most cases, the end justifies the means.

Related to this concept is the fact that the corporate game is played out not so much in the "formal" organization but in the informal one. It is, therefore, important to find out how the organization really works: Who are the power people? Who really makes the decisions? What are the true relationships in the organizational chart? Where are the factions? Where are the rivalries?

Remember that different games and situations have different sets of rules and styles of play. Be clear as to what they are. Be very careful when, where, and how you play. The more you control these factors, the more likely you are to be successful.

Also remember that, as in all games, you will lose some and win some. Whether you win or lose, you should use those experiences to refine and better your game. Do not allow yourself to sulk or become defensive. Don't let the game get you down; it is, after all, just a game. If you can't take the heat, you should seriously consider leaving the corporate "kitchen."

Corporate Politics

Most corporate executives, especially those at the upper levels, do not like to admit that politics exist in their company. However, politics exist in every company and at every level, varying only in degree. A number of writers have acknowledged this. Allison and Allison argued: "No chance. . . . Wherever there are people, there is influence, power, and competition. Add to this brew personality clashes, differing leadership styles, conflicting goals, limited budgets, and rapid change, and you have politics, corporate politics."[15]

The sources of such politics were first identified by Machiavelli centuries ago. He believed that political action is motivated by one's own ambition, followed by the fear of another's ambition. Both are fueled by greed, the desire for more than one has, and the belief that one deserves more than one gets.[16]

Politics, to me, is a double-edged sword; it can be both productive and destructive, and its value (and danger) are largely in the eyes of the beholders. The political process in itself is not harmful. Productively, politics can motivate a person to attempt to gain power, control, and influence so that he or she will be able to achieve work and/or personal career goals. Good political game-playing is constructively persuading people through fairly open, straightforward, honest dialogue, through various reward systems, and through the constructive use of power to do what one wants them to do.

The destructive aspects of corporate politics are exploitation, apple-polishing, backstabbing, lying, sabotaging, cheating, and so on. These negative manifestations of politics occur when people become willing to do whatever is necessary to get ahead. Sad to say, most people frown upon such activities, deny any involvement in them—but do them anyway. In fact, I would caution you to be very wary of those who protest that they do not engage in politics, that they are always honest, straightforward, fair, and on the up-and-up. If they are truly all of that, they will not need tell you so, certainly not more than once. Those who do so continually "protest too much."

Part of playing the game is learning how to disarm people, to throw them off balance. People often develop "second-hand" images of us through the judgment of others. If you perceive that your image is a negative one (for example, people believe that you don't listen, or that you are argumentative), try to do the opposite of what is expected. If people are able to predict your behavior, reactions, and thoughts, they will find it easy to develop strategies that will render you powerless, and you will lose the political game. Don't let this happen. Another crucial point to remember is that there is not one corporate political game but thousands, and the games change as the actors and actresses change. The rules, patterns, and traditions are modified by the actors and actresses in different groups and areas of a corporation. You cannot learn corporate politics in a classroom; you will learn only by experience and through coaching by knowledgeable political players.

A final, important factor to recognize is that you cannot ignore corporate politics or exclude yourself from them. The question is not whether to play but what *kind* of game to play.

Manipulation

Another technique that most corporate managers will not admit to using is manipulation. J. P. Kotter argued that many people think it is wrong to try to manipulate people and that doing so invites retaliation. He suggested that people who gain the reputation of being manipulators seriously undermine their own capacities for developing power and for influencing others. "Few people will want to identify with a manipulator and virtually no one accepts, at face value, a manipulator's sincere attempts at persuasion. In extreme cases, a reputation as a manipulator can completely ruin a manager's career."[17]

Maccoby believes that all manipulation is bad and that people resent managers who use their power "to manipulate, rather than motivate them." Manipulation, according to Maccoby, is to seduce, give false promises, mislead people in relationships, deceive them about opportunities, and provide unequal rewards and punishments. Companies hire those who demonstrate their motivation to work hard, and managers must nurture and develop this motivation, not frustrate it. Employees welcome the opportunity to express and develop themselves as members of a winning team and winners as individuals.[18]

Maccoby's distinction between manipulation and motivation is somewhat strained. To motivate, according to the dictionary, is to "provide a person with something . . . that causes a person to act."

To manipulate is to "control or play upon by artful, unfair, or insidious means especially to one's own advantage, to change by artful or unfair means so as to serve one's purpose."

Obviously, manipulation can be either artful or insidious. Motivation, on the other hand, involves no value judgments as to artfulness or insidiousness. In simplest terms, motivation and manipulation are ways of getting people to do things. The difference is a matter of semantics.

N. V. Iuppa lists a wide range of manipulative tactics and gives them names that most corporate types would reject, despite the fact that all corporate managers use the tactics themselves. For example, he puts forth these definitions: (1) *bribery*—something that is used to induce or influence; (2) *guilt*—feeling of culpability, especially for imagined offenses from a sense of inadequacy; and (3) *seduction*—leading astray, usually by persuasion or false promises.[19]

From the day we were born until we die, we are manipulated by our parents, television, peers, government, schools, and society, to name just a few. Manipulation, like politics, can be good or bad;

either way, it is part and parcel of the human condition. Being a successful member of a corporation is nothing more or less than being a successful manipulator!

Recognizing that manipulation is a natural part of human interactions, you must become very adept at using different strategies to manipulate different people. Iuppa made this important observation: "People tend to be more complex than you could ever imagine, and the things that motivate them are extremely hard to define. People's desires keep changing, and your employees may not ever be sure what they really want."[20]

You must also acknowledge that not only do you attempt to manipulate others psychologically but others try to and do manipulate you. Whether you call the process motivation or manipulation depends, in most cases, on whether you are the giver or the receiver, and that is often difficult to determine, depending on the level of the "game." There are not only thousands of games and players; there are various levels to each game.

Power

Power is another "dirty" word in America. A. Zaleznik and M. Kets de Vries wrote: "'Power' is an ugly word. It connotes dominance and submission, control and acquiescence, one man's will at the expense of another man's self-esteem. . . . Yet it is power, the ability to control and influence others, that provides the basis for the direction of organizations and for the attainment of social goals. Leadership is the exercise of power."[21]

McClelland has observed that "Americans, in general, are proud of having a high need to achieve but dislike being told they have a high need for power, at times to the point of neurotic obsession."[22] This is because people think of power in terms of exploitation and corruption. They therefore distrust those who openly seek power. In *The Greening of America*, Charles Reich argues, "It is not the misuse of power that is evil; the very existence of power is evil."[23]

Despite the general "dislike" for power, Machiavelli and those who write after him acknowledge that power is an essential ingredient in the climb up the corporate ladder. People use laws; beasts use force. The art of politics consists of combining the two. "Study and books do not suffice to rule a State," Machiavelli wrote. "Even Moses, although considered the instrument chosen by God to carry out His orders, was forced to resort to means not so far removed from those used by pagan princes."[24]

Iuppa wrote: "This most difficult and dangerous of all management techniques combines the logic and foresight of the chess player with the intelligence of the genius and the ruthlessness of Attila the Hun. Power is the name of the game, and your goal is to maneuver employees into situations where they have no choice but to do things your way."[25]

M. L. Loden believed that power is derived from two sources: position and personal characteristics. Power of position includes the allocation of resources (including financial, human, and technical) and hierarchical position (including organizational title, rank, contacts, and status). Personal power is derived from intrinsic qualities within an individual—skills, talents, and personality—rather than from external roles.[26]

According to Kotter, the degree of power needed to survive in corporate America depends on managers' job-related independence. This refers to the resources at their disposal for getting their job done. The more dependency, the more power-oriented behavior the manager needs to achieve success. In other words, "as job-related dependence increases, the relative frequency with which managers engage in the more "negative," riskier forms of power-oriented behavior tends to increase."[27]

Manipulating people and being political are both necessary to achieve what corporations and most of society respect most: power. To survive in corporate America, you must have the ability and willingness to acquire and use power. Most people understand that personal power is not granted but acquired. However, few people understand that they can assume more power if they just dare to go for it. More explicitly, I have seen people who, according to the organization charts, did not have authority, position, or "power" accomplish, initiate, or stop things only because they assumed the power and dared to take a risk. Corporate American culture, however, is not known for risk takers.

How do you assume power? One way is to create a perceived

or real dependency of others on yourself for resources, information, or emotional support that only you can give. Even if you do not actually have the resources or information, you can gain power if people believe that you have power. The bottom line to gaining power is that you must clearly understand the formal and informal networks. You must use many strategies, techniques, and resources and must realize that, in the end, the judgment of whether a tactic is moral or immoral rests with you. Others will try to persuade you that a tactic you are using to gain power is immoral—but they are often the very people who have used or will use the same tactic themselves. The more you limit the range of the tactics you will use to gain power, the weaker and the more vulnerable you become to other power plays.

Still another technique you can use is to give up some power in order to gain more at some future date. To do this you must be secure in yourself and clearly understand what you are giving up and what you expect in return. The old ward politicians in Chicago provided excellent examples of giving up some power to gain more.

Kotter wrote: "Managers who are effective at acquiring power tend to calculate the consequences of any action not only in terms of its organizational impact but also in terms of its effect on their power. . . . They recognize that power is too valuable to be wasted."[28]

M. E. Dimock noted that power relations are inherent in any managerial situation. Managers must be aware, ready to fight openly for survival. Whether in business or in government, leadership means a constant struggle against other power wielders; "fair contests fought along constructive lines." However, fighting as an end in itself is no longer socially useful. If competition and in-fighting are to cause social good rather than harm, power must be used as a legitimate means of effective management.[29]

Survivors, as I noted earlier, are those who not only have power but who recognize the other players and why they have power. One important but frequently overlooked source of power is secretaries. Nonmanagement in most cases, and low in the hierarchy, they are usually women, and many men refuse to believe that women have power or know how to use it. Secretaries in fact have power far beyond their positions and their gender. This is because most smart bosses trust, confide in, and depend on their secretaries much more than on anyone else. Secretaries, through their knowledge of their bosses' business and personal dealings, can be very helpful to others—or very unhelpful.

Recognizing the inherent power of the secretary holds two strategic implications for those who want to survive and move up in the corporation. The first is: Make your secretary your ally. Be sensitive to his or her needs, treat him or her as a colleague and not as a slave, and help him or her grow and advance professionally. The second is: Treat other secretaries, including those who work for your supervisors and top management, with respect and consideration. They are not only the gatekeepers to the executive suites; they often can speed up approval processes, and their comments about you—behind closed doors—can strongly influence the boss's opinion of you.

I conclude with two important cautions about power: One, be careful about how you treat people; someday one of them may be your boss. Two, as Machiavelli wrote, there is such a difference between how men live and how they ought to live that he who abandons what is done for what ought to be done learns his destruction rather than his preservation, because any man who under all conditions insists on making it his business to be good will surely be destroyed among so many who are not good.[30]

Loyalty

One of the most serious mistakes an employee can make is to buy into the corporate propaganda that an employee's first loyalty should be to the company. Many have believed that logic. However, just as you must be honest with yourself and know yourself, you must be loyal, first and foremost, to yourself. If the corporation gets in trouble and is forced to lay people off, you can be sure that your "company loyalty" will not protect you. The company's loyalty is to its own survival; yours should be to self-preservation. Furthermore, recognizing that vulnerability, you should consciously develop skills that will be marketable outside your own company. AT&T, which for over 100 years offered what amounted to lifetime employment, has in its recent "downsizing" terminated thousands of employees with many years of service, employees who were middle-aged, without advanced education, and with no real transferable skills. Despite AT&T's tradition of lifetime employment, it quickly moved to lay off these loyal employees when it felt they were a drag on the company's success. Even though most received what corporate America believes were substantial "exit packages," the personal toll of ending careers in mid-life has had a tragic impact. One needs to look no further than the Pittsburgh steel industry or the New England textile mills for similar examples.

A black, male craftsworker wrote: "Being a team employee for over twelve years now, I feel my dedication to the company is going to be rewarded by my ending up without a job."

Honesty

Once I would have recommended a consistent, straightforward, and honest approach to everyone in the corporate environment. My advice now, however, is that it does not always pay to be honest. To survive the corporate game and the political game, you must learn that, unfortunately, total honesty says only that you do not understand the reality of corporate life and you will doom yourself to failure.

Although candor and emotional honesty can be valuable assets in personal relations, "letting it all hang out" in a work setting is unwise, inappropriate, and often damaging. J. La Rouche and R. Ryan argued that, in order to achieve their goals in the work place, employees need to be selective about the specific truths they reveal, to choose their words wisely, and to choose carefully to whom they reveal information. Some people can't accept honest, straight talk. You have to make crucial decisions about honesty.[31] To avoid being dishonest, simply say nothing or decline to comment. Supporting this concept of limited openness and the need for tact and discretion, McCormack wrote: "Everyone's heard the twist on the cliche, 'Honesty is not always the best policy.' I think that's misleading, implying that sometimes in business it's okay to lie. It is more appropriate, and more accurate, to say: 'Honesty can be mitigated.' The truth can be couched in such a way that it is neither insulting nor self-destructive."[32]

In three instances, however, you should always be honest. The first is when you make a promise. If you make it, keep it. If, for some reason beyond your power, you can't keep it, explain honestly why you cannot do so. Do not simply ignore the matter. The second instance is when you make a mistake. Admit it. Never be defensive. Never point a finger at other people to protect yourself. If the company is going to block your progress, management will find a way to do so, and trying to cover up your mistakes won't prevent their action. Mistakes, in themselves, are not fatal. In fact, if you are not making mistakes, you are not trying hard enough. Iacocca, discussing one of his bosses, made some crucial points about mistakes:

> He accepted mistakes, provided you took responsibility for them. "Always remember," he would say, "that everybody makes mistakes. The trouble is that most people just won't own up to them. When a guy screws up, he will never admit it was his fault, not if he can help it. He will try to blame it on his wife, his mistress, his kids, his dog, the weather—but never himself. So if you screw up, don't give me any excuses. Go look at yourself in the mirror. Then come see me."[33]

Finally—and probably most important—you should always be honest with yourself.

Trust

Most of us have a natural tendency to trust other people. However, in the corporate fishbowl trusting too many people is foolish and naive. Trusting people before you have a very good understanding of them is also foolish and naive. If you are really in tune with yourself, you can after a short period of time identify the few people whom you can really trust. John Petrillo, a director at AT&T, noted: "We must trust each other personally before we trust each other professionally." While this statement is absolutely true, the bureaucratic structure, the limited opportunities and rewards, the competitive individual culture, and the corporate game make it difficult for trusting relationships to form on a personal, let alone a professional, level.

As you progress in your career, one reasonably reliable, tried-and-true method of ensuring that you have trusting people around you is to develop your own team.

Building Your Team

One of the first things you should do on a new job is to determine who in the organization should be on your team and who should not. Begin to develop a cadre of loyal team members whom you will bring along as you move up the corporate ladder; long-term working relationships and teamwork bonds people together. Remember, a great many of your personal successes will depend on your team. I strongly suggest that you begin by selecting your own secretary, who will be loyal and beholden to you and to no one else. In order to build an effective team and network, you must ignore the corporate hierarchy and the chain of command. By building your team, made up of people from all levels in your organization and from outside, you will establish a network to gather information from the various levels, information that will allow you to protect yourself, advance your career, and get your job done in a more effective, efficient fashion. The wider your support team, the more likely you are to survive. Many people rely on only one or two people, but people can die, get transferred, or leave the company. A multilevel, diverse team increases your access to information from the various levels and gives you a better view of the total company. If your team is made up of only subordinates, you will get only information from below, much of it filtered by those who are protecting themselves. If you rely only on a network of peers, most of them will consider you the competition, and their information will be unreliable at best. Information from the top in most cases is controlled, and—unless it originates at the top—it, too, is subject to filtering. When you have multilevel input, you have a better chance to evaluate and "flush out" the various reports.

Finally, your team should not be made up of your "clones." You don't want a lot of yes-men and yes-women. Your team should be diverse in terms of race, gender, age, political philosophy, and so on. Diverse work groups come up with better solutions because of their varied backgrounds and perceptions.

Managing with Equity

Some managerial social scientists will argue that you should treat all people equally. In my opinion, that is hogwash. If all subordinates were equal in talent, ability, and mental healthiness, you might be able to treat them all equally. However, in most organizations there is a key group of employees that all managers depend on, more so than on others. This group (which is generally, but not necessarily, the top performers) is composed of the creative types, the dependable ones, the ones who protect you. It makes no sense to treat the members of your team in the same way that you treat those who are not part of your team. Some people will call this favoritism, but I call it reality—and a crucial step in team building and trust building.

Your Attitude toward Work

I have seen, and our data show, that many people who feel they are not treated fairly and equitably by their company begin to perform below their abilities. While excellent or outstanding work is not a sure way of getting to middle and upper management, performing below your ability is a sure way of *not* getting the chance to make it to those levels. My strongest advice to anyone, no matter how unfairly you are treated, is always to perform to the best of your ability or voluntarily leave the company. If you do not, you are giving the company a reason not to promote or reward you and, in some cases, to fire you.

One way of doing an outstanding job is to approach your job in the opposite way from what normal corporate culture dictates. It is assumed, in corporate cultures, that those people are most valued who always make their jobs seem difficult, who say how much they are working and how busy they are. I believe, on the contrary, that your responsibility is to take complex problems and make them simple, not to make simple problems complex. It is extremely important to have a "can-do" attitude. You are not hired to explain why a job can't be done; you are hired to solve corporate problems and get the job done—at a profit for the stockholders.

An ongoing debate centers around the controversy of too much direction versus too little direction. It seems that many corporate employees continue to play out the parent/child role in work. When there is too much direction from above, they complain about the overly controlling boss; when there is too little direction, they complain that the boss (parent) doesn't have an interest in their work. Unless you were hired to do routine work, your chief value lies in your ability to direct yourself. If you want to advance in your career, you have to be able to take initiative. I discount the complaint that the boss doesn't give direction. In reality, that makes for an ideal situation. Your basic training for full responsibility is learning how to direct yourself in any situation, and the boss who allows you to do this—with nothing more than an occasional "go-ahead"—is doing you a tremendous favor. You have the opportunity to go full steam on your own, within, of course, some minimal parameters of the boss's thinking, and you will learn how to exercise your own independence.

In addition, I come from the school that says that you never turn down an additional work assignment, especially if you have people working for you. Your job as a manager is to figure how to get the work done. That is part of the excitement and challenge of the job. If, on occasion, you or your people simply cannot take on an additional task, your refusal will be understood if your previous responses have been to readily accept additional assignments. Saying that you should never turn down an assignment does not mean, however, that you should never ask for help. Only fools with oversized egos will never ask for help. Just be certain that you really need additional help and that you can justify it to those who will authorize it.

Similarly, saying that a task or problem is not your job is foolhardy. If the task or problem comes to you, it is ultimately your responsibility to see that it is completed. It *is* your job. If, however, you need additional information to do the job, don't hesitate to ask for it. If you pretend to know and blunder ahead, there is a very good chance that you will regret it.

This does not mean that you must never take risks and must know all the answers before you act. Being decisive is especially crucial when you first enter a job. You must establish your authority and your position, and the best way to do that is to be decisive. It is better to make a decision today, knowing 89 percent of the facts, than to delay the decision for a month to have 100 percent of the facts. Facts are a decision maker's tools, but they can't replace your intuition and your powers of interpretation. It is better to make a hundred decisions and risk being wrong twenty times than make ten decisions and be wrong twice. When you make more decisions, you accomplish more. If you make a wrong decision, don't dwell on it. Learn from it and try not to repeat mistakes.

Townsend gave additional valid advice on decision making: "Make every decision . . . in the light of this question: 'How would I do this job if I owned the company?' And then do it that way, to the extent that you can. Most of your competitors will be making decisions based on the question: 'What will make me look good to my boss?' or 'What does my boss want me to do?' or even 'What exactly did he tell me to do?' None of these questions will lead to effective action.[34]

Managing Your Career

To enhance your chances of making it in corporate America, you must not follow the traditional view that says you should be a passive player in your performance and potential evaluations, career planning, and training and development needs. I say you must be an active player; you must take control of your career and of your responsibilities. Let's look at this suggestion in more detail.

You must first take the responsibility of getting candid, honest feedback about your performance and potential. Many bosses will avoid giving this; however, if you fail to get it, you could harbor false hopes and expectations for years. It is your responsibility to judge whether your boss is being honest with you or not.

Only with accurate judgments on your part will you be able to make the correct career decisions. One way to tell whether you are getting accurate feedback on your performance and potential is to see how honest and straightforward your boss is on little, noncontroversial issues. Then move to bigger, controversial, and sensitive issues. Where does your boss begin to give you "dishonest, corporate or evasive" responses? Another signal as to how honest your boss will be with you is how honest he or she is with other people in and outside the organization.

Other telltale signs indicate the integrity of your boss and the type of feedback you can expect. If you are very observant, you may begin to notice a change in the boss's behavior about three months before the formal yearly appraisal. If you have had a good relationship and, in September or October, he or she begins to question your vouchers, disagree with you more frequently than in the past on little things, and magnify minor incidents into "federal cases," you will very likely be in trouble with your appraisals. The boss is trying to justify in his or her mind why your rating will not be as high as you expect it to be. At the same time you will begin to notice less frequent interaction, less eye contact, and less camaraderie. If you pick up these signals, you should begin to develop your case without letting your boss put you on the defensive. In all likelihood, your boss will try to "save face" with you by saying that he or she tried the damnedest to get you a high evaluation but his or her peers and superiors were not supportive. Whatever the boss has to say about your performance and potential, he or she is likely to encourage you to do better in the coming year and promise that you will be justly rewarded.

Any time your performance or potential evaluation is a shock to you, you have let yourself down by allowing your boss to avoid giving you honest feedback throughout the year, on an ongoing basis.

A strategy that you can use to take power away from your boss, or from a small group of superiors who have total control over your performance and potential, is to promote yourself to others on every occasion. Rewards and promotions almost never go to those who believe that their quiet, hard work will get them ahead.

Many employees are reluctant to promote themselves because they feel it is not "polite" or "appropriate"; however, if you do not promote yourself, who else will? Remember that everyone in corporate America is deep down inside looking out for number one. One way to promote yourself is to become visible. Try to get into a key job that will gain exposure for you to people inside your department and outside of it. While there is no sure way of getting these jobs, you can enhance your chances by knowing which jobs give a lot of visibility, developing your skills for these jobs, quite openly lobbying (depending on the situation) for these jobs, and finally by making a concerted effort to form relationships, both personal and professional, with people who have control over these jobs. Do not wait for the job to come to you; go after it. You might not get it, but you will maximize your chances of getting it.

Another visible and also self-protective strategy is to gain as much exposure outside of the company as possible, through writing, speaking, teaching, community activities, and political activities. Join professional organizations and become an active member and leader. While these activities are usually thought of as incentives for promotion, they are also ways to protect your livelihood in case of the loss of a job. What is more, such exposure can open up competitive job opportunities while you are employed, providing in some cases an opportunity for career advancement or, at least, leverage within your own company to negotiate for a promotion or raise.

Visibility always comes to those who see change as an opportunity rather than a problem. You can become visible if you help to lead change, and change is occurring more rapidly in the 1980s than ever before in corporate America. Change should be viewed by managers who want to succeed as exhilarating and refreshing. Kanter also notes that:

> Change brings opportunities when people have been planning for it, are ready for it, and know what to do when it comes. What is more, change also provides an opportunity for entrepreneurs to offer "change-management" products and services, turning other people's confusion into profitable business.[35]

In most cases, success depends upon distinguishing yourself from the crowd, whose members are about as qualified as you are and who are your true competitors. The one sure, but risky, way to stand above the crowd is to manage with a flair and to do things in a creative way.

You must be a risk taker and create change—especially if you do not fit the corporate image. However, distinguishing yourself from the crowd does not *guarantee* you a promotion. In fact, in many instances being a risk taker, creating change, and managing with a flair may detract from your chances. Change can be threatening, particularly to people who are insecure. The down-side risks, however, are fewer than the up-side rewards.

As Machiavelli wrote: "Results are often obtained by impetuosity and daring which could never have been obtained by ordinary methods."[36]

Despite our discussion of daring strategies, more career goals will be reached if you simply manage your career and develop realistic career goals and plans. London and Stumpf give some excellent advice in this area:

> Few people systematically investigate and collect extensive information on target jobs and the possible career paths to attain them. . . . Establishing career objectives is more than stating a possible target job. It is knowing: (1) the work-related activities one is seeking, (2) the social and political aspects of the position, (3) the demands the position will place on one's personal time and family, and (4) the series of possible positions which would prepare one to perform effectively.[37]

London and Stumpf note that three things are essential for effective career progression. First is a clear perception of one's current knowledge, skills, interests, life-style, and preference. Second is an individual definition of success, including activities that bring positive feelings and future positions that will satisfy psychic and social as well as economic needs. Third is a realistic plan of action including short- and long-term goals. London and Stumpf noted, "To the extent that the plans and actions are flexible and sensitive to organizational opportunities and constraints, they are more likely to result in effective career progression." The three elements of self-assessment, establishment of objectives, and career planning are the essence of career management. Each element interacts with the others. According to London, these form the framework for pinpointing opportunities as well as constraints upon success. Self-assessment means generating and analyzing information about oneself in relation to career and overall life themes. A job-seeking strategy helps in assessing whether prospective employers and positions fit with one's primary work and life-style goals.[38]

London and Stumpf's book on career development and planning, *Managing Careers,* gives a detailed analysis of how to develop career plans. They also give useful suggestions on how to manage your career.

No one has outstanding abilities in marketing, production, personnel, planning, research, and all other functions. However, concentrating on your weaknesses instead of strengths can cripple your career. Career plans should be developed in the same way that specialists develop corporate plans, beginning with an analysis of assets and liabilities. An intelligent self-growth strategy must contain a realistic appraisal of your individual assets and liabilities, followed by a plan that makes the most use of your assets, and either changes or compensates for your liabilities.[39]

Career plans are *your* responsibility. Bosses do not implement career planning for their subordinates because most do not have the training and the time to do so, or so they say. In reality, there are few rewards for doing so. Managers point out that when they are evaluated by their superiors, their performance is measured for a wide range of responsibilities but that little, if any, weight is given to how conscientiously or effectively they attend to career counseling for their subordinates.

Taking charge of your own performance potential, career planning, and training and development needs will not guarantee your success, but it will certainly give you a better chance of achieving your goals. It will also allow you to evaluate more realistically your next course of action, whether that is to leave the company or to stay.

One final piece of advice: Your work will take up the majority of your waking hours and a large number of your most productive years. A mistake that many young, eager people make is that they are too impatient. They do not recognize that staying on a job at the same level for two to three years is a very short time in one's career. A good employee will outlast any bad work situation—or leave the company.

Waiting need not be passive. You should do anything you can to improve your situation or to get out of it. However hostility and a negative attitude will only worsen your situation and lessen your chances of moving up or out under positive conditions.

It is crucial that you recognize that patience is truly a virtue. In my sixteen years as a consultant and thirteen years in corporate America, 85 percent of my successes have involved, in some way, the need for patience, and 85 percent of my failures have been caused in part by a lack of it.

Conclusions

The basic concept put forth in this chapter is that employees will enhance their chances of making it into middle and upper management if they understand the realities of bureaucracies and of human nature. This means developing the skills to understand and know the people we are dealing with—and ourselves.

Surviving in the corporate fishbowl means understanding that, in most cases in corporate America, the end justifies the means. Corporate America is a political power game, in which the key strategies are manipulation and control.

Most people are out primarily for themselves despite what they might say—and rightly so. If you do not look out for yourself, no one else will. Because of the competition for limited opportunities, it is crucial that individuals trust few people and be selectively honest and forthright. (Note, however, that a policy of "selective honesty" does not imply a license to be *dis*honest. It means exercising the wisdom to leave some things unsaid, particularly in tempting moments.) I suggest that you must take control of your own career. More explicitly, the ultimate responsibility for getting accurate information on performance, potential, and career objectives rests with you. Only through accurate information can you make realistic career decisions and plans.

Iuppa summarizes what it takes to survive in corporate America:

Management is a complex task, friends. As complex as life. So why not draw on the tools humanity has developed to cope with life? As I say, control tactics are deeply rooted in all of us. To understand them, all we have to do is recognize them. Plotting and scheming are part of management. Admit it. So is honesty. So is dishonesty. Setting a good example is an important management technique, so is the Zen of letting go. To be a good manager, you have to know how to listen, how to be sensitive, how to insult, how to bribe, how to use rumors, and how to run a baseball team.[40]

Let me conclude by strongly urging all ambitious corporate employees to read Douglas LaBrier's book, *Modern Madness: The Emotional Fallout of Success* (Addison Wesley, 1986), on the negative psychological—and ultimately physiological—impact that corporate success has had on an increasing number of employees.

6
Socialization: Racism and Sexism

To write a book on surviving in the corporate fishbowl without dealing with the issues of racism and sexism would be to ignore two of the most powerful forces affecting the efficient functioning of corporate America. These forces have severely curtailed corporate America's full use of the female and minority work force.

This chapter clarifies what we mean by racism and sexism and explains how we are all socialized to be racist and sexist. Comprehensive data demonstrate that racism and sexism exist in society and in all facets of our lives, and that presumably rational, objective corporate managers harbor a large supply of racist and sexist stereotypes. Women and minorities have special, painfully unique problems in trying to make it up the corporate ladder. Moreover, these two forces profoundly affect corporate life and bureaucratic processes in general. The negative impact of racism and sexism on the corporate bottom line is evident throughout the next four chapters. As a black, male, upper-level manager wrote: "Many whites who think they are not prejudiced unconsciously engage in offensive acts and display attitudes that are not conducive to a productive working environment."

Employees' Views of Women and Minorities

The following comments by the study participants reflect the views of employees in corporate America about women and minorities. Even though they were randomly selected, most comments express attitudes and experiences of a racist and sexist nature.

The first series of responses reflect some of the racist views of employees. As the reader will see, many of the old stereotypes are still alive and well in some employees' minds.

> I don't believe in interracial marriage (God doesn't allow robins to mix with crows). Only animals that man has domesticated cross over the lines of their own kind.
>
> —white, male, craftsworker

> A person of color is thought of more as a 'group member' and less as an individual, which leads to negative self-esteem, promotes behavior problems—late to work, inadequate performance.
>
> —white, female, lower-level manager

> When I started here, I did not feel I was prejudiced. This company has made me that way. The blacks tend to stick together and exclude whites. The company promotes blacks because of their color when many times they have no seniority, qualifications, or ability.
>
> —white, female, lower-level manager

> In my 21 years with this company I have worked with only three people of color. Is this just coincidence or an indication of numbers of people of color being hired?
>
> —white, female, lower-level manager

> Most people think blacks are lazy and dumb until they really prove themselves differently.
>
> —white, female, craftsworker

> I believe whites should be with whites (married I mean) and colored with colored.
>
> —white, female, craftsworker

> I'm quite mixed up on the issue of whites marrying blacks and vice versa. I don't really know if we should mix the races. Only God can say and I haven't met him as yet. When I see it, I don't feel that it's right.
>
> —white, female, upper-level manager

As we shall see in a great detail in coming sections, these racist attitudes and stereotypes are translated into racist behaviors. One employee put it this way:

Pre-conceived notions about different races or genders are most often private, subjective feelings and are hard to correct. But they impact people's behavior tremendously.

—Asian, female, lower-level manager

Several comments of our study participants about racist experiences gives the reader an idea of how racist views come out in corporate America:

I was at a meeting recently, and racist comments were made by a lower-level management in the presence of a middle-level manager and craftspeople. The references were to a black woman ("everyone should own one") and children: ("I'll adopt a little black athlete who'll make me rich.") I brought to the attention of the group that such remarks offended me, and then the middle-level manager endorsed my concern.

—white, female, craftsworker

Racism is not only alive and well but flourishing at our company. To cite the instances I have seen and heard over the past 12 years would take me well into retirement, if I could remember all of them and planned on staying that long. One of the better ones I have heard lately come from two white males and two white females referring to their female boss as a black bitch. You see, she is a black first and bitch second; however, they referred to their white female middle-level as a bitch, not a white bitch.

—white, male, craftsworker

Although sexism and racism in the workplace are minimal, outside the workplace the same people go back to the "old" ways. Cultural change of this nature moves very slowly. Even though our top management professes commitment to EEO values, they still use terms like "Chinese dollars." Signatures on documents professing those beliefs would seem to ring hollow when compared to their actions.

—Asian, male, lower-level manager

Whites are very slow in accepting people of color as equals. They outwardly appear to be playing fair, but "some" are "very" prejudiced and only do what is necessary to keep from being caught at discrimination. But most of them practice it.

—black, female, lower-level manager

Some of the sexist stereotypes and attitudes of the participants are reflected in the following comments:

Women managers can't handle it when the going gets tough. Women are too emotional.

—American Indian, male, lower-level manager

Some parts of the company are further ahead than others. I work in a highly technical area. Racism and sexism (covert) are rampant. There is not one person of color on my floor. Women and people of color are still viewed as being unable to succeed in a technical area.

—white, female, lower-level manager

It seems totally evident that the men of this company feel that only *good looking, slinky* and *sexy* women should be advanced if any are advanced at all, and that a woman's brain should *not* be taken into consideration.

—white, female, lower-level manager

Women seem to be harder on women working under them than on men who work under them. They seem to have less flexibility. Case in point is how the business office is treated compared to other departments within the company.

—white, male, craftsworker

Equal pay for equal work is fine, but when the work is not equal and the woman is getting away with doing less, it's a problem.

—Hispanic, male, craftsworker

Some women use their gender as a ploy for men to help them in a difficult task. Also many women have trouble coping due to emotions at home and physical problems due to premenstrual stress.

—white, male, craftsworker

There always will be sexism and racism to a certain degree. It's the nature of man; to believe differently is absurd. The very nature of clubs is to eliminate certain people. I find no harm in this. When women started working, divorces increased: enough PROOF!

—white, male, lower-level manager

As is the case with racist views, sexist views are translated into sexist behaviors, as the following quotations demonstrate.

The fact that an upper level male sent flowers to female managers on National Secretary's Day indicates a real problem in the upper management levels. Did the male managers get flowers? No!

—white, female, lower-level manager

True racism and sexism are not at all blatant in our society or company; yet they exist and they will continue to exist. Why? Because they both exist on a very insidious, downplayed level. We, the employees and citizens, cannot fight intangibles that exist as a gentleman's (note: gentle*man*, not woman, nor person) agreement. Even our language is structured to reflect and reinforce that vague kind of prejudice inherent in our society.

—white, female, upper-level manager

If you view any type of group activity that combines men and women, you'll notice by body language alone that the men don't listen and respond to what the women say. I've been in a situation where I did a job jointly with a man; yet everyone, including my female boss, deferred to him. I'm sure it was something my male co-worker didn't even notice.

—white, female, lower-level manager

Racism is practiced undercover. By that I mean, no one is going to tell you he is a racist; however, his actions and talk show it. Sexism is practiced more openly. I think the biggest problem here is that everyone was raised with the idea this is a job for men and this is a job for women. Women are homemakers; men are the breadwinners.

—black, female, craftsworker

In times of social or economic stress, racism seems more rampant as if it were an exercise, which it *never* is. At work during stressful times, the comments seem more frequent and more derogatory. Sexism is apparent in an office where women are called "girls."

—Hispanic, female, lower-level manager

I feel one of the areas that needs the most emphasis is language. I can't count the number of times I have been referred to as a girl. That really offends me because I am a 30-year-old woman.

—white, female, craftsworker

I hear a lot of lip service paid to diversity in the workforce, but I don't see enough minorities/women in the technical jobs or at upper management levels. I also hear a lot of bigoted talk from people at all levels in the company.

—white, female, craftsworker

Before going further, it is important to define racism and sexism.

Racism and Sexism Defined

I define racism and sexism as cultural ideologies that view whites and males as inherently superior to minorities and women solely because of their race and gender. Whites and men, and thus most strongly white men, wield the power in societal institutions to develop, evolve, nurture, spread, impose, and enforce the very myths and stereotypes that are basic foundations of racism and sexism, in the minds of not only white males themselves but many women and minorities. These myths and stereotypes are used to maintain and justify white men's dominant social, economic, and political positions.

Racism and sexism are rooted deeply in the very structure and fabric of society. They are not solely a matter of personal attitudes and beliefs. Indeed, it can be argued that racist and sexist beliefs are but accessory expressions of institutionalized patterns of white and male, especially white male, power and social control.

A black, male craftsworker aptly wrote: "Racism and sexism are creatures of habit and so intertwine with American society. Many people don't know or consciously realize they are officially members of a racist or sexist group. The company reflects this awareness."

A white, female craftsworker concurred: "I don't think any amount of training and/or awareness groups will correct attitudes of men towards women. I think it is a basic attitude built in by culture, society, area of country the person grew up in, family values and prejudices."

Underlying racism and sexism are power struggles between dominant white men who seek to maintain their privileged positions in society, and minorities and women who are determined to change the status quo. Even while they control society's major institutions, white men have great fear of losing their hegemony. This drives them, consciously or unconsciously, to nurture myths and stereotypes about women and minorities in order to preserve the status quo.

I suggest that racism and sexism are defensive adjustment mechanisms used by whites and males to deal with psychological and social-status insecurities and anxieties. Put another way, while I have argued that we are all mentally unhealthy in varying degrees, I believe that racism and sexism are severe mental disorders that more often afflict those with the most interest in preserving the systems than those interested in tearing them down.

History of Racism

Racism is an old problem that divides people into superior and inferior races. A number of writers have argued that racism had its origins among Western Europeans during the sixteenth century with the rise of nationalism, and that it was applied first to class conflicts and then to national conflicts. Other researchers find evidence of racism much further back in our history.

The biblical story of Noah and his son, Ham, has been used as justification of racism. Ham saw Noah lying naked and asleep in his tent, and Noah, upon discovering this, put a curse on Ham's son, Canaan: "Cursed be Canaan, a slave of slaves shall he be to his brothers." Canaan, according to the Old Testament, was the progenitor of the early Egyptians and other African tribes.[1] Therefore, although no reference to skin color occurs in this passage, the phrase, "a slave of slaves," was used as righteous justification of the enslavement of black Africans, the supposed descendants of Canaan. This passage and others have led present day racists to justify their racism. (For example, Bob Jones University, a fundamentalist Protestant school, prohibits interracial dating. They lost federal funding in a Supreme Court decision because of this racist rule. Our present Supreme Court chief justice William L. Rehnquist was the only Supreme Court justice to support the continuing of federal aid for Bob Jones University.)

Interpreters of the Bible associated the blackness of people with things that mean evil, sin, death, despair, and ugliness. B. Schwartz and R. Disch stated that the English colonists brought to the New World an association with the word black that: "became important as men put language to use in first defining and later justifying the status they desired for the nonwhite. Before the close of the fifteenth century, the words soiled and dirty first became linked with black. By 1536, black connoted 'dark purposes, malignant, deadly;' by 1581, 'foul, iniquitous;' by 1588, 'baneful, disastrous, and sinister.'"[2]

W. Jordan agreed that these negative associations with the word black preceded any contact between the English and black Africa.[3]

With such negative connotations of blackness, and positive connotations of whiteness as symbolizing purity, goodness, and holiness, the English had no difficulty in justifying the enslavement of black-skinned people. Today the negative connotations of black have been expanded to include concepts such as blacklisted and blackballed. In business, the "black knight" is an unfriendly takeover of another corporation; a "white knight" is a friendly takeover. A best-selling book on corporate culture noted, "cultural change is still a black art as far as we are concerned."[4] With all these negative connotations of black, it is not surprising that, as we shall see, many present-day blacks are trying to change their "blackness" through plastic surgery.

J. Kovel makes a number of relevant statements about white Americans' reasons for focusing on blackness. He claims that the "random clustering of assortments of genes that are the human evolutionary heritage has led to certain easily perceived differences among groups of men." Scientific evidence has unequivocally demonstrated that, whatever the unresolved biological problems of race, such superficial characteristics do not in themselves explain racism. Rather, "fantasies of race" account for the tradition of racism; a symbolic meaning is assigned to "the blackness of black skin (even if it's really brown)."[5]

Racist ideology in the United States is aimed not only at blacks. While Europeans were encountering the "uncivilized," non-Christian culture of Africans, a similar meeting occurred between the Puritans and Native Americans, with similar attitudinal results. As the

Puritan population increased and the demand for land and resources grew, the Puritans' intolerance of native Americans increased. This led to the development of racist attitudes and behaviors toward Native Americans, culminating in the view that "the
only good Indian is a dead Indian."[6]

Using the Bible as a justification, early legislators in this country
passed laws to make racism a reality in practice as well as in
thought. The preamble to South Carolina's code of 1712 said that
"blacks were of barbarous, wild, savage natures, and . . . wholly
unqualified to be governed by the laws, customs, and practices of
this province. They must be governed by special laws as may re-
strain the disorders . . . and inhumanity to which they are naturally
prone and inclined."[7] The tension created by the presence of a large
and degraded black population in a nation founded on democratic
ideals of equality has haunted American dialogue, ideas, and leaders
for more than three hundred years. Thomas Jefferson believed that
a harmonious biracial society was inconceivable. "Deep rooted prejudices entertained by the whites," he wrote, and "ten thousand rec-
ollections, by the blacks, of the injuries they have sustained," com-
bine to make equal, peaceful coexistence between blacks and whites
impossible. Jefferson believed that free blacks and whites could end
up in a conflict which would lead to "the extermination of the one
or the other race."[8] Sixty years after South Carolina's code, when
the U.S. Constitution was first written, a black man counted as only
three-fifths of a white man for apportionment purposes. Black
women, of course, were not considered to be even three-fifths of a
person. Almost a century later, Chief Justice B. Taney concurred
and wrote in his opinion of the *Dred Scott* v. *Sanford* case (1857):

> The question before us is whether the class of persons described
> in the plea for abatement compose a portion of this people and
> are constituent members of this sovereignty. We think they are
> not, and that they are not included, and were not intended to be
> included, under the words "citizens" in the Constitution, and can
> therefore claim none of the rights and privileges which that in-
> strument provides for and contrary, they were at that time consid-
> ered as a subordinate and inferior class of beings, who had been
> subjugated by the dominant race, and whether emancipated or

not, yet remained subject to their authority and had no rights or privileges but such as those who held the power and the government might choose to grant them.[9]

This antiblack trend continued through the 1860s until the Thirteenth, Fourteenth, and Fifteenth amendments to the Constitution granted blacks equal rights of freedom, due process, and the vote. Yet, legal discrimination against blacks and other minorities, especially Asians, did not stop. Thirty years after the Civil War, in *Plessy* v. *Ferguson,* the U.S. Supreme Court ruled that "separate but equal" facilities were permissible. This precedent was not reversed until 1954 in *Brown* v. *Board of Education.*[10] However, during Chief Justice William L. Rehnquist's 1986 confirmation hearings the Democrats brought out a 1968 memo in which he seemed to argue that *Plessy* v. *Ferguson* was a correct decision. Although Rehnquist denied such a belief, a Louis Harris poll found that a majority of Americans questioned Rehnquist's honesty and straightforwardness.

Judge A. L. Higginbotham quotes from Mark Twain's parody in *Huckleberry Finn* to show that "as late as 1884 many white Americans still failed to perceive blacks as human beings." This is the dialogue.

Good gracious. Anybody hurt?

No'm. Killed a nigger.

Well, it's lucky because sometimes people do get hurt . . .[11]

Article XIX of the California Constitution, passed in 1879 and in effect until 1952, extended legal racism to include the Chinese. The article prohibited the hiring of Chinese by corporations and by "any state, county, municipal, or other public work, except in punishment for crime."[12]

The American resentment of the Japanese culminated in the Johnson Immigration Act of 1924, passed by Congress, banning the immigration of persons "ineligible for citizenship." This act was directed against the Japanese and was not repealed until 1952.[13]

Only twenty-two years ago nonwhites were first guaranteed the right to public accommodations, and fifteen years ago interracial marriages and cohabitation became legal in the fifteen states with laws against miscegenation, after the ruling in *Loving* v. *Virginia*. These laws were originally directed against blacks and Asians.

That racism could become part of our laws once again can be seen from the number of congresspersons and senators who have tried to pass laws on the immigration of illegal Mexican aliens into the United States. President Reagan and some of these same congresspeople have not seen fit to support legislation to stop U.S. corporations from supporting directly through investments and indirectly through moral support the racist regime of South Africa. Can anyone imagine Reagan and Congress not supporting legislation or maybe even sending in the Marines if South Africa were ruled by a black majority that killed over 2,000 whites in a little over two years?

Much racism and sexism has been founded in our academic institutions. One of the most insidious concepts coming out of academia is the intellectual inferiority of blacks. Soon after the Civil War and still today there is a group of academics who believe in eugenics, the science of heredity. Not an inherently racist science, eugenics has been made racist by prominent "scientists," beginning with Sir Francis Galton in "Hereditary Genius: Its Laws and Consequences." In current academic America, there are still Galtons. William Schockley, one of the inventors of the transistor and an avowed eugenicist, has been noted for his claim that blacks are intellectually inferior to whites as determined by IQ tests. He has suggested that black people below 100 IQ level volunteer themselves for sterilization.[14]

Dr. A. Thomas and Dr. S. Sillen noted that academia does not even train psychologists and psychiatrists to deal with their racism:

> Probably the most disturbing insight obtained from the relentless clarity with which this book documents the case of racism in American psychiatry is the ironic fact that the students, research workers and professionals in the behavior sciences—like members of the clergy and educators—are no more immune by virtue of their values and training to the disease and superstitions of American racism than is the average man.[15]

In brief, in our history, in our religion, in our laws, in our language, and in our academic institutions are the seeds, the soil, and the fertilizer of racism.

History of Sexism

Sexist attitudes originated tens of thousands of years ago, as noted by M. Harris: "Male-supremacist institutions arose as a byproduct of warfare, of the male monopoly over weapons, and of the use of sex for the nurturance of aggressive male personalities. And warfare . . . is not the expression of human nature but a response to reproductive and economic pressures. Therefore, male supremacy is no more natural than warfare."[16]

Long ago, war was conducted with hand weapons whose effectiveness was a function of physical strength. The less-rugged anatomy and child-bearing duties of women rendered them less physically powerful, so males dominated in war and hunting for food. Male babies were preferred since they added to the defensive team, and they had first choice of available resources. Women did drudge work and provided food not requiring vigorous hunting. Their subordination and devaluation followed automatically from the need to reward men at the expense of women and to provide supernatural justifications for the whole male-supremacist complex. Thus, the origins of sexism are tied to the exigencies of cave and village life. Later sexism was culturally induced, made permanent by laws, and when necessary, rationalized with religion.[17]

A biblical passage used to show that men are superior to women is 1 Corinthians 11:3–9: "But I would have you know that the head of the woman is the man, and the head of Christ is God. For a man indeed ought not to cover his head for as much as he is the image and glory of God, but the woman is the glory of the man. For the man is not of the woman, but the woman is of the man. Neither was the man created for the woman but the woman for the man."[18]

The ideological distortion has woman only of man and created for man, and man not of woman but of God.

This definition of women as inferior and subservient to men was reflected in early English law. The oldest written English law, Ethelbert's Dooms of 600 A.D., and the laws that followed it in

Western civilization were developed, written, and interpreted by men who subscribed to this definition of women and who used the Bible to justify their sexist outlook. We also should remember that over the centuries the Bible has been written and translated by men, many of whom were not married.

Even in 1873 the U.S. Supreme Court found that the State of Illinois could deny a woman a license to practice law in the state. Notice the biblical influence on Supreme Court Justice Joseph Bradley's words:

> the civil law, as well as nature herself, has always recognized wide differences in the respective spheres and destinies of man and woman. Man is, or should be, woman's protector and defender. The natural and proper timidity and delicacy which belongs to the female sex evidently unfits it for many of the occupations of civil life. The constitution of the family organization, which is founded in the divine ordinance, as well as in the nature of things, indicates the domestic sphere as that which properly belongs to the domain and functions of womanhood. . . .
>
> It is true that many women are unmarried and not affected by any of the duties, complications, and incapacities arising out of the married state, but these are exceptions to the general rule. The paramount destiny and mission of women is to fulfill the noble and benign offices of wife and mother. This is the law of the Creator. And the rules of civil society must be adapted to the general constitution of things and cannot be based upon exceptional cases.[19]

The attitude conveyed by Bradley in "noble and benign offices of wife and mother" was still in effect in 1961 when the Earl Warren Court upheld a Florida law (similar to laws in many other states) that gave women special immunity from jury duty in order that they be allowed to remain at "the center of home and family life."[20] This decision was overturned by the Warren E. Burger Court.

It is well known that the Civil Rights Act of 1964 included women only because some Southern congresspeople thought that such a ridiculous idea would easily defeat the bill. However, their strategy backfired. During the 1970s many state laws that discriminated against women were challenged, often upheld at the state level, and sometimes overturned at the federal level.

For example, in the 1970 case of *Reed v. Reed,* a woman challenged an Idaho statute that stipulated that men must be given preference over women as administrators of estates of persons dying intestate (without making a will). The Idaho Supreme Court found the statute constitutional and, calling upon nature, gave this feeble opinion:

> Philosophically it can be argued with some degree of logic that the provisions of I.C. 15–314 do discriminate against women on the basis of sex. However, nature itself has established the distinction, and this statute is not designed to discriminate but is only designed to alleviate the problem of holding hearings by the Court to determine eligibility to administer. . . . The legislature, when it enacted this statute, evidently concluded that in general, men are better qualified to act as an administrator than are women.[21]

The most recent and important proposed legislation pertaining to the rights of women is the Equal Rights Amendment to the U.S. Constitution. This amendment states simply and succinctly, "Equality of rights under the law shall not be abridged or denied by the United States or by any state on account of sex." Not only men but millions of women opposed the passage of this amendment. Years of promale socialization prevent women themselves from seeking legal protection of their right to equality.

Legislators have had not only the Bible but the dictionary to assist them in justifying their sexist positions. Like textbooks, the dictionary contains words that apply sex-role stereotypes to both sexes. Lee H. Gershuny cited numerous examples of this in *Sexism and Language*:

> She burst into tears upon hearing of his death, but it was only a grandstand play.
>
> She always wears a crazy hat.
>
> She depends on her father for money.
>
> Women with shrill voices get on his nerves.
>
> You could see him turn off as she kept up her chatter.[22]

In addition to the sexist tone of language in the dictionary, one author found that women are generally described in terms of sexuality. She noted that there are approximately two hundred words to describe a sexually passive woman and only twenty to describe a sexually passive man.[23]

While dealing with the daily expressions of sexism in a legal system that designates her a "he" and recognizes her by her husband's surname, a woman becomes still more frustrated when dealing with the societal institutions that have given her labels and definitions, relegated her to an inferior position, and reduced her to a second-class status. It is one thing to cope with the men in the office who call her "doll," or "toots," or "baby" and quite another thing to get rid of the stereotypes when the courts and the legislatures of the land make them a part of their judicial opinions and legislations.[24]

As is the case with racism, a great deal of sexism is rooted in our educational institutions. The same psychological leaders who branded blacks as inferior to whites declared women inferior to men, and mentally ill as well if they were not dependent, emotional, and passive. In other words, women who display "male" characteristics like independence, stoicism, and aggressiveness are considered mentally unhealthy.[25]

In sum, this nurturing and legitimizing of the inferiority of minorities and women by law, religion, language, and education is ancient. R. Benedict aptly summed up the historical perspective of the power struggle that is the cause of racism and sexism when she observed:

Persecution was an old, old story before racism was thought of. Social change is inevitable, and it is always fought by those whose ties are to the old order. Those who have these ties will consciously or unconsciously ferret out reasons for believing that their group is supremely valuable and that the new claimants threaten the achievements of civilization. They will raise a cry of rights of inheritance, or divine right of kings, or religious orthodoxy, or racial purity, or manifest destiny. These cries reflect the temporary conditions of the moment, and all the efforts of the slogan makers need not convince us that any one of them is based on external verities.[26]

Forms of Racism and Sexism in the 1980s

Racism and sexism continue to be two of the most powerful and complex social forces affecting American society. Their form, however, has changed drastically, especially since 1964. Our present laws are trying to correct the obvious forms of discrimination—*overt* racism and sexism—but have made little impact on the more subtle forms of discrimination that influence policies, practices, and patterns of decision making—*institutional* racism and sexism—or on the still subtler, covert, more devious, and sophisticated neoracism and neosexism. Comments of some of our participants demonstrate that the less blatant neoracism and neosexism of the 1980s are more difficult to see than overt discrimination but are just as real:

> The problems are less visible today than they were 10–15 years ago but I believe they have just gone "underground."
>
> —Hispanic, female, middle-level manager

> There is still discrimination, it is just "in the closet."
>
> —American Indian, female, craftsworker

> We have forced verbal/physical signs of racism and sexism underground. We have not changed the attitudes, only prevented them from being obvious. Nothing else has really changed.
>
> —white, female, lower-level manager

> Eliminating racism and sexism is a wonderful idea, but unfortunately, there are a few bigots and chauvinists who will not allow themselves to view each person as an individual. These people will continue to humiliate, debase and ridicule others. Then we have the bigots and chauvinists who do a great job of masking their feelings and attitudes. Only a major slip will show their "true color." These people can be more dangerous than those who do not conceal their feelings. They can erect invisible barriers as *in the company.* EXAMPLE: A white female is told she is not qualified for a company tech job, after she has passed all required tests, then the job is given to a white male hired *off the street!!* BELIEVE IT. IT REALLY HAPPENED, I KNOW!!
>
> —white, female, craftsworker

Not only are neoracism and neosexism difficult to perceive, but as the following three quotations demonstrate, institutional racism and sexism are not even considered discrimination but are just as damaging as overt discrimination to women and minorities:

> They don't discriminate. They just keep on using the old boy network for promotion candidates. It discriminates for them.
>
> —white, male, middle-level manager

> Our company very seldom recruits at black colleges—this is institutional racism.
>
> —black, female, lower-level manager

> They have women's jobs, black jobs, Hispanic jobs, Asian jobs and Indian jobs. Ninety-nine percent are not mainstream jobs to help you advance your career. Then you have white male jobs. Ninety percent of them are the right jobs to advance your career. I don't care what you call it—racism/sexism—it is unfair and it is discriminatory.
>
> —white, male, middle-level manager

Despite the covert forms of neoracism and neosexism, these forces are no less destructive than overt discrimination to the profitability of corporations. Vast numbers of employees continue to be underused and underdeveloped because of their race and/or gender.

Development of Racist and Sexist Attitudes and Behaviors

Racism and sexism are developed and nurtured by all of the societal institutions controlled by the dominant white male group. Babies begin their lives with a sense of kinship to all humans, regardless of skin color or other physical features. Most infants and very young children are open, loving, and comfortable with people who show them love, attention, and caring. However, children learn racist and sexist attitudes and behaviors at an early age. Families, schools, churches, government, the media, and other social groups and institutions socialize the population by communicating what is "good" behavior and what is "bad." They teach us what to expect of ourselves, our friends, and our families. They teach us how to relate to society.

As a result of their socialization, children learn how to be minorities or whites, men or women. They acquire a sense of the worth of their social group and of themselves from their earliest contacts with other members of their family, their peers, and teachers; from what they see in the movies, on television, and in advertisements; from what they read; from conversations they overhear; and from their daily observations.

A black, male, lower-level manager observed: "Until white parents stop instilling in their children that they are superior and have more intelligence than black people, race/ethnic discrimination will always have a base at this company."

Innumerable studies have explored the development of racist attitudes in white children at very early ages. One study found that very young children strongly prefer the color white over black and that their regard for the color black is transferred to their perception of black people.[27]

What many Americans do not want to recognize or admit because they have developed such elaborate rationales for their views is the issue of interracial dating and marriage. I believe that this is one race-related issue that most white Americans believe is appropriately dealt with in an overt manner. More specifically, most white parents believe it is appropriate to tell their children not to date persons of other races, especially blacks. They rationalize this overtly racist position by saying that interracial couples have a much more difficult time because of the social hostility they face. Others say that children of interracial couples suffer because "neither race will accept them." These two "rationales" often emerged in my research on employee attitudes about interracial dating and marriage:

> They have to live with their decision and like any other marriage, make the best of it. Where I do have a problem is with their offspring. Say for instance one parent is black and one parent is white, it seems to me neither white nor black want to accept them.
>
> —white, male, craftsworker

> I have a problem up to a point about mixed marriages because of the pressure society puts on these people. I am sympathetic with

these people for I believe a person should have the right to marry whomever they choose. Yet society can make life hell for their children and I don't like watching children suffer because of ignorant people. It tears me apart even to see an adult suffer because of ignorance of people.

—white, female, craftsworker

Although I personally would like to allow my daughters to openly date whomever they choose, their father is totally against it. I know that they meet members of the opposite race and sex away from the home for dates without their father's knowledge. They come to our home if they are with other friends who are white, but not usually by themselves.

—white, female, lower-level manager

No matter how nonracist white people believe they are, if they cannot look at minorities as potential family members, then they do not accept minorities as equals. These same "nonracist" whites at some time in their lives will act in a racist manner if they perceive minorities as a threat to their dominant position. My study found that a majority of employees oppose interracial marriage and dating. The highest percentage of employees who *do not* at all oppose interracial marriages are black men (75 percent). They are followed by other women of color (53 percent). The lowest percentages of employees who do not at all oppose interracial marriages are the white men (22 percent) and women (28 percent). In the middle are the other men of color (39 percent) and black women (46 percent). Some readers may question whether minorities who oppose interracial marriage are not also racist. I say no. The majority of the minorities who oppose interracial marriages do so not on the basis of perceived racial inferiority or superiority but because of feelings of hatred toward whites because of white racism or, especially in the case of black women, because of anxiety about the limited number of available black men. Do I believe these attitudes are right? No, but I do not define such attitudes as racist. Let's look at other comments of the study participants on interracial dating and marriage.

I'm opposed to interracial marriage only to the extent that those individuals involved should have a thorough understanding of each other's culture and what the sociological consequences may be for them and their children. Only then would I condone it.

—American Indian, male, craftsworker

I'm making an attempt not to let my kids become as biased as I am.

—white, male, craftsworker

In raising my child, I am very conscious of sex typing, the behaviors and attitudes he develops. I also am very conscious to make an extra effort to associate with people from all races and try hard not to have him develop in a racist environment. Most of all, I'm trying hard to build a sense of high self-esteem and self-confidence in him.

—Hispanic, male, lower-level manager

It really does not matter what race or background you may have. A person is a human being, and if you take the time to get to know the other person not only can you learn from them, but you can also like the other person for him/herself, not because of race.

—black, female, craftsworker

My children can date whomever they choose. Color has nothing to do with it, as long as the dater respects me as a parent and honors my rules while dating my child.

—black, female, craftsworker

Somewhere in the Bible it states not to mix races in marriage—it causes heartache. An innocent date in public, no matter what race or cultural background, may be beneficial to a teenager to understand life better—the whys and why nots.

—white, female, craftsworker

In my opinion, there are a lot worse things a person can do than marry someone of another race and if it bothers people, they probably have an empty life and nothing better to worry about.

—white, female, craftsworker

A 1964 study found that white four-year-olds had already internalized feelings of superiority to blacks.[28] Another study found very young black children already entrenched in negative concepts about their blackness.[29] These studies clearly show that the control of society's institutions by whites dominates children's perceptions.

No matter how strongly the black community says "Black is Beautiful," the Hispanic community says, "Brown is Beautiful," or the Native American community says, "Red is Beautiful," few of society's members will believe it unless most of society's institutions support these propositions.

That even in the mid-1980s there is self-dislike among many minorities can be demonstrated by the fact that an increasing number of blacks are having plastic surgery to make them look more white. Pattie LaBelle and Michael Jackson are among the most famous of blacks who have decided that black can be *more* beautiful by having such surgery.[30]

A noted black plastic surgeon in Philadelphia said: "Ten years ago, blacks were holding up clenched fists in anger and defiance. Today we are seeing a turn to 'normalcy,' an attempt to blend into the woodwork. If you are going to climb the career ladder, to land a position with a Fortune 500 company, it pays to look as good as you can. Generally, these patients find the wide saddle-bridge nose and the large lower lip unglamorous in today's environment."[31]

A black woman in her mid-40s who lives in an upper-middle-class integrated neighborhood of Philadelphia said she had her lips and nose remodeled because, "I'm looking for a new position in private industry, and both looks and skills count there, so I'm putting my credentials in order. What the doctor did for me is just like what a parent does when he buys his child braces for his crooked teeth. We buy cars and furs and jewelry, and so I think to invest a few thousand in your looks isn't exorbitant."[32]

The previous paragraphs tied in with the historical perspective gives the reader some sense of how the socialization process affects the opinions of minorities, especially blacks, about themselves, and the opinions of whites about minorities.

With regard to gender socialization, little boys are aware of their sex role as early as age two, according to H. Lewis. She observed that they seem compelled to show that they are different from their mothers and to renounce all characteristics that may be considered unmanly. She wrote: "No wonder they have more trouble with the gender identity than little girls. And no wonder men are more prone than women to obsessional neurosis and schizophrenia."[33]

Experimenting with the role of the opposite gender is much

more acceptable for little girls than for little boys. Girls learn young that the male role is to be envied and imitated. Girls are free to dress in boys' clothes, but the reverse is certainly not the case. Parents who are amused to see their daughters become a "tomboy," are genuinely distressed if they have a son who is a "sissy."[34]

In my 1986 study, we asked the following two questions about the employees' children:

How frequently do you:

Encourage girls to do activities other than those which have been considered to be only for girls.

Encourage boys to do activities other than those which have been considered to be only for boys.

We found that 50 percent of other minority men, 39 percent of white men, and 35 percent of black men never or infrequently encourage girls to do activities not normally considered for girls. Between 24 percent and 29 percent of the women never or infrequently encourage girls to do "boys'" activities.

Between 58 percent and 64 percent of men never or very infrequently encourage boys to do activities that are not normally considered masculine. The women's responses range from 32 percent to 36 percent. These findings indicate that we as a society still have considerable problems in socializing our children, not as boys or girls, but as human beings. In addition, the data show that it is more acceptable, especially to men, to encourage girls to do boys' things than vice versa.

Through role-modeling techniques, the woman's need to achieve is, ever so gently, sublimated into a need to nurture and serve: "She is discouraged and protected from taking risks by her parents. At the same time she is subjected to peer pressure to fit the mold. 'If you take chemistry, you won't have time to date'; 'If you really swim, your hair will look a fright and your muscles will bulge'; 'If you get good grades, you're a drag'; 'If you always win at tennis, no one will want to play with you.'"[35] The result of all of this is that girls follow tradition:"She doesn't plan for the long range and doesn't recognize choice points but begins to back into or avoid decision making. She becomes more dependent on others because it is easy and comfortable. She ceases her formal education, takes a job, finds a man, and becomes the role model."[36]

It is not surprising that when women enter the corporate world, they begin to adopt male styles of management, dress, behaviors, and language, much more so than men adopting women's ways. Several comments from women in my studies acknowledge this fact.

> Women have been socialized to defer to men as authority figures. No matter how far we think we have gotten from these attitudes, we sometimes unconsciously hold back when put in the position of giving orders to men. For this reason I checked 'agree' to the question saying assertiveness training is valuable for women to overcome this stereotype. Women managers sometimes go too far in the other direction and become domineering.
>
> —white, female, upper-level manager

> Many women could improve their career opportunities by majoring in more technically oriented fields in college. They are just as capable as men are in these fields, but are not encouraged by their parents and society as they are growing up.
>
> —white, female, middle-level manager

While many people acknowledge this socialization pattern on an intellectual level, many also believe that somehow they have escaped or dealt with the evil forces of racism and sexism and that it is always "the other person" who is racist and sexist; not themselves. Few people understand the severely negative consequences that these forces have on themselves as well as on the people who are the object of racist and sexist oppression.

Impact of Racism and Sexism on Society

With such strong forces operating to socialize people, many believe that a racist and sexist society is the natural consequence of human behavior. A consistent message about race and gender from the church, family, peers, schools, government, newspapers, and television instills in people an unconscious or conscious ideology, a set of beliefs and attitudes that many accept implicitly as the natural state of the universe. Everyone has heard a family member, school-mate, coworker, friend, or political, social, or economic leader say, "Of course I have racist/sexist attitudes. Everyone has them. One cannot help it. We were brought up this way."

Racism and sexism as unconscious ideologies have debilitating effects on people's psychological and physical health. For example, the U.S. Commission on Mental Health declared in 1965 that Americans' racist attitudes, which cause and perpetuate tension, are a compelling health hazard, severely crippling the growth and development of millions of citizens. The commission diagnosed racism as a form of schizophrenia, "in that there is a large group gap between what whites believe in and actually practice."[37]

A white-centered superior attitude leaves the people who adopt it isolated, confused, and mentally underdeveloped. Racism produces false fears in whites and allows this fear to control where they live, where they go to school, where they travel, where they work, with whom they socialize, where they play, and whom they love and marry. Whites develop unhealthy mechanisms such as denial, false justification, projection, disassociation, and transference of blame to deal with their fears about minorities. J. Katz pinpointed this by declaring that "racism had deluded whites into a false sense of superiority that has left them in a pathological and schizophrenic state." Further, it has produced "miseducation about the realities of history, the contributions of Third-World people, and the role of minorities in present-day culture. In short, it has limited the growth potential of whites."[38]

As the ideology of white male supremacy has its negative impact on whites, sexism has its negative impact on men. J. Harrison stated that the socially prescribed male role requires men to be uncommunicative, competitive, nongiving, and inexpressive and to evaluate success in terms of external achievements rather than personal and interpersonal fulfillment. A man is caught in a double bind because to fulfill the prescribed role requirements he has to deny his human needs. If he meets these needs, he could be considered unmanly.[39]

The negative consequences of the male sex-role stereotype on the male life expectancy have been increasing for some time. In

1900, life expectancy in the United States was 48.3 years for women and 46.3 years for men. In 1975 it was 76.5 years for women and 68.7 years for men. During this period the life expectancy for both men and women increased by more than 20 years, but the difference between their respective life expectancies increased from 2 years in 1900 to 7.8 years in 1975. In 1980 the gap increased to 10 years.[40]

Harrison cites evidence that implicates male-role socialization for men's early deaths: "Recognizing the multiplicity of variables within the chain of causality . . . three-fourths of the difference in life expectancy can be accounted for by sex-role-related behaviors which contribute to the greater mortality of men."[41]

Dominant groups, of course, are not the only ones to suffer the far-reaching effects of racist and sexist attitudes. Black Americans show symptoms of disturbances resulting from the arduous emotional conditions under which they are obliged to live. Researchers have observed that even four-year-old patients were able to perceive themselves as black, different from white, and also displayed signs of some emotional disturbance as evidenced by the vagueness of responses to the "Who am I" question.[42]

A number of black social scientists have stressed the negative effect of racism on blacks' ability to compete successfully as adults. Some psychological results are aggressive behavior, professional anxiety, and escape from reality through alcohol and drugs. Some negative physical effects of racism are higher rates of hypertension, high blood pressure, and suicide among blacks than whites.[43] Racism's negative effects on the mental and physical health of Native Americans has also been well documented.

While Harrison argues that sex role socialization is one factor affecting the health of men, others argue that it also negatively affects women. For example, a greater incidence of mental illness among women than men has been reported. Some researchers attribute it to the greater stress of women's roles. They also report a correlation between sex and marital status, which suggests that marriage is related to a decreased risk of mental illness for men but an increased risk for women. This is due in part to the fact that men report great social support from wives while women must go to friends to talk about feelings.

Racist and Sexist Stereotypes

The past 100 years have seen new political and social values gradually taking hold in the United States. A steady progression of laws has challenged white men's preferred positions and monopoly on power. Although these laws contain the mechanisms for putting some of the new values into practice, they cannot eradicate the pervasive, unconscious ideologies that have a tremendously negative effect on all people, both morally and psychologically. In addition, the attacks by the Reagan administration on civil rights have created a generally hostile attitude nationwide against affirmative action, which has weakened the effectiveness of these laws in assuring women and minorities their deserved place in society.

As children we have little, if any, control over how we are socialized; thus racist and sexist attitudes and behaviors might come to seem normal. As teenagers and adults we become better able to determine what our own value systems and beliefs should be. Nevertheless, as a white, male craftsworker correctly notes, much of the information we are given as teenagers and adults is also very racist and sexist: "Sexism and racism are everywhere. We are bombarded daily with peoples' attitudes, prejudice, advertising, TV, movies, tales of liberation and integration: it goes on being used and abused." Let's first focus on sexist stereotypes and attitudes, then on racist stereotypes and attitudes, of the participants in my study.

Specific Stereotypes about Women

Numerous studies have shown that society's negative stereotypes about women are carried into the corporate structure, where they grossly affect women's careers.[44] Let's look at some comparative information over the past ten years. In my 1976–78 study 43 percent of men and 21 percent of women agreed with at least one of the following sexist stereotypes: most women are not as qualified as most male managers; women use their gender as an alibi for difficulties on the job; women are too emotional to be competent managers; and women are not serious about professional careers.

Alarmingly, there has been an increasing trend toward stereotyping between 1976–78 and 1986. For example, when we compare the responses about women's seriousness about their careers, we find that in 1976–78, 16 percent of the men and 7 percent of the women agreed that women were not serious about their professional careers, and in 1986, 22 percent of the women and 31 percent of the men agreed. This significant increase in such a negative stereotype flies in the face of the increasing numbers of women in the permanent full-time work force and the findings by an unpublished study of high tech companies that 82 percent of the men and 85 percent of the women categorize their careers as either extremely or very important. In addition, 68 percent of the women compared to 53 percent of the men said career development was their top priority in life.

I believe this increase in employees who believe that women are not serious about a professional career is tied into the belief that women should not work; several comments of our participants reflect this view.

I believe women should be at home and men should be the breadwinners.

—Hispanic, male, lower-level manager

If my company would use *men* for work instead of all *married* women who do not need to work, there would be better work relationships and more output. Bitchy women just create problems throughout the company. Look around you for yourself.

—American Indian, male, craftsworker

I do feel women in the working force competing with men has caused more divorces.

—white, female, craftsworker

I don't think I am racist or sexist with two exceptions. I personally believe that a mother should be at home to rear her own children if at all possible. I also believe a person should be promoted regardless of sex or race only if he/she is the best qualified.

—white, male, lower-level manager

Another belief that drew a number of comments is that of women using their sex as a tool. As we noted earlier, this male-dominated society places a lot of emphasis on sex but blames the women for using sex. These comments reflect this stereotype:

> I lost a chance of being sponsored to a blonde, blue-eyed, big breasted woman—and I had been in my job much longer and had more experience. I am brown-haired, brown-eyed, small-built.
>
> —Hispanic, female, craftsworker

> I have twice seen women (less qualified and with less service than myself) come to my male boss, shake and flaunt it until you could see him in a state of excitement. Needless to say, these women got the job I was up for.
>
> —white, male, craftsworker

> I feel women are as effective as men. However, I feel women are not promoted based on performance, but more on looks and having to fill quotas.
>
> —Hispanic, male, lower-level manager

A large number of the sexist responses revolved around women not being "good" managers:

> In 12 years of service, my supervisors have always been women. About 85 percent of the time, they shouldn't have had the position they did (incompetent), but because of their position, they employ political pressure, reverse discrimination, sexual harassment, etc.
>
> —white, male, craftsworker

Most comments about women lacking managerial ability came from women, a clear indication that many women stereotype their own gender:

> I find that most female bosses I work with are moody and seem to stab employees in the back more often than the laid-back attitudes of male bosses.
>
> —white, female, craftsworker

As a female employee who has worked for both male and female supervisors—I greatly prefer a male supervisor. They approach the job more realistically.

—white, female, craftsworker

I am a woman and I prefer to work for a man due to pettiness and jealousies coming from a woman supervisor; however, I feel women are equally qualified as managers on any level.

—black, female, craftsworker

A whole host of stereotypes characterized women as being lazy and too weak to do their job:

Women are basically lazy in the workplace. They need to be led at every turn. Most have a tendency to visit with other women and gossip when the boss is away.

—white, male, lower-level manager

I feel women are sometimes more petty and vicious by nature than are men.

—white, female, craftsworker

Women tend to "visit" more than men and generally are more negative to company goals and objectives.

—Hispanic, male, craftsworker

Women want to work 9:00–3:00. Men, in most cases, work 11 hours a day.

—white, male, lower-level manager

Is a pregnant manager an effective manager?

—white, male, craftsworker

Although women can be as capable as men, they do not take the right courses in school or think seriously about a career. I see this slowly changing.

—white, female, lower-level manager

The majority of women managers I've worked under do one hell of a good job. Some of them are too emotional and scare easily.

—Hispanic, female, craftsworker

Women managers tend to take things to heart, react on a personal level. If something goes wrong, they take it as a personal attack against them. They also let personality conflicts become involved with the judgments they make.

—Hispanic, female, lower-level manager

Women are capable of doing any job a man can do, but no matter how strong a woman is, she'll never be as strong as a strong man. Anyone saying man and woman were created equal hasn't seen a woman in a bikini lately.

—white, male, craftsworker

These comments express the underpinnings of the sexist stereotype that women are not qualified to be managers. The views of an Hispanic, male, lower-level manager reflect this attitude.

Affirmative action is a good thing if used properly—especially with women. But if things keep going as they are, the company is going to lose a lot of good male and female employees who are frustrated by all the incompetence in female managers. It is not a state of female overkill to raise them into low and high management ranks even if they're not qualified.

Many men have been categorized in the same fashions; however, the difference is that in this sexist society, if one woman has the stereotyped trait, then in the minds of many men and some women, they all have these traits. Put another way, women are much less likely than men to be perceived as individuals.

Lee Gershuny made some cogent observations on the negative effects of gender stereotypes:

The trouble with stereotypes is that they restrict behavior and understanding by constructing a static image of both sexes. Furthermore, assigning verbal qualities to each sex creates an illusion of biologically determined traits instead of suggesting their sociocultural origins or even an interplay of biology and environment. It is as though emotionality and passivity, usually assigned to the female stereotype, are qualities inherently absent in men. The passive man and the assertive woman are "unnatural" anomalies and are urged into psychotherapy to remedy behavior unbecoming the stereotype.[45]

Let's look more specifically at the questions about stereotypes that we asked in our 1984–86 study. As most responses of over 12,000 employees in the past three years were similar, I shall only use the 1986 data in the tables.

To demonstrate the strength of sexist stereotypes in 1986, I formed the responses to a series of questions into an index. The questions are as follows:

To what extent do you agree or disagree that:

Pluralism will force us to lower our hiring and promotion standards?

Many women are too emotional to be competent employees in the company?

In general, women are as qualified as men?

Many women need special training to be successful managers?

Private men's clubs have a right to exclude women?

Many women got their current position only because they are women?

Many women are not really serious about professional careers?

The increasing employment of women has led to the "breakdown" of the American family?

Chester I. Barnard, a former Bell System president, wrote in his book *The Function of the Executive* (1940) that a culturally homogeneous group of managers was necessary for the smooth, efficient functioning of a corporation. To what extent do you agree or disagree with his statement?

How opposed are you to women smoking in public?

How often do you wish for the "good old days" when "women were women" and "men were men"?

How frequently do you do the following:

Encourage girls to do activities other than those which have been considered to be only for girls?

Encourage boys to do activities other than those which have been considered to be only for boys?

While 8 to 14 percent of the women from different races agree to at least some sexist statements, 37 percent of the men, except for black men (21 percent), also agree to at least some sexist statements. Table 5 in the appendix shows the details of the employees' responses by race, gender, and occupational level. It illustrates that craft employees are more likely than management employees to hold sexist views. White male and other minority men are most likely to have sexist attitudes and stereotypes. Women managers are least likely to have such views.

Level of management fairly consistently influences responses to this index. The higher the level of the employees, the less likely they are to have sexist attitudes and stereotypes. For example, 24 percent of the white men at lower management and 39 percent at upper management agree with no or just a few sexist statements. This is a positive sign that, at least in these companies, upper-level managers' stereotypes and attitudes are being affected positively by the affirmative action programs that they have been putting in place in the past ten years. Another positive sign, which was not as evident in my 1976–78 and 1972 studies, was that younger, more educated employees seem to have fewer racist and sexist attitudes and stereotypes than older, less-educated employees. For example, 53 percent of white males with no college and 24 percent with at least a college degree agree to some sexist statements. Seventy-one percent of all men age thirty and under, compared to 51 percent over age fifty, agree with no or just a few sexist statements.

The more frequent contact employees have with women on the job, the less likely they are to have sexist views. However, the impact of contact is significantly greater for men than women. Of men, 47 percent who do not have frequent contact with women on the job compared with 80 percent who do have frequent contact hold only a few sexist views or none.

A denial mechanism operates in people with respect to "owning" their racist and sexist views. We found that people who express the most stereotypes are the most likely to say that women are no longer looked at in a stereotypical fashion. Only 23 percent of those who agree that women are no longer looked at in a stereotypical fashion do not agree with any sexist stereotypes. Sixty percent who express at least a moderate number of stereotypes believe that women are no longer looked at in a stereotypical fashion.

Let's look at a few of the stereotypes specifically.

Stereotype: Working Women Lead to Breakdown of the American Family

A number of the quoted comments suggest that working women lead to the breakdown of the American family. In the 1986 study, more men (45 percent) than women (24 percent) agree with this proposition. People who believe this proposition are unfamiliar with the history of working women. While it is true that women have been joining the active work force in increasing numbers over the past two decades, the majority of women have always worked; only the location and conditions of their labor have varied.

Even a cursory review of women's participation in the work force shows that they have played a crucial role in the economy and have performed far more than menial tasks within the home. Prior to the industrial revolution, little differentiation existed between men's work and women's work. Most jobs were performed by both sexes, and all members of the family had to work. "No work was too hard, no labor too strenuous to exclude women. Among the masses of people emerging from serfdom and existing in terrible poverty, the family was an economic unit in which men, women, and children worked in order to survive."[46]

Anyone who believes that working women are a significant factor in the breakdown of the American family will not give women a fair and equitable chance in present-day corporate America.

Stereotype: Women Are Not Qualified

Many of the stereotypical comments about women relate directly or indirectly to their abilities and qualifications. The data suggest that, while most people will say that they believe that women in general are as qualified as men, many believe that the particular women they are working with are not as qualified as men. For example, 98 percent of the women and 81 percent of the men believe that in general women are as qualified as men, but 36 percent of the women and 60 percent of the men believe that many women got their current positions only because they are women.

Anyone who believes that women got their current positions just because they are women, or that men have a right to exclude women from private clubs, or that many women use gender as an alibi for difficulties they have on the job, or that many women are not serious about professional careers, or that they are too emotional to be professional managers, cannot treat women fairly and equitably in any aspects of their job. As we saw from table 5, few employees are without sexist stereotypes and attitudes.

What are some positive comments from nonsexist employees in these studies? The following are representative. Fewer positive comments are listed for the simple reason that the study participants wrote far fewer positive than negative comments about women.

> In meetings, women tend to be able to cut through the traditional male chest beating to achieve a workable compromise.
>
> —white, male, lower-level manager

> Many women quietly demonstrate skills and abilities and earn promotion and respect.
>
> —white, male, lower-level manager

> Many men feel that women cannot manage effectively because they lack technical skills. My observation is that women in general are more attuned to organizational skills and tend to be more sensitive to the employees' feelings. I see these skills as more important than technical skills.
>
> —white, male, lower-level manager

> I think women bring very important experience to the job in the form of: time management, open emotions, honesty, hard work, determination, kindness, friendship.
>
> —white, female, craftsworker

Years ago many of these questions could have been answered "agree," however, the female employees today have, by and large, earned their positions.

—white, male, lower-level manager

Most women work harder than their male counterparts and are more *dedicated* and *loyal*.

—white, male, upper-level manager

My current workforce has 135 women and 7 men. It's one of the best management jobs I've had. Women are great (all of my assistant managers are women).

—black, male, lower-level manager

Be it president or janitor, generally women are . . . harder workers than men. The higher the position, the harder the woman works.

—Hispanic, male, craftsworker

In my opinion, the women that I have worked with have better self-discipline, and work steadier towards finishing their work. But sometimes their strength limits their ability to perform in some situations, and many men will pounce on that to degrade them not to their face but to other men or their boss.

—American Indian, male, craftsworker

I have worked for two women during my glorious career and they were excellent. The men I have worked for ranged from mediocre to a total jerk.

—white, male, lower-level manager

I believe women are quickly becoming a strong positive force at this company.

—white, male, lower-level manager

I have had several women bosses and they were very good supervisors.

—white, male, craftsworker

I have been fortunate to have worked in open work groups populated by mostly highly visible, independent and very effective women who have enjoyed a solid working relationship with all but two males who have since left due to early retirement incentives but believe difficulties for women exist throughout our business.

—white, male, upper-level manager

I have been a "non-traditional" employee my entire career. The men and women who think that women are, by virtue of their sex, inferior are in the majority. The people who don't think that way are often our high performers. They are wonderful. Their results are highly competitive. You show me poor results in a mixed workforce, and I'll show you sexism and racism at work. How long can we afford to "humor" these attitudes?

—white, male, lower-level manager

Let me reiterate an apparent contradiction. While few employees have no sexist stereotypes and attitudes, 62 percent of men and 34 percent of women believe that women are no longer viewed in stereotypical ways by male employees. This denial of the sexist atmosphere is one of the biggest problems women face in corporate America.

Specific Stereotypes about Minorities

While whites have developed negative stereotypes to justify the exploitation of and discrimination against all minorities, negative stereotypes are most common and resilient about blacks and blackness. Positive concepts of blacks have not prevailed in any period of white history, although other minorities have been viewed negatively and positively at different times. The following passage illustrates such fluctuations:

In 1935, most Americans thought of Japanese as "progressive," "intelligent," and "industrious"; by 1942 they were "cunning" and "treacherous"; and by 1950 the image had changed again. When there was a need for Chinese laborers in California, they were portrayed as "frugal," "sober," and "law abiding"; when labor was plentiful and they competed with white workers, they became "dirty," "repulsive," "unassimilable," and "dangerous."[47]

Now, especially on the West Coast and in the Texas area, a trend of anti-Asian sentiment is rising, in part because of the large influx of Asians after the racist immigration laws were changed to a more equitable, but not totally equitable, position. This has caused a great deal of resentment because of the successes of the many Asian immigrants.

Another factor contributing to the increase in anti-Asian feeling is the success of the Japanese, and to a lesser extent of the South Koreans and Nationalist Chinese, in producing quality products much more cheaply than the American labor force. Loss of jobs to Asian countries and the importation of large amounts of Asian goods have fueled the negative reaction to Asian-Americans. I say Asian-Americans because many Americans do not distinguish between Chinese or Japanese or Vietnamese: they all "look alike." A case in point was the death of a Chinese man in the Detroit area several years ago at the hands of an irate auto worker who thought the young man was Japanese.

Another very diverse group of minorities who are at times considered all the same is the Hispanics. As with the Asians, views of Hispanics, especially Mexicans, have varied over the years. Prior to the Los Angeles "zoot-suit riots" during World War II, newspapers stressed Mexican-Americans' positive traits, including the romantic qualities of their heritage; their brave temperament; their dance, arts, and music; and their devout religious values and strong family ties. However, during the riots the imagery changed to a clearly negative portrayal of Mexican-Americans as law violators, violent, lazy, cowardly, superstitious, backward, and immoral.[48]

Since World War II the number of Hispanics in the United States has not only increased rapidly but has moved out from Texas and California to places such as Miami and Hartford, Connecticut, causing increasing resentment and concerns among some of the populace. An article titled "A Melding of Cultures" noted that the Hispanic population could surpass the black population in the United States by the year 2000. Some whites have expressed fear that this growth of Hispanic culture will make parts of the United States into an extension of our southern neighbors. "But this fear is much more mythology than fact, in part because the Hispanics are anything but a unified force."[49]

This great influx of Hispanics, especially Mexican Americans, and the "Latin Dope Connection" has brought out new racist stereotypes. For example, one hears increasing hostilities about Hispanics not assimilating: "If they do not want to speak English send them back!" Another is the perception that all Hispanics are drug pushers or on welfare having lots of babies. These stereotypes are contradicted by the so-called rational argument that Hispanic aliens are taking jobs away from Americans. How can Hispanics take jobs away and still all be on welfare? This is the mind of a racist at work.

The story with blacks is slightly different. White society has never wanted to be black. In America the old saying is, "An ounce of black blood makes one black." This adage applies to no other minority group. White and Asian is Eurasian. Hispanics were classified as whites until 1970. At various times in the history of this country, whites have taken "pride" in finding a little Native-American blood in their family. However, whites will go to no end to prove that they do not have black blood. Susie Phipps, "a white woman" from Louisiana, has spent tens of thousands of dollars desperately trying to change her race identification from black to white. While she is very white in features, her great, great, great, great grandmother was an African slave.

Estimates show that now more than 36 million white Americans have some degree of black blood and that the vast majority of black Americans have white ancestors. Therefore, notions of biological or racial purity and superiority are as invalid as saying that only English-speaking people are Americans.[50]

Many Americans led by Ronald Reagan believe that this country has shed almost completely its negative racist stereotypes and attitudes. However, it is not that antiblack attitudes are no longer widespread among white Americans, but that society has been better socialized not to express many attitudes openly. It has found new stereotypes that are much more acceptable than old stereotypes; for example, "We won't hire blacks" has become "Blacks do not have the right qualifications." The suppression and refinement of racial attitudes have given us hope of change. However, the behaviors exhibited towards blacks have not been modified to the extent of the change in language, according to studies that use sophisticated techniques to measure both attitudes and behavior.

In 1980 J. Crosby et al. reviewed "unobtrusive measure" studies: research that looked at people's behavior without their knowing it. An array of studies showed up significant amounts of racial bias in interpersonal behavior among black and white Americans. For example, whites were consistently more inclined to help a person in need if that person were white rather than black. Moreover, given the opportunity to deliver an electric shock, white subjects tended to be more aggressive against blacks than against whites. Furthermore, the aggression was more likely when the target was in no position to retaliate. Since whites are in the dominant position of power in this society, it follows that white aggression toward blacks rather than black aggression toward whites would be more frequent. Finally, in spite of positive attitudinal statements made about a person, the underlying "affective tone" implied negative emotional content when the target person was black.[51]

T. I. Pettigrew wrote that approximately 15 percent of adult whites in the United States are vehemently racist out of "authoritarian" impulses. Another 40 percent constitute a population of "conforming bigots," who reflect racist norms that remain as historical vestiges even as they embrace the newer, equalitarian norms. Only about 25 percent of white adults predictably support equal rights and fair treatment for people of color and refrain from exhibiting antiblack behaviors under most circumstances.

We know from our research as well as other studies that the most racist people tend to be older, less educated, and more traditionally religious. They also tend to have lower self-esteem and higher anxiety, and to be more authoritarian, intolerant of ambiguity, and likely to conform to group pressures.

Let's now look at some of the racist stereotypes that employees in my studies expressed about minorities in response to neutral, open-ended questions. Then we will examine data from specific questions asked about racist stereotypes and attitudes.

The following quotations relate in large part to the attitude of minorities. One frequent comment in corporate America is that minorities have "bad attitudes." These "bad" attitudes are frequently used as reasons to hold up the careers of minorities.

Black managers are not as learned or as qualified as white managers. Blacks with positions get arrogant and are hard to work with, want to become personal and if rejected, they intimidate you.

—American Indian, female, lower-level manager

Some colored people are very bold and selfish, while others are very pleasant, intelligent, and a joy to work with. They are different as white people are different.

—white, female, craftsworker

There seem to be two kinds of people of color—dependable and capable or undependable. There does not seem to be the middle quality of people that is typical of some white employees.

—white, female, lower-level manager

There is good and bad in all races; however, in my experience, most minorities have a very bad attitude towards work and whites.

—white, female, craftsworker

Rather than improving work habits, some minorities threaten discrimination to the union or EEOC, and therefore, do not have to conform to the same rules as others.

—white, female, craftsworker

Many blacks that I have supervised have had very different attitudes concerning attendance and following rules for non-pay time, vacation days off, family problems and being at work but when they are here, their work is fine. For the number of blacks I've supervised (few), attendance has been much worse than whites; percentage-wise, but the work has been equal.

—white, male, craftsworker

A number of employees commented on the perception that minorities, especially blacks, are lazy:

I like working with and having contact with the opposite gender in the workplace. For me it makes the job very pleasant. I wish people of color, particularly blacks, would work harder at achieving a good performance, therefore, improving their reputations.

—white, female, craftsworker

Many black minorities use the excuse of being black in order to be lazy. They don't work and when you tell them they're lazy, they cry discrimination. It's a shame!

—Hispanic, female, craftsworker

The few black employees I've had contact with have been good workers and wonderful people. There are many out there who get by with murder knowing the company won't do anything for fear of discrimination charges. Everyone should be made to produce. There are many freeloaders of every color. Many blacks have been brought up with a "lazy" attitude.

—white, female, lower-level manager

There are a few "good" people of color, but the ones I have worked with are very lazy and can get away with reading books, being late or anything because the supervisor doesn't want them to say he is biased because of their color. This makes coworkers dislike these people.

—white, female, craftsworker

The next two comments reflect whites' beliefs that minorities are clannish, cling to their culture, and have defensive attitudes.

America is a "melting pot" of many cultures and races; many people of color have not "melted in" and cling to many of the cultural behaviors that lead to discrimination. (Being different in any race or gender causes discrimination). It is important to hold on to your heritage, but unfortunately, the most successful people of color have "melted in" just as many other cultures have in the past.

—white, male, lower-level manager

The only real problem I see is how they stick together and always feel they are picked on because of their race. They never think whether they are doing the job or not, just their race.

—white, female, lower-level manager

Obviously anyone with any of the characteristics described above does not have the proper attitude and background to be successful in business:

> People of color don't have the same business background as whites. It is more difficult for them to adjust.
>   —American Indian, female, lower-level manager

Finally, a white, female, middle-level manager sums up the ultimate belief that most minorities are not really qualified for corporate jobs:

> This company's practice of meeting "quotas" hurts the company and everyone involved. Excellent qualified people are overlooked because they are the wrong sex or race. Very often lazy incompetent people are kept on strictly because they are a minority or a non-traditional. This is unethical and immoral and should be stopped.

To weigh the strength of racist stereotypes, I formed an index from responses to questions measuring employees' racist stereotypes and attitudes. The questions are as follows:

To what extent do you agree or disagree that:

Pluralism will force us to lower our hiring and promotion standards?

In general, minorities are as dependable employees as whites?

Many minorities got their current positions only because they are minorities?

In general, minorities are as qualified as white employees?

Many minorities use their race as an alibi for difficulties they have on the job?

Many minorities come from different cultural backgrounds which are not conducive to their success in the company?

Many minorities need special training to be successful managers?

In general, minorities could not be demoted, even if inadequate in his/her role, without undeserved charges of discrimination being made?

Many minorities do not have the intelligence to be effective as managers in the company?

Chester I. Barnard, a former Bell System president, wrote in his book *The Function of the Executive* (1940) that a culturally homogeneous group of managers was necessary for the smooth efficient functioning of a corporation. To what extent do you agree or disagree with his statement?

How opposed are you to interracial marriage?

How often do you wish for the "good old days" when there was not such an emphasis on minorities?

How frequently would you allow your child(ren) to have friendships with children not of your racial background?

How frequently would you allow your teenager(s) to date people of a race other than yours?

Only 11 percent of the employees do not agree with any racist questions. Equal percentages of black men and black women (4 percent) agree to at least some racist stereotypes and attitudes. Twenty-six percent of white men, 21 percent of other minority men, 7 percent of the other minority women, and 19 percent of white women agree to more than a few racist statements.

Thirty-six percent of the white women who express no racist views and 55 percent who express a great deal believe minorities are no longer viewed in a stereotypical fashion. These data show how much white women deny the reality of their own racism. However, the opposite is true for white males. The more racist comments they agree with, the less likely they are to believe that minorities are no longer looked at in a stereotypical fashion. For example, 65 percent who express no racist views compared with 45 percent who express a great deal believe that minorities are no longer looked at in that fashion.

Table 6 in the appendix shows the responses to these questions about racist attitudes by race, gender, and occupational level. A higher percentage of black managers than any other group do not agree with any racist statements. White craft males are most likely to agree with racist statements.

As was the case with sexist stereotypes, white women and men at the higher levels of management are more likely than those at lower levels to agree with no racist statements. For example, 29 percent of the women and 23 percent of the men at upper-level management compared to 16 percent of the women and 11 percent of the men at a lower level do not agree with any racist statements. The figures for minorities show similar trends.

Education does not seem to have a significant impact on the racist views of minority employees, but it does have on whites: 8 percent with no college compared to 17 percent with a college degree agree with *no* racist statements. In addition, there is a tendency among older minorities and a significant trend among older whites to agree with most racist statements. Of whites, 14 percent age thirty and younger compared to 34 percent over age fifty agree to at least a moderate number of racist statements.

Social contact with minorities, but not work contact, moderates racist stereotypes and attitudes. For example, 28 percent of whites who have very frequent social contact with minorities compared to 8 percent of those who have no social contact with minorities do not agree with any racist statements.

Stereotype: Minorities Lack Intelligence
A national study of white racist attitudes found that 31 percent of whites believe blacks are less able as a race than whites. I have found that between 10 percent and 15 percent of the corporate employees believe that minorities do not have the intelligence to be effective corporate managers. Few whites today will agree with an out-and-out racist statement; however, a few will make comments such as the following:

Regarding relative "intelligence" of black people: black culture is a problem in that it does not value intellectual development in reading, math as opposed to being streetwise. Black men are often obsessed with maintaining a macho image and tend to be extremely sexist, especially young black men. Latin and Indian cultures tend to be highly sexist as well.

—white, male, lower-level manager

All of my past experiences with colored co-workers indicate they are lazier and slower learners than other non-colored peers.

—white, male, craftsworker

As we have seen, there are still socially acceptable ways of being a racist. For example, 55 percent of whites believe that the only reason many minorities got their current positions is because of their race. This statement in a very direct way questions minorities' abilities, if not intelligence.

*Stereotype: A Minority Background Is Not Conducive
to Business*
Another question we asked employees was whether minorities come from a background not conducive to their success in corporations. One out of four white employees believe this. A related question was: "Do minorities need special training to be effective managers?" About three out of ten whites believe this, and about the same percentage of minorities concur. A similar question in a national survey found that 52 percent of the whites agree that black Americans teach their children values and skills different from those required to be successful in American society. It is obvious that white managers who agree with any of these racist questions will have a very difficult time being objective about the abilities and thus the upward mobility of minorities. I have argued in previous writings that minorities who want to enter the corporate world have the same skills as whites for being successful in business. In addition, because of the mass socialization process, most Americans have many more similar than dissimilar values and backgrounds.

As with women, if one minority behaves in a lazy, arrogant

manner, then many whites project that to all minorities. The reality is that minorities are not given the opportunity to demonstrate their learned business skills in the corporate world and, even when they are, white racist stereotypes and attitudes get in the way of positive acknowledgment of these skills.

A few—very few—positive comments were made about minority employees:

> There are very few people of color in our office so it's difficult to be comprehensive in evaluation and giving opinions. However, the ones we do have are top-notch, intelligent and hard workers.
>
> —white, female, craftsworker

> I think socializing with people of different races and color is very important. These values must be instilled in our children now to make them productive adults in the future.
>
> —black, female, craftsworker

> I have worked under both black and white managers. In some ways the black managers have been more qualified and more understanding or approachable with problems.
>
> —Native American, female, craftsworker

> I have only experienced good things with such people. They seem to be a lot more outgoing for the little guy and understanding. But you'll always have the few that use their color as a device.
>
> —white, female, lower-level manager

> As a white male who has visited clubs (taverns) and attended social functions where people of color are the majority, I am encouraged by the acceptance and friendliness that I usually find.
>
> —white, male, craftsworker

In conclusion, employers who believe that minorities got their jobs because of their race, that minorities lower standards, that their background is not conducive to business, and that they are not dependable and smart cannot treat minorities fairly inside or outside the corporate world.

Racism and Sexism in Society

Ninety percent of my study participants believe that racism and sexism exist at least to some extent today in this country. Less than 5 percent believe that there is no racism and/or sexism—a clear indication that few corporate employees believe that we live in a color- and gender-blind society. A white craftswomen said, "Racism/sexism exist everywhere in society. Why should this company be different?" While this acknowledgment of the existence of racism and sexism is positive, the problem is that many of the participants who say it exists are part of the problem but do not recognize it.

The following news headlines substantiate the existence of racism and sexism throughout society:

"Whites Remove Dead from Cemetery Now Owned by Black Man" (*Jet*, 1985)

"When Blocks Battle To Stay Lily-White" (*U.S. News and World Report*, Dec. 9, 1985)

"Michigan May Limit Race as Factor in Adoptions" (*New York Times*, Dec. 15, 1985)

"Prosecutors, Prejudice and Handpicked Juries" (*New York Times*, Dec. 15, 1985)

"Boston Realtors Acting to Detect Housing Bias" (*New York Times*, Dec. 15, 1985)

"Racial Tension Is Not Limited to S.W. Phila." (*Philadelphia Inquirer*, Dec. 8, 1985)

"Violent Incidents against Asians" (*New York Times*, Aug. 31, 1985)

"Boston Case Revives Past and Passions" (Racism in the Boston Red Sox Baseball Team) (*New York Times*, March 3, 1986)

"Plight of Black Student at Penn State Tested Anew" (*Philadelphia Inquirer*, March 12, 1986)

"School Desegregation Isn't Faring Very Well in Washington Today—Justice Department Argues against Busing in Court, to Dismay of Minorities" (*Wall Street Journal,* Oct. 22, 1985)

"Racial Issues Called Factor in Democratic Defections" (*Philadelphia Inquirer,* May 6, 1985)

"Justice, HUD Oppose Housing Segregation, but Enforcement Lags—Critics Charge Indifference; Officials Argue Overwork, Budgets Are the Problem—No Vacancy for Chester Chin" (*Wall Street Journal,* Oct. 28, 1985)

"Bias against Orientals Increases with Rivalry of Nation's Economies" (*Wall Street Journal,* Nov. 28, 1986)

"State Facing 45-Day Limit on Bias Plan" (With Regard to Segregation in Pennsylvania University and Colleges) (*Philadelphia Inquirer,* July 4, 1985)

"Bias against Asians Follows an Old Pattern" (*Philadelphia Inquirer,* 1985)

"Unfair Shake? Women Charge They Don't Get Their Share of White House Jobs—Chief of Staff Denies Sexism, but Even Some in GOP Complain of Backsliding—The 'Bank-Teller Syndrome'" (*Wall Street Journal,* Sept. 10, 1985)

"Still Hostile to a Woman's Right" (*Philadelphia Inquirer,* July 18, 1985)

"Companies Want to Talk with Men—Not Women" (*Philadelphia Inquirer,* Oct. 10, 1985)

"Price Waterhouse Cited in Sex Bias" (*Philadelphia Inquirer,* Oct. 10, 1986)

"A Male Club Tries to Keep Women Out" (*Philadelphia Inquirer,* June 9, 1985)

What these newspaper and magazine headlines say is that racism and sexism permeate all aspects of our lives, from the grave to the White House.

Conclusions

We and our children are socialized into racist and sexist views from the day we are born. Our society continues to reinforce these views throughout our adult life in thousands of ways.

As our society has become more sophisticated about racism and sexism, it has acquired new, insidious forms of them: institutional racism and sexism, neoracism, and neosexism. These forms are even more detrimental than overt discrimination. Until this society develops an overall strategy to deal with racism and sexism in all of our institutions; until white and male America recognize that the problems of racism and sexism are theirs, not problems of the oppressed; until we get moral leadership from the White House to the corporate board room; and until this society understands that racism and sexism are severe symptoms of mental illness; this country will never rid itself of racism and sexism.

Gunnar Myrdal, in his monumental work, *An American Dilemma: The Negro Program and Modern Democracy,* points to the fundamental contradiction between America's cherished values of liberty, equality, justice, and equal opportunity and the degraded position of blacks in American society:

> The American Negro problem is a problem in the heart of the American. It is there that the interracial tension has its focus. It is there that the decisive struggle goes on. . . . The "American Dilemma" . . . is the ever raging conflict between, on the one hand, the values preserved on the general plane which we shall call the "American Creed," where the American thinks, talks, and acts under the influence of high national and Christian precepts, and, on the other hand, the values on specific planes of individual and group living, where personal and local interests; economic, social, and sexual jealousies; considerations of community prestige and conformity; group prejudice against particular persons or types of people; and all sorts of miscellaneous wants, impulses, and habit dominate his outlook.[52]

The contradiction between American values and actions can be seen in these comments:

I am married to a white woman and I still prefer this for myself. I am not opposed to my friends' mixed marriages. I do feel that I might have a difficult time of it if any of my three daughters were to enter a mixed marriage. I am quite comfortable working with other races and ethnic people and do not know of anyone on the job who has any problem this way either. One's qualification for a job should not be the ability to do the least because it could become that we all should have to do no more than the worst.

—white, male, craftsworker

I have no problems working in a pluralistic environment. I feel the diversity of a workforce adds to everyone's character. All races and all genders have competent, incompetent, ambitious, lazy, conscientious, and apathetic people. I do have a problem with hiring practices when they involve the hiring of an obviously less qualified individual.

—white, male, craftsworker

A black, female, craftsworker points out where most whites are coming from:

Racism/sexism still exist—the sorry thing is that the people who still practice this don't see themselves as in this category. They have been in this mold so long that they don't see where they are wrong and are unwilling to have anyone tell them they have a problem."

Corporate America and American society would be better if we had more people like the following:

I would like to say very honestly that when I came to work for this company 21 years ago, I was extremely racist and sexist and this company has changed me through education. I have learned that you judge the individual and not their sex or race. I can very honestly say I enjoy working with and for the opposite sex and people of color. I know I go home at night feeling very good about that. Even though I have changed, because of the feeling I had 20 years ago, I'm sure I will die with some prejudices. I am raising my family so they are starting out where I am today. I am hoping that some day these prejudices are gone from this earth.

—white, male, lower-level manager

I went to a junior high and high school with almost 50 percent black enrollment. They have the good and bad just like the whites but people have to mix with them in order to learn how to deal with them.

—white, male, craftsworker

The costs of prejudice and discrimination, Simpson and Yinger suggest, include personality distortions, economic inefficiency due to wasteful use of labor resources, depression, derisiveness, and civil and international strife.[53]

Racism and sexism are not only attitudes but behaviors that are the major detriments to women and minorities making it to middle and upper management and surviving at those levels.

7

Special Career Problems of White Males and Their Solutions

M any white males believe that they, rather than women and minorities, are the true victims of discrimination. Is "reverse discrimination" the primary problem white males face in achieving their career goals, or are other factors involved? Let's explore this question in more detail.

White Males' Perceptions of Reverse Discrimination

When white males in my survey were asked about their career goals and opportunities, it was evident that many of them at all levels of the hierarchy place a great deal of blame for their lack of mobility on "reverse discrimination" and affirmative action programs. They believe that many qualified white males are losing out to unqualified women and minorities. Let's look at some of their comments.

> I feel that I'm being discriminated against because I am a white male. I have an above-average work record that I'm proud of but it doesn't seem to give me any advantage. Discrimination against a white male is still discrimination, and it won't make EEO right because a different group is being affected.
>
> —white, male, craftsworker

> The Affirmative Action Program epitomizes discrimination and should be terminated. Affirmative action is an unconscionable

concept, perpetrated by the element which intends to subjugate and ultimately destroy us. On the other hand, equal opportunity epitomizes the fundamentals of our society; that an individual's work performance should be solely judged on merit, without consideration to race, ethnic background, gender, etc.; the equal opportunity concept should be fully supported and maintained.

—white, male, upper-level manager

The most discriminated-against class of employees is probably the white male. I know I am a victim. I feel the best qualified person should be the one selected regardless of gender, race, color . . .

—white, male, craftsworker

This company has nothing to offer a white male. I feel that all white males are discriminated against in order to avoid discrimination against people of color and women. There are many white men who are more deserving of promotions but don't get them because they are white.

—white, male, craftsworker

Female managers are as competent or as incompetent as male managers; gender has very little to do with competency; only qualifications do. There is no discrimination against female managers in this company; if anything, there is discrimination against male managers due to EEO/AAP considerations.

—white, female, upper-level manager

Pluralism must equate to equitable treatment from this point in time FOR ALL—not just those who may have been slighted in the past. I'm afraid those who feel pluralism is a pleasant euphemism for quotas, smacking of reverse discrimination, may be right. I am ready to defend everyone's inalienable right to equal treatment and opportunity. I am equally as ready to defend my rights against racist reverse discrimination. Establishing quotas is unfair. It is wrong. Don't attempt to absolve past sins by committing more. Wipe the slate clean! Reward ability not categories. (DON'T CATEGORIZE PEOPLE.)

—white, male, middle-level manager

A misdirected effort. A better idea would be to focus efforts to surface and advance the real contributors, without all this flap about having a social, ethnic, gender, etc. "rainbow coalition" as an end in itself. Pluralism is just another word for the socialistic concept of egalitarianism, a concept of dubious value and no proven benefit.

—white, male, upper-level manager

Are these white males accurate in their assessment? Is the company treating them unfairly and giving the opportunities to unqualified women and minorities? Or do these white males, harboring a sense of entitlement perhaps, in Machiavelli's terms "expect more than they deserve"? What can white males do to enhance their career opportunities?

A Change in White Males' Advancement Opportunities

Whenever I give a speech on mobility in corporations, I like to start out by asking, "Would you prefer to compete for a promotion with thirty-three people or one hundred people?" Ninety-nine percent of the respondents say they would prefer to compete with thirty-three people rather than one hundred because they will have a much better chance for the promotion. To understand those two numbers is to understand the problem white males confront in their desire to move up the corporate ladder and the psychological turmoil that they increasingly experience as corporations move toward greater commitment to equal employment opportunity.

Until the Civil Rights Act of 1964, white males in corporations had to compete against only 33 percent of the population, for that is the percentage that white males comprise in America. However, after 1964 white males, at least by law, had to compete on a more equitable basis with the other 67 percent, that is, women and people of color. Essentially what this means is that white males who were average and below average in abilities have a more difficult time in advancing because they are now competing with the entire population, which includes many with credentials and abilities far superior, let alone equal, to theirs.

A lower-level white male accurately wrote: "While I understand the concept and agree with it, it limits my opportunity. Being a white man, if there are 10 openings and 5 are reserved for minorities, then only 5 are available to me. It limits my opportunities."

Despite this, however, white males who are above average—especially those who fit the "image of the promotable manager"—have little trouble. The most numerous and powerful decision makers were and are white males and, given the "cloning" tendency, even the average and below-average white males still, in many cases, have an advantage over above-average women and minorities.

K. W. Terry made some astute observations about racism that also apply to sexism. He pointed out that, although white male managers currently face greater competition for fewer jobs as a result of affirmative action policies, racism (and sexism) have sheltered them from the need to test their skills. The tacit discrimination practiced by upper-level management created the need for affirmative action, he explained. This discrimination leaves white males ill-equipped to deal with pluralistic competition once it is forced upon them.[1]

Greatly increased competition with large numbers of people whom white males believe, in large part, to be inferior or deficient in some way to them naturally leads to severe psychological dislocation, and cries of unfair treatment and reverse discrimination. Corporations should recognize this as a normal reaction of people who are at risk of being displaced from a privileged power position. This is especially painful because white males, always a minority of the population, have perceived themselves to be a majority. As a white, lower-level manager said: "The company in effect has produced a new minority—the white male."

Let's use an analogy to put the problem white males face into perspective. Assume that you and your immediate friends controlled this society for 500 years. During those years you and your ancestors were brought up to believe that you are in control because you work hard, have the necessary credentials, and have the right values and attitudes. You were also taught that those other people (not your friends) failed to make it into the power positions not because of discrimination but because they were essentially inferior and did not have the right skills, values, and attitudes to control. Now, after 500 years, you and your friends are told by law you have to share your privileged position with large numbers of "inferior" people who greatly outnumber you. Do you think you would willingly share your position and power? Would you immediately stop believing, after 500 years of discriminatory socialization, that the others were inferior? Would you think that the law was fair? The answer to all of these questions is no. Neither you nor I would willingly give up or share something that we have been conditioned over 500 years to believe was rightfully ours because we had the right values, intelligence, and work ethic. Neither would white males.

What we would do, given the above scenario, and what white males have done, is to become fearsome toward people and programs that challenge our privileged position. In addition we would begin to develop, consciously or unconsciously, an array of strategies to defend our place in the status quo. The news media tells the populace about how terrible things are for the white males and how women and minorities have it made. Academics write books about the terrible consequences of the new meritocracy and how this has negatively affected corporate efficiency and productivity.

By developing such theories that blame the victims and encourage them to accept the blame for their oppression, the white males can feel more comfortable that they indeed deserve their privileged positions. In this way they can concentrate on maintaining their bastion of power and privilege and avoid looking at their own deficiencies.

A crucial way in which white males have maintained their privileged position has been by keeping the women and minorities divided, fighting among themselves for the small piece of pie. This keeps the oppressed occupied.

Some comments by white males in our survey were:

Any attempt to right a previous wrong is going to stir negative reactions. That's life—you don't win them all. White males must know that the best white male was not always chosen for promotion in the past. In short, the psychological consequences of being a minority and recognizing that your privileged position over the majority (women and minorities) is being slowly but surely erased leads to increasing insecurities, cries of unfair treatment, complaints about the qualifications of the oppressed and just a victimized mentality.

—white, male, middle-level manager

Any injustice that is allowed to occur or is enacted to remedy a past injustice will only lead to more of the same. Trying to cure one sickness by spreading another will never solve anything. Past injustices to non-whites and women were wrong but occurred in a different time and climate. Allowing the burden to fall on today's society only adds to the burden. The burden of solving past injustices by committing more of the same (reverse discrimination) is not productive.

—white, male, craftsworker

I feel as a white male my days are numbered. I know the technical aspects of our business like the back of my hand. This company can't survive without me and my 115,000 other mates.

—white, male, craftsworker

I am outraged that a person, like myself (a 31-year-old college grad with a B.A. in journalism) should be stuck in a job as a customer representative, along with people of similar backgrounds for 7+ years in a growing, profitable company like ours, being continually told that the chances for "movement" are highly limited at best.

—white, male, craftsworker

I believe the company discriminates against the white male as a matter of policy. Intellectually, I understand and agree with the policy, but, as a white male, I have a problem dealing with it emotionally.

—white, male, upper-level manager

White males in the 35–49 age bracket are the most discriminated against group in this company. There is no meaningful future for these people in terms of an advancement. The only positive action that can be taken is for the white male to find employment elsewhere. Those of us that have too much invested (or are too conservative) to do so have the other option of accepting conditions as they are, with no hope of advancement.

—white, male, middle-level manager

> I find that the only group being discriminated against is the white male. On his shoulders the past is trying to be rectified. His skills are ignored for the sake of others. . . . If people are hard workers, friendly, and respectful, there are no problems no matter what the sex or race. Your goal is hire that type of individual.
>
> —white, male, lower-level manager

Some of these comments reflect a siege mentality. This insecurity seems due in large part to the white male's upbringing, in which he was taught that he is the superior being and will never have to compete with people of color or women. Many white males are like fish out of water in the emerging, more equitable environment. They are trying to figure out how things are changing.

The most important step that white males can take to enhance their career opportunities is to accept reality so that they can better develop their strategies. Regardless of race and/or gender, if one insists on living in a world of illusion, one cannot effectively cope with the real world. Listed below are some of the realities that white males must recognize.

Reality No. 1: Corporate America Is Unfair to All

Corporate America is an unfair bureaucracy that has never given promotions, jobs, rewards, or anything else strictly on the basis of merit, even to white males. In addition, it does not offer unlimited opportunities, as most white males have been brought up to believe it does. The comments of the following white males are based on myths:

> White males are now, once again, being blatantly discriminated against. The meritocracy is dead.
>
> —white, male, upper-level manager

> I have felt severely handicapped by being a white, well-educated male in this company and feel frustrated that more emphasis on sex and color *versus* ability is the criteria for advancement within the company.
>
> —white, male, lower-level manager

Promotion of minorities should be considered right along with
any other group, but it seems we have lost track of job knowledge
and ability along the way. If a person wants advancement, it is his
or her responsibility to make the effort to learn everything possible about the business. Nothing came easy for anyone without
hard work.

—white, male, upper-level manager

My main concern is that the criteria used to decide who gets the
promotion does seem to be standard. Some highly qualified people
are being overlooked because of our effort to achieve a pluralistic
work force.

—white, male, lower-level manager

Many white males have a quite difficult time coming to grips with
the inherent unfairness and limited opportunities in corporate
America because they developed, own, and run the system.

One white, male, middle-level manager has a perspective that
few white males have and more should adopt: "Pluralism has very
recently 'slowed down' my advancement; however, it is the right
thing to do. I'm making a good living, have a challenging job and
have two daughters that I want the same opportunities for. So, it's
worth it."

A white, male, craftsworker recognizes that a lot of the white
males' complaints are self-serving: "If you try to please everyone,
you're a failure. No matter who got that last promotion, 50 other
people could do just as good a job. I'm happy with my job. I know
that, if I want to progress in this company, I must make my own
breaks."

Reality No. 2: Image Is Vital to Success

The higher a white male goes in the corporate structure, the more
likely he is to be discriminated against by the white males in power
if he does not fit the image of the promotable manager.

It is essential for white males to recognize on not only an intellectual level but a gut level that there are numerous subjective reasons why people get ahead. Over sixty years of systematic research
support this view.

Again it seems that white males, because the system is theirs and because they see many successful role models, find it hard to see reality. As developers and owners of the system, most have totally bought into the rhetoric of meritocracy and as a result are having extreme difficulties with their perceived "limited" career opportunities.

Reality No. 3: Competition Is Keen

White males must recognize that most of them will not get their promotions or the jobs they desire—not because of reverse discrimination but simply because the selection pool has increased from thirty-three people to one hundred people. The odds against the thirty-three people are greatly increased, especially those who are average or below average in ability.

Despite the prevalent belief among many white males that they are members of the superior group, each race and gender has a small percentage of outstanding people, a larger percentage of below-average people, and a very large percentage of mediocre people. The vital question for white males is, now that they are competing with a larger pool of people, which of them will lose out to the increased competition.

Reality No. 4: White Males Are Still Advantaged

In most cases, the below-average and average white male still has significant advantages over women and minorities of the same ability. The same advantage applies to above-average white males who compete with above-average women and minorities. Chapters 8 and 9 present considerable data to support this position. Mediocrity is still the privilege of the white male.

A case in point is President Richard Nixon's nomination of B. Clement Carswell to the Supreme Court. Carswell was opposed by numerous groups, including civil rights groups, for diverse reasons. However, the primary reason he was not confirmed was that he was a mediocre judge. A white male senator nevertheless argued that Carswell should be confirmed despite his mediocrity "because mediocrity also needs representation on the highest court."[2]

Can you imagine a senator proposing that a mediocre minority or a mediocre woman be confirmed for the Supreme Court? Women and minorities have long needed to be better performers to get ahead.

As R. L. Jones wrote:

> Much of the expressed antagonism toward affirmative action is based on the belief that standards are lowered by allowing "less qualified" minorities and women in entry positions ahead of "more qualified" white males. The historical fact is that minorities and women have had to be overqualified in order to obtain opportunities. An implication of the overqualification requirement is that, historically, white males have obtained positions with substantially weaker qualifications.[3]

Why is this the case? White men still dominate corporate America. They set the cultural tone, the standards, and the criteria for advancement. As was shown in previous chapters, human beings are most likely to select their "clones" to replace them, in this case white males. Considerable research supports this view. Researchers have clearly demonstrated that competitive choices favoring in-group members tend to dominate all other choices available to the study participants.[4] In other words, despite white males' concern that they are at a great disadvantage because of affirmative action, the basic concept of in-group bias suggests that, until the corporate hierarchy has many more women and minorities, white males will still be the favored group.

One would suppose, with all the cries about reverse discrimination over the past twenty years, that women and minorities have made substantial inroads into the corporate hierarchy.

I developed a model chart with information from some of the companies I consult for about the percentage of minorities and women in their managerial ranks. Figure 7-1 shows that corporate America at the middle and upper levels is still a white male reserve.

Comments from three white, middle-level, women managers state the reality for white males:

> The "good old boy" network is still alive and well.

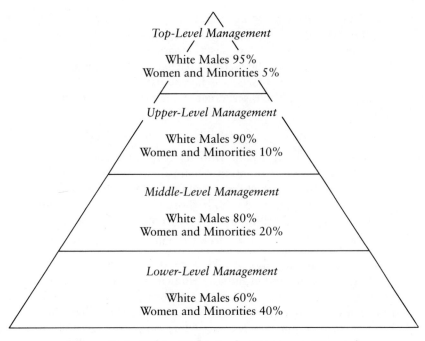

Figure 7–1. *White Males in the Corporate Hierarchy*

Majority of employees (white males) that see only women and people of color being promoted are blind to the white males' movement.

Look at the numbers; the company only wants diversity at lower management. After that, it's white males (with very few exceptions.)

Reality No. 5: "Reverse Discrimination" Is Based on Lies

White males' sense of reverse discrimination is based in large part on the lies they hear from their own corporations, from the media, and from educational institutions.

Several comments from white males bring this point into focus:

I am proud to be a white male and I appreciate people who are proud of who they are. My parents immigrated to this country from Germany and I knew discrimination during the second World War because of the German background. Consequently, I have empathy for people who are discriminated against; however, I don't feel I should be discriminated against in the "interest of parity."

—white, male, middle-level manager

As an upper level white male who supports pluralism, I suspect that my chances for promotion remain the same. In all candor, however, I could very well be passed over to remedy deficiencies and prior behavior and I do think about that from time to time. However, I do not dwell on it and I try to focus on my strengths.

—white, male, upper-level manager

I think this company should take a good, hard look at how its emphasis on hiring and promoting women and people of color is holding back more qualified employees. Being a white male who has been passed over for promotion because of this, I have first-hand experience and am not just expressing "sour grapes." By continuing this practice of promoting less qualified individuals, the company is setting itself up for many organizational problems in coming years. I am all for equal opportunity and affirmative action, but the company has gone well beyond the bounds of fairness to near discrimination of white males. Don't be surprised to see legal action taken to resolve this problem. I would encourage top management to closely examine its almost blind approach to this growing problem. I realize that women and people of color feel very strongly about the discrimination they've faced, but their positions today are no worse than that of the white male.

—white, male, middle-level manager

Over the past sixteen years I have observed many white males who believe that they are victims of reverse discrimination, because their companies and managers implicitly or explicitly lie to them. Some are directly told that their careers are going nowhere, or that they did not get a promotion or a lateral job, because of women and minority quotas. In fact, none of the companies in my studies ever had quotas; they had goals and timetables for management positions up through middle management. The goals and the time-tables were minimal, and there was no penalty for failing to meet them. Most managers or craftsworkers who believe they were dis-criminated against actually were not promoted because of lack of skills, ability, or potential, or because of some subjective evaluation on the part of their bosses or the corporation. Also, corporations promise many more opportunities than they are able to deliver and have not developed ways of satisfying the high expectations not only of the white males but of others. As most white males believe they are being discriminated against, it is much simpler and easier to tell them that they are not going anywhere because of women and minorities than to tell them about their own limitations. White males, who feel much more membership and in-group loyalty to the corporation than other groups, are less likely to take formal action against perceived discrimination than women and minorities.

The following comments illustrate this process:

> I was hired as a management trainee. I have been on the high potential list for many years but am still at middle level. My bosses have all said that I have potential and ability but still I get no opportunities because of the need to promote women and minorities.
>
> —white, male, middle-level manager

> My boss was really pushing me for promotion in the Marketing Department, but he told me a woman got the job. I was going to file a complaint until I found out another white male got it. My boss said he had only told me what he heard.
>
> —white, male, lower-level manager

Blame for the lack of mobility of white males on women and minorities should be a red flag. White male candidates should rec-ognize that, by allowing their superiors to shift blame, they are al-lowing them to avoid discussing the employee's actual ability to do the job. Most bosses want to avoid uncomfortable situations, es-pecially those related to giving employees bad news—like why they are not getting a promotion.

Therefore, bosses will pick the easiest way out. White males can commiserate with one another about how terrible it is now for them because of "reverse discrimination"; however, there is no commiserating when one white male tells another, "I am not supporting you for a promotion because you just don't have it. I don't like your style, your dress, your height or your personality."

Corporations have done a disservice to white males by not explaining the true facts about their opportunities; society, which is controlled by white males, has done the same. News media, books, and articles have basically presented an image that all it takes to succeed is to be a woman or a minority. The statistics, however, show just the opposite. Probably the one factor that has caused more psychological trauma in white males than any other is the Reagan administration's constant attack on equal employment opportunities and affirmative action. How can white males believe they are getting a fair shake when the most popular president in recent history says that they are being discriminated against? B. Bowser and R. Hunt summarize the impact of the Reagan administration. In public signs an erosion is evident in the federal commitment to initiatives and programs that, for almost fifty years, assisted the advancement of racial equality. Moreover, a number of occurrences reflect a mood of backlash and hostile reaction to the insistence on racial justice in America: "our nation seems quite willing to countenance an era of benign neglect on contemporary racial issues."[5]

To deal constructively with the potential for reverse discrimination, white males should insist on quarterly written performance evaluations. They should also seek yearly written potential evaluations with career plans and development plans as integral parts of the evaluation process. My book, *Racism and Sexism in Corporate America,* has chapters on performance, potential, and career planning, which contain good common sense advice on how to ensure that you are getting at least a somewhat even chance of being treated fairly in these processes. This advice is useful not only to white males but to anyone trying to advance and survive in the corporate world.

White males should ask for a breakdown of all promotions by race, gender, and level. They should also demand to know specifically why they did not get a particular job. If they believe they are truly the better candidates and that they have been discriminated against, they should pursue the matter to higher levels. Sitting around complaining about reverse discrimination instead of insisting on the full story from the company is shortsighted and not productive for anyone's career.

Having said this, let me also say that white males, who say that women and minorities are "always crying" about discrimination, are themselves some of the worst offenders. As a white, male, lower-level manager said: "People of color and women have it made. We white males have absolutely no promotion opportunities."

To focus constantly on race and gender as factors holding up a career is to waste a lot of energy. White males, to be successful in the emerging heterogeneous corporation, must begin to face reality. If they continue to attribute their lack of success to reverse discrimination, they will not focus on getting the true story from the company and thus they will be unable to develop realistic strategies to reach their goals, revise them according to the realities, or develop plans to correct them. They will doom their careers because competition will get tougher as more people compete for fewer positions.

Reality No. 6: Nothing Excuses Poor Performance

With the increasing competition and limited opportunities, white males must not allow their frustrations to affect their performance. If they do this, as was noted in the previous chapter, it will give the corporation another solid reason to block them from reaching their desired positions.

The following employees are setting themselves up for failure:

> Corporate efforts towards pluralism have gone way too far towards female. Almost every promotion is now female. The future for talented males is disappointing and I expect more turnover or poor performance of the male as a result. The young/middle aged male is being penalized for the sins of the past.
>
> —white, male, upper-level manager

It's all show. Open your eyes—you've bypassed a heck of a lot of good working men that used to give only 50 percent or less for you.

                                        —white, male, craftsworker

If white males or anyone else really believes they are not being treated fairly, they should either adjust their goals or leave the company. Poor performance benefits no one.

As a white male, rated "high potential" for many years, I feel I will continue to be passed by for promotion opportunities as officers need to meet their objective of numbers of female directors and above. It is becoming clear that I may have to choose to leave the company to advance.

                                        —white, male, middle-level manager

Reality No. 7: Adjust for Success

White males who attempt to change their racist and sexist attitudes and behaviors will have greater promotional opportunities than those who do not.

In 1981, I wrote:

Although many of the problems just discussed are caused primarily by the creation of a younger, more affluent, and better-educated workforce, another set of factors—race and sex—also has made an impact on the conflicts and stresses of the corporate workplace. Corporations are changing from homogeneous organizations dominated by white men to heterogeneous organizations.[6]

Many minorities and women have been socialized differently from white males. They have diverse cultural backgrounds, different value systems, and different expectations than do the white males who presently dominate corporations. The coming together of these people of diverse backgrounds, in some cases for the first time in the corporate setting, has created great tension for everyone.

This is not to judge which group has the correct background, values, expectations, and so on. Each group has some unique good and bad qualities and there are more similarities than differences because of the American socialization process. What is important for white males to understand is that because of their power and dominant position, they have not had to adjust to others; others have always had to adjust to them.

Corporate America, out of competitive necessity, will become increasingly heterogeneous. The employees who will have the greatest chances of making it will be those who can accept and feel comfortable working with this new work force. White males who are racist and sexist will never be able to work effectively with truly heterogeneous work groups. As a result they will never be able to help their organizations achieve their best results.

The white males who can operate effectively in this new heterogeneous environment will have a definite advantage over racist and sexist white males, professionally and personally. As the previous chapter demonstrated, while racism and sexism have negative consequences for those who are victims of these evil forces, they also have negative consequences for the oppressors. Numerous researchers have documented that racist and sexist people are much more mentally unhealthy than nonracist and nonsexist people.

Conclusions

The most important advice I can offer to white males who want to "make it" in the coming years is that they must be more honest about who they are, what they are, and what the realities of corporate life are all about. Terry made these comments about people in general:

> Authenticity operates along two vectors—true to self and true to world. To distort either vector, or both, undermines our capacity to act knowledgeably and effectively. Inauthenticity destroys our groundedness. It substitutes a false foundation for a solid one, and guarantees a false understanding of the world. Thus if I am untrue to myself, I say one thing and do another. Not only do I cease to be trusted by others, but eventually, if not immediately, I cease to know myself as well. I became uprooted, subject to external pres-

sures, and unsure of my direction and my ability to act on my deepest insights about life and myself.

If I am untrue to the world, I lose my grasp on what is happening around and to me and thus make judgments that lead to behaviors that are inappropriate to situations in which I find myself. I distort what is happening to me and, because of this false diagnosis of my situation, continually make erroneous judgments.[7]

Put in corporate terms, if white males want a better chance of making it in the bureaucratic structure, they must understand themselves and be realistic about the unfair bureaucracy and the natural unhealthiness of people. Some comments from employees sum up the more healthy, realistic views that white males should begin to adopt in order to be successful in the late 1980s and 1990s.

I feel the management has adjusted, however, I also feel we need a lot of work in our white male "traditional" jobs to have them more supportive. I feel the company has a very positive attitude in accomplishing a pluralistic force and, even though I feel I have been held back because of it, it is the right thing to do.

—white, male, middle-level manager

I applaud it. It's fair, honest. It's human. It's right.

—white, male, lower-level manager

I'm white and male and to some extent I believe what is happening is hindering my chances. On the other hand, the cards in the past were stacked in favor of white employees. My gut reaction is that the company is doing an admirable job in improving its pluralistic mix and I don't think we have suffered talent while doing it.

—white, male, lower-level manager

White males who do not focus on the realities of the corporate bureaucracies and their inherent unfairness will increasingly doom themselves to failure as this society strives to become more equitable.

8
Extraordinary Problems of Women Employees and Their Solutions

The pervasive sexist stereotypes and attitudes of society in general and corporate America in particular translate into special difficulties that corporate women must face, over and above the normal bureaucratic problems, concerns, and difficulties encountered by all employees. As women move up the corporate hierarchy, the intensity of these problems increases. This is partly because the criteria for higher advancement become increasingly subjective and there are fewer and fewer candidates to observe.

The Situation of Women in Corporations

Let's review some basic facts. Between 1970 and 1980, women moved into management jobs at a much faster rate than men. A Census Bureau report showed that women increased their representation in executive, administrative, and managerial jobs from 19 percent in 1970 to 31 percent in 1980. In the managerial ranks alone, the presence of women almost tripled during the decade, particularly in such fields as financial management, the top echelons of state and local government, educational administration, and self-employment.[1]

While on the surface these statistics seem impressive, a report on the economic progress of women conducted by Stanford University economics professor Victor Fuchs noted that, despite gains in the labor market and in antidiscrimination legislation, women were no better off economically in 1983 than in 1959. The report noted that women's income had doubled in the past twenty-five years; however, their average hourly pay was still 50 percent less than men's.

S. Fraker wrote in a 1984 article, titled "Why Women Aren't Getting to the Top," that a decade after U.S. corporations began hiring more than token numbers of women at low levels of management, these women have not progressed nearly as far as their male counterparts. Despite impressive progress at entry and middle levels, women are having a great deal of trouble even breaking into senior management. Only one company of the Fortune 500 has a female chief executive. That woman, Katharine Graham of the *Washington Post,* openly states that "she got the job because her family owns a controlling share of the corporation."[2]

J. Alter and D. Weathers in *"In Women: Give Us Some Air"* noted how little progress women have made in the past years in the electronic news media. Even after lawsuits and federal regulations, "white males still fill the airwaves." Alter and Weathers summarize, "Somewhere along the line the gallop toward equal time turned into a crawl." While much better off than fifteen to twenty years ago, women are only marginally better off than five to ten years ago.

In television news, hiring is not so much the issue as power sharing and air time. Marlene Sanders became the first woman vice president for a news division. Almost ten years later, there is still only one woman vice president at ABC News, one at CBS News and two at NBC News. Local management is even more male dominated. There are no female general managers, station managers, news directors, or assistant news directors at CBS. Despite the fact that CBS has the highest proportion of female correspondents (25 percent), only 14 percent of the air time is given to women.[3]

The explanations for this lack of mobility, Alter and Weathers noted, vary from one extreme to another. Many women and some men see blatant sexism as the cause. Many men and a few women see women's lack of skills or their commitment to their children as incompatible with the world of television broadcasting. A large group of both men and women believe that women are the victims of discrimination, but are not sure exactly what they mean by the term.[4]

While many people cannot define precisely what they mean by discrimination, we have some very clear indications of the mindset that causes discrimination from the evidence presented in chapter 6. We explore in this chapter how such a sexist mindset affects in precise discriminatory ways women's careers, and the solutions that women have found for surviving and making it in the corporate fishbowl. Many of these solutions, like many of the suggestions for white males, will be equally applicable to other race/gender groups in corporate America.

Overview of Gender Discrimination in Corporations

All the data I have collected over the past sixteen years indicate that sexist attitudes and stereotypes, such as "Women are too emotional to be effective managers," "Women are not really interested in a professional career," and "Women working leads to the breakdown of the American family," are translated into discriminatory actions against women. The protestations of many corporate managers that they can hold these beliefs privately without acting them out in the work environment is pure fantasy. Some social scientists such as Kanter suggest that women and men are equally to blame for women's lack of progress. I disagree. Some women may be, in part, responsible for their own lack of progress, but I believe most women deserve very little blame. Kanter wrote:

> Lack of support systems for women, lack of adequate integration into a world of mostly men, lack of female role models, and lack of feedback, then, were among the circumstances making it harder for a woman in sales. The successful women indicated that those who had left the sales force had to bear their share of the responsibility for the problems, either through ignorance or inappropriate behavior, but they also felt that many of the situations could have been eased or avoided.[5]

M. Loden puts forth the position that my data support:

"When asked if a woman who has the same ability as a man has as good a chance to become the executive of a company, 71 percent of the women with a college education said that they did not. From a very personal and pragmatic standpoint, women can no longer afford to ignore this issue if they hope to realize their full professional and earning potential."[6]

Let's review *some* of the problems women have in corporate America as seen by my study participants. A number of participants indicated that they saw a great deal of discrimination because of the few numbers of women above lower-level management:

> In this work environment, women are lower management. Middle level and above are all males.
>
> —Asian, female, craftsworker

> Upper management is still overwhelmingly white, male, over 40.
>
> —white, female, craftsworker

> The employee profile shows that women in positions of authority are tokens, only one is qualified for officer.
>
> —American Indian, female, lower-level manager

> Within the last five years I have seen six white men promoted in my department and one white woman downgraded as far as pay is concerned. So I definitely question the effects of pluralism.
>
> —black, female, craftsworker

One comment expressed concern that women are "type-cast" in particular types of jobs:

> Key decision-making positions are still unavailable to women, as a rule. Women are still relegated to less significant or less impacting positions. . . . women generally fill positions in "maintenance" modems of our business-positions which do not permit innovation or direction setting, where one implements what others have decided—the structured, regimented arenas.
>
> —Hispanic, female, middle-level manager

Many believe that the criteria used to judge women for any position are very different from those used to judge men. The standards for women are higher than for men:

I must be five times better than my male peers.

> —Hispanic, female, lower-level manager

The number of women with degrees in management positions has increased tremendously. Unfortunately, research shows: (1) women make less money than men with the same job titles; (2) women have to work harder than men to prove that they got the job because they were qualified; (3) women tend not to have the same power as men in "equal" management positions.

> —Hispanic, male, craftsworker

I am tired of "cannot let you go at this time" phrase. I could have been promoted in 1980–81 instead of 1984. It took a woman boss to upgrade my job. My male bosses gave me nothing but personal praise and good appraisals—no action—no promotions. I made them look great; *they* got a bonus.

> —white, female, middle-level manager

A very serious problem in advancement of women in corporations is that they are not part of the "old boy network." A number of comments reflect this view:

Women are seldom part of the men's internal work groups, not because we do not want to belong but because they do not want us to belong.

> —white, female, lower-level manager

Women have a much more difficult time finding sponsors or mentors. Men want to help the "good old boys."

> —white, female, middle-level manager

The "good old boys" make it very difficult to prove yourself, to show that you really do deserve recognition and advancement on the job.

> —white, female, lower-level manager

The working conditions for women are from the dark ages. They are treated as if they don't have the brains they were hired for.

> —white, male, craftsworker

If the emphasis to "be like one of the boys" is not totally eliminated, we stand to lose valuable numbers of women who don't want to be like "one of the boys."

—black, female, lower-level manager

Not only are women excluded from the old boy network but, as we noted in chapter 6, there are considerable negative feelings about women working at all. Men who have these feelings are not about to make women part of their network.

Women are placed on surplus lists because they are not "head of their household!"

—Hispanic, female, middle-level manager

I have often seen a man selected for promotion before an apparently qualified woman because his career aspirations were taken more seriously.

—white, female, craftsworker

Lower-level males do not like female middle level managers. This has been very apparent in the department. I believe they feel intimidated by a woman middle manager; many of them still feel a woman's place is in the home and the bedroom. I feel they would resent a person of color even more—especially if she were female.

—white, female, craftsworker

One of the many things as far as income or promotions of men or women is that miserable excuse that a man has a "family to support." Well, so do millions of women, but besides that "fact," levels of income and promotions should not be based on gender.

—white, female, craftsworker

Some of the other problems women face are related to authority:

Men—especially white men—do not respect women's authority. Their wives have no power and authority at home so why should women in work?

—black, female, lower-level manager

Some participants see women's intentions being misinterpreted as a problem:

> I believe that, in general, men find it easier to express their feelings to a man. If both the manager and the supervisor, for example, are men, they can become better acquainted by going to lunch, without people thinking there is hanky-panky in the office—versus the male manager and a female supervisor.
> —black, female, lower-level manager

One man sees only attractive, slim women getting ahead:

> Show me a fat, homely woman in a high level job.
> —white, male, upper-level manager

Others believe that women's attitudes influence their ability to get ahead:

> Sexist language ("girls," "gals," "manned," etc.) is very prevalent. Activist women must be careful to be low-profile. Only certain "acceptable" women get promoted—those who are non-confrontational on feminist areas or unaware themselves.
> —Asian, female, middle-level manager

The following comments express how sexism has lowered women's morale and leads women to consider quitting—two deadly consequences for companies.

> This is extremely candid—but, I think the company should take a serious look at management employees—especially middle-upper level males. Most tend to hold sexist views and some are racist as well. Women are not taken seriously by their bosses even though their bosses may like and respect them personally. Most lower-level women feel frustrated and angry in dealing with these men. Morale seems to be very low among women.
> —white, female, lower-level manager

I have only seriously considered quitting my job when my boss
has been unsupportive and malicious toward me as a woman
employee.

—white, female, upper-level manager

These comments vividly illustrate the wide range of discriminatory behaviors confronting women in the work place, a burden
so great that it is truly a credit to women that they have come as
far as they have. This statement will become clearer as we examine
the hard data and analyze some of these problems in detail.

Gender Discrimination over the Last Ten Years
Between 1964 and 1972 the percentage of employees who believed
that being a woman would be harmful to advancement in their
company decreased. For example, Bowman found that 77 percent
of employees in 1964, compared to 58 percent of the white managers and 72 percent of the black managers in 1972, believed that
being a woman was harmful in business.

Between my 1976–78 and 1986 surveys I changed the question
about the effect of gender on advancement to relate specifically to
the respondent's own career. In 1976–78, 19 percent of the women
and 47 percent of the white men believed their gender was harmful
to their career advancement. In 1986, 43 percent of minority
women, 30 percent of white women, and 29 percent of white men
believed their gender was harmful. The responses of minority men
were similar: 15 percent in 1976–78 and 14 percent in 1986 believed their gender was harmful to their careers. This is a clear sign
that affirmative action efforts have slipped under the Reagan
administration, and that white males are feeling less threatened by
even a perceived emphasis on preferential treatment for women.

Responses from the 1976–78 and 1986 surveys show a general
trend toward increased discrimination against women, especially as
perceived by women. Men's responses remain fairly constant on
most issues.

In 1976–78 about 63 percent of the women and 57 percent of
the men agreed that women were excluded from informal work
groups. In 1986, 75 percent of the women compared to 51 percent

of the men agreed with this statement. In 1976–78 about seven out of ten women surveyed believed that women must out-perform men to get ahead. By 1986, this percentage had increased to more than eight out of ten. In both years about one in four men concurred.

For some specific activities, men also see things as getting worse for women. For example, only 20 percent of the men in 1976, compared to 39 percent in 1986, believe that many men are unable to work comfortably with women and that they often bypass female supervisors to go to their male superiors.

These data clearly demonstrate that, despite claims that corporations have made tremendous progress in advancing women, many female corporate employees perceive women as having a more difficult time advancing because of their gender in 1986 than in 1976–78. The data also show that men do not believe that there has been any decrease in gender discrimination in the past ten years.

Gender Discrimination in 1986

When asked specific questions about the extent of gender discrimination in 1986 in their companies, 78 percent of the women and 63 percent of the men responded that it exists at least to some extent. Several comments are illuminating:

> Efforts to place women and minorities in Director and Officer positions have been only nominal. We have few women and minorities at upper middle levels and no efforts have been made to develop middle levels to assume these positions in the future. We have good pools at lower levels to move into middle level positions, but there is little support to move women/minorities in to the "Old Boy Power Network".
>
> —white, female, middle-level manager

> Take a look at the "numbers" in the officer and upper level ranks of our company.
>
> —white, male, middle-level manager

> Even though our company claims to be sexually unbiased, very few inroads have been made by women into jobs that have traditionally been considered male-oriented. Also, the higher up the

ladder in management you go, the fewer women you find occupying these jobs.

—white, female, lower-level manager

To obtain a clearer perception of employees' views of gender discrimination, I posed a series of questions and formed participants' responses into an index. The questions were:

Today to what extent do you believe sexism exists in your company?

How frequently do you hear sexist language in your company?

To what extent do you agree or disagree that:

Other employees accept a woman manager's authority as much as they accept a man's in a similar situation.

Many men in work groups listen to work-related opinions of women managers less than they do to those of other men managers.

Many women are often excluded from informal work networks by men.

Many women managers have a difficult time initiating informal work-related activities such as lunch and socializing after work because men misinterpret their behavior as a "come-on."

Women have a much easier time finding a sponsor or mentor than men do.

Women managers have to be better performers than men to get ahead.

Many men are unable to work comfortably with women; they bypass them and go to their superiors.

Many women are faced with some type of sexual harassment on the job.

Responses revealed that only 3 percent of the employees believe there is no sexism in the company.

Women, regardless of race, are more likely than men to perceive a great deal of gender discrimination in companies. Sixty-two percent of black women, 50 percent of other minority women, and 47 percent of white women believe that there is a great deal of gender discrimination. Black men (42 percent) are much more likely than other minority men (25 percent) and white men (12 percent) to believe there is a great deal of gender discrimination in their company.

Table 7 in the appendix shows responses to the questions about gender discrimination by race, gender, and occupation. Women managers and black male managers are more likely than other groups to believe that women face a great deal of gender discrimination in their company. It is not surprising to find that white male managers are the least likely to see gender discrimination in the company. They own and control the system. It is difficult to be critical of one's own actions.

A disturbing finding is that the higher whites go in the corporate world the more likely they are to believe that there is a great deal of discrimination. (While not statistically significant, the same trend exists for minorities.) For example, 53 percent of lower-level compared to 66 percent of upper-level white women believe that women face a great deal of discrimination. Of white men, 11 percent at a lower level and 16 percent at an upper level agree. However, of white men at the very top, only 2 percent agree. One might expect that the higher women advance, the more they would perceive the system as being fair to women. In reality, however, the higher they go, the less support they receive from other women because they are usually alone or among very few women in the fishbowl. In addition, while they have been successful in moving up the hierarchy, the jobs they hold are generally out of the mainstream of business activity; they are not as powerful and influential as their male counterparts—a situation they readily observe. Furthermore, as they move up, they become more privy to the thinking of top management, which includes them but not as full members.

Many dissatisfied women may leave the company and thus become a drain on corporate resources and the bottom line. In fact 38 percent of the women who say that there is at least some gender discrimination in their company, compared to 22 percent who believe that there is only a small degree of gender discrimination, are seriously considering quitting. As it costs corporations $25,000 to

$50,000 to train employees, losses of this magnitude are simply not good for any corporation.

Even before women take the drastic step of leaving the company, discrimination affects their performance. Of the women who say that their performance is negatively affected to a great extent only 9 percent believe that there is little or no gender discrimination in their company, compared to 25 percent who say that their performance is not at all affected.

A Serious Contradiction Women Face

In stark contrast to the tremendous amount of gender discrimination employees acknowledge that women face in corporate America is a perverse sexist notion held by 69 percent of men and 35 percent of women that women got their jobs only because they are women. A white, female, lower-level manager stated: "As a female, everyone says I'll be promoted quickly. I do not want to be promoted just because I am female. I want to be promoted because I earned it."

She wants to earn her position (on the basis of merit, obviously), but this concept does not fit the realities of corporate America. Sooner or later, women (as well as minorities) must wake up to the fact that there is no way in hell the white male is going to promote them only because of their gender or race unless they are legally required to do so. Situations in which corporations are legally liable to promote by gender or race are very few. Only 5 percent of all court cases mandate a quota system; all others order goals, timetables, and only a good-faith effort to balance the work force. Therefore, those who run corporations will grant few, if any, promotions to women simply because they are women. Their sexist psychology will not allow them to do so even if they insist that they are making every effort.

It is extremely important for women to recognize that the most important barrier to their advancement is not their ability but gender discrimination. They must adopt a more positive attitude about their abilities and, like men, believe that they have earned what they get. They must confidently reject the sexist notion that the only reason they got the job was because they were women.

J. La Rouche and R. Ryan observe that women often seriously

underestimate how much they accept the chauvinistic view, without realizing that their accomplishments, seen through prejudiced eyes, are reduced to a distorted notion of "the way women are." For example, "the woman accountant is mistaken for a bookkeeper; the woman with an important title is said to have slept her way to the top; the woman executive is said to be just a figurehead who doesn't really do the job—the important work is handled by someone above her." This demeaning of women's accomplishments is automatic. Not only does a woman have to do twice as well in her work as a man to be successful; she also has to put twice as much effort into image building.[7]

Unless women recognize the severe impact of discrimination on their careers, they will allow men to continue to blame them for their lack of success, to keep them feeling insecure about their abilities. Women spend enormous time and energy getting the right credentials and experience without understanding that sexist men will never give them due credit, recognition, reward, or value.

One of the major reasons women have not been as successful as they might be in corporate America is that many have bought into the concept, as most men have, that hard work, keeping your nose clean, and ability are the keys to advancement in corporate America. Many women want and are encouraged by males to believe that, if there is discrimination, they will somehow be exempt; it certainly will not affect their own careers, only those of less fortunate women. They even rationalize the failure of other females by buying into the idea that these women must not have been good enough.

Should Women Conform?

A very serious problem women face in corporations is conformity. "But doesn't everyone have to conform?" you ask. "Why is this more difficult or different for women than for men?" The fact is that from their earliest days of life most women are socialized differently from men. As a result, women's operating and managerial styles are, in general, "naturally" different in some crucial aspects from those of men. Rather than understanding and attempting to adapt some of these positive qualities to the corporation, the male-dominated hierarchy attempts instead to make women conform to the male image. This effort has been helped immensely by business schools and self-help literature that tell women managers that they must be "one of the boys" to be successful. It is obvious at first glance that the most successful women in corporate America are those who have adopted the "male" style down to the pinstripe suits and ties, the types of questions they ask, the mannerisms and language they use, and the "survival-of-the-fittest" mentality that characterizes most corporate men's cultural philosophy. A black, female, lower-level manager noted: "Many of the women currently in power conduct themselves like the 'good old boys.'"

Loden wrote that, instead of valuing the varying styles women and men offer in their managerial roles, we have redefined equality to mean exact sameness according to traditionally masculine standards. "The result is that women who succeed in management often do so by adapting to male norms. Masculine bias, whether conscious or unconscious, continues to be the major obstacle." The feminine is often unappreciated by male bosses and colleagues because they are not used to dealing with "the nontraditional approach."[8]

A white, female craftsworker wrote: "I have noticed that women in management positions tend to have a hard exterior because they have to prove they are as tough as the men."

A white, female, lower-level manager also noted: "Most of the upper level women managers I have dealt with have been single, or have no children. They all seemed to be trying to act like a man and have no feelings or understanding for a woman who has children."

Women should not conform to meet male expectations. Yes, refusing to conform might for the time being be detrimental to some women's advancement, but it will do wonders for mental health, theirs and that of the narrow-minded males around them. And in the long run, refusal to straight-jacket talents (whether innate or culturally conditioned) will be to the benefit of the corporation and society as a whole. I have seen hundreds of women trying to become male clones and doing a very good job of it; however, at what cost? Most of them will not be rewarded for behaving as male clones, because they will never *be* males, and men will continue to change the criteria for becoming a "true clone" and/or they will ridicule women who are trying. It is a double-bind. How many times have you heard men say, "Why doesn't she act like a woman and stop trying to be a man?" The definition of being one of the "boys" is one that the "boys" can always change if they want to keep women focusing on their problems. In addition, the definition varies from corporation to corporation, department to department, work group to work group. Anyone who spends her time trying to fit someone else's image cannot be spending as much productive time on her job as if she were concentrating on doing the job well.

Another risk is that the more time women spend trying to become one of the boys, the more likely they are to fall into the trap of believing that they *are* one of the boys when, in reality, no matter how much they fit the image, the "boys" will eventually side with one another, except in the rare instances when the man believes it is to his personal advantage to support a woman. What is more, having been lulled into a false sense of security that they are one of the boys, such women often neglect the lessons discussed in previous chapters that the rule of the corporate jungle is survival of the fittest. This sense of being a "special" woman with the corporate hierarchy prevents many women from seeing danger signals in their careers. If men rewarded all the women who have forsaken their unique, positive, feminine styles for the male image, the number of women in middle and upper management would be significantly higher than it presently is.

A white, male, middle-level manager noted: "Women need to realize they are women and adopt a management style to fit their gender. Male management styles, which many women imitate, make them look silly and ineffective. Women are not little men. They need to capitalize on the qualities that make them female and incorporate them into their management style."

Loden supports this position. She wrote that many of the so-called feminine skills women are encouraged to develop are the very same talents needed to be successful in the new competitive corporate world. These include intuitive management, interpersonal skills, and creative problem solving. Recently there has been growing appreciation of people-oriented skills—which "most women are taught to value and utilize from the time they are little girls."[9]

The male hierarchy's tacit purposes in pushing women to conform to the male image is to be able to control them, to make men feel more comfortable with women, to make certain women focus on themselves rather than on male sexist attitudes as the problem, and to establish a screening mechanism to exclude large numbers of women from the power positions. "Cloning" themselves justifies men's own sexism. Conformity to male standards will assist only a very few women in making it and surviving in the corporate fishbowl. The fact that only one Fortune 500 company has a woman CEO also means that conforming to male standards does not bring the ultimate in advancement and power to women; for men, however, it is a different story.

In sum, *not* conforming to male standards may cost a few women the opportunity to advance. In the long run, however, if more women stand by their own uniqueness, many more opportunities for advancement will occur because the "boys" will recognize that they can no longer control women, and women will recognize they collectively have the power to change the system.

Social-Interaction Problems Caused by Sexism

Another area in which women must be realistic is that of social interaction in corporate life. I asked the survey participants the following three questions:

> *To what extent do you agree or disagree that:*
>
> Many women are often excluded from informal work networks by men?
>
> Many women have a difficult time initiating work-related activities such as lunch and socializing after work, because men misinterpret their behavior as a "come-on?"
>
> Many women are faced with some type of sexual harassment on the job?

Some men will argue that men, too, are excluded from informal networks by other men, and they are right; however, men are much more likely to exclude women simply because they are women and not because of some factor that, as in the case of men, can often be changed. Even in the matter of sexual harassment, I am amazed at how many men and even a few women are now saying that men, too, are victims. While a few men have been sexually harassed by women, the reality is that 95 times out of 100 women are the object of sexual harassment by men. This denial of women's special social-interaction problems in corporate America is a symptom of the rampant sexism that exists in the fishbowl.

When responses to the three social-interaction questions were formed into an index, I found that more than double the percentage of women (40 percent) than men (17 percent) answered all three questions positively. Correspondingly, almost three times the percentage of men (28 percent) than women (10 percent) answered none of the questions affirmatively.

Exclusion of Women from Informal Work Groups
As noted earlier, the past ten years have brought no improvement in sexist attitudes in the corporation, according to the women in my survey. In 1976–78, 63 percent of the women and 57 percent of the men believed women managers were often excluded by men from informal work groups. In 1986, the figures were 75 percent and 51 percent. What is happening here is that men are almost always automatically brought into the informal "how to" network, while women have to make a conscious effort to establish themselves. However, even when women try to establish themselves, some men are too insecure and sexist to allow women to become part of the network. Some of the participants' comments are illustrative:

> Women are not allowed the shared knowledge or brainstorm benefits by their male peers because they are women first and not acceptable as peers in the corporate community by most men.
>
> —white, female, craftsworker

> It is difficult at times to find your support group. Men "click" together. Still a lot of "good old boy" philosophies.
>
> —white, female, middle-level manager

> My middle-level manager is a woman, but her peers and boss are

men. I see her constantly struggle to be treated as an equal. It does
not encourage the rest of our work group.

—white, female, lower-level manager

Women are just not part of the "in" group. Men have such a
strong close-knit network and most want it to stay that way. Most
men don't understand women's style of management and they
either fear it or brand it as ineffective.

—white, female, lower-level manager

I believe that upper managers still belong to the good old boys'
club and until that changes, women and persons of color will remain at a disadvantage.

—white, male, middle-level manager

Women have not been provided support groups in work areas,
and men gang up on them to get rid of them. Lousy treatment of
women. Solo women. We come off strict when attacked. Women
are under a great deal of pressure to be perfect.

—Asian, female, middle-level manager

This commitment to exclusivity is backed up by the fact that 46
percent of the men in the 1986 study believed that private men's
clubs have a right to exclude women! As we all know, to exclude
women from private men's clubs where many crucial business decisions are made is to put women at an extreme disadvantage.

Kanter made some astute observations about why men may exclude women from their informal work groups. She wrote that because men have to deal with women in traditional male territory,
"routine encounters become problematic: opening doors, pulling
out chairs, shaking hands." Language is another problem, Kanter
noted, for example, are women girls, ladies, gals, or females? Kanter concluded that because of such new awarenesses in the relations
between men and women and because behavior that was once taken
for granted can no longer be automatically invoked, men sometimes
feel on edge around women in new situations, particularly if they
want to make a good impression.[10]

Women's Difficulties Finding Mentors

An issue related to work-group exclusion is the difficulty women have in finding mentors or sponsors. In 1986, 73 percent of the women and 44 percent of the men believe women have this difficulty. In 1976–78, the figures were 54 percent of the women and 37 percent of the men. A middle-level, white, woman manager wrote: "Position makes you feel isolated. It gets lonely standing by yourself. Frequently you have no department role models. Mentors are hard to find. It takes a lot of effort to establish relationships. Once established, the mentors retire, get moved, or die. You start again. You have to prove yourself over and over, your performance level must be head and shoulders above male competition."

Men Misinterpreting Women's Intentions

Another social problem that women face is subjective interpretation of their motives. How are women's actions interpreted when they try to include themselves in informal gatherings or initiate informal work-related activities such as lunches, dinners, or drinks after work? Do many men create a problem for women because they misinterpret women's actions as a "come-on?"

In 1976–78, 47 percent of the women and 43 percent of the men believed that men misinterpret women's work-related social actions. In 1986, 59 percent of women and 34 percent of men believed this. The managers' responses illuminate a very serious problem that confronts women within corporations. Since many important decisions take place in informal settings, women are at a tremendous disadvantage as managers if they cannot initiate such contacts. While this question does not directly probe managers' views of sexual harassment, it indirectly indicates that many women might be confronted by such harassment if men misinterpret their initiatives of informal contacts.

Sexual Harassment of Women

The heightened consciousness of working women and the evolution of EEO case law have resulted in recent court decisions that bring sexual harassment out of the realm of social rights and into the realm of sex discrimination. Recent articles and books indicate that sexual harassment has been the rule rather than the exception for all women who work. In 1976–78 I did not ask any questions about sexual harassment but I have since incorporated them. The 1986 survey found that 71 percent of women and 51 percent of men believed that women face some type of sexual harassment on the job. In the words of the participants:

> Harassment is alive and well. A new management hire showed me a 'diary' (documentation) of the times, dates, places a district level manager asked her to lunch, what she was doing over the weekend . . . and so on.
>
> —white, female, middle-level manager

> Sexual harassment is alive and well. It is covert. In our organization, the director's feeling about women in management is widely known and nothing he has done proves differently. Even the men feel it and are appalled. The company is not as progressive towards upgrading women as it was in previous years.
>
> —black, female, craftsworker

> The sexual harassment level in this company far exceeds most males' comprehension. I have found it to be frustrating, annoying and just plain humiliating.
>
> —white, female, lower-level manager

> Early every day at work a man touches me. One day while I was washing the coffee pot in a small enclosed area, the man approached me and wanted me to kiss him. He used to call me and make sexual remarks. He often referred to the clothes I wore— making suggestive remarks about them. After such a remark one day, I told him to go to hell. He hasn't bothered me since. There is a man in our office who is always staring at women. Some of us feel as if we are on parade if we cross the room.
>
> —white, female, craftsworker

> In my office, there is still frequent sexual harassment directed at women: sexual comments, men touching women, men commenting how women are stupid, etc. Sometimes I want to be sick.
>
> —white, female, craftsworker

Some harassment still exists in the office environment in the form of suggestive materials or remarks. In general these are being suppressed and will hopefully disappear eventually. I don't see any examples where gender interferes with employee cooperation in the job performance.

—white, male, lower-level manager

I worked with a man who was suspended for sexual harassment but was reinstated as a district manager with women subordinates. This is a good example of lip service. I would think that the woman (or women) who turned him in would feel betrayed by the company.

—white, male, middle-level manager

It's no secret that sexism runs wild here at this company, especially when known offenders are not punished. What does a woman have to do to convince you that these people should be fired?

—black, female, craftsworker

Some (both men and women) blame women for sexual harassment problems:

Don't close your eyes to the fact that women are normally as attracted to men as men are to women and they purposely "come on" to men just as men do it to women. It is not always the man who "comes on" to women.

—white, male, lower-level manager

Some women "ask" for sexual harassment even if they deny it. They dress provocatively, and then if a comment is made, look out. Women want to be admired but won't admit it.

—white, female, craftsworker

Many women seem to bring on sexual harassment by "going along" with jokes, etc. They try to be "one of the boys" until it backfires.

—Hispanic, male, lower-level manager

Women will do anything to get to the top including going to bed with a superior.

—white, male, craftsworker

These comments basically blame women for a male problem. The realities of this society are that we socialize men into seeing women primarily as sexual objects. On TV, we see everything from cars to cake being sold by sexy, attractive, skinny, usually blonde women. In my survey, more than 70 percent of the employees believe that there is too much sex in advertisements. The view of women primarily as sexual objects does not begin or end at the corporate doorstep. It is acted out millions of times a day—sometimes on a conscious level, often subconsciously—because men have been socialized to see women chiefly in sexual terms.

Some women manage to handle the problem delicately. Of course, the question remains as to why they should have to handle this type of mistreatment at all. Others reinforce male chauvinism by an almost fanatical opposition to the feminist movement. They are known by a variety of names, such as the "fascinating womanhood." The modus operandi of these women is to appear helpless while artfully manipulating others. These women see life as being full of rewards for which their sexuality can be traded. Feminists condemn this approach as similar to, but more dishonest than, prostitution.[11]

Other women, particularly young and inexperienced ones, are genuinely flattered by attention and flirtation. These women usually, consciously or subconsciously, need male attention but are often not prepared for or interested in the more serious need for sexual attention on the parts of some men in positions of power.[12]

Men who treat women with expectations of a sexual response tend to become enraged if rejected abruptly. Can you get fired if you refuse a superior's pass? You can. La Rouche and Ryan explain:

> Some women are hired for a dual function. The boss hopes to obtain not only an assistant but also a sexual companion. If the woman is cooperative, he can have his sex paid for by the company. He can offer his employee a salary increase for her sexual services without its costing him a personal dime. In such circumstances, excellent performance at work and in bed are part of the job requirement, and if you won't do both jobs, you get fired. In most cases, however, you are likely to be fired only if your rejection is demoralizing or hostile.[13]

Yielding to sexual overtures can also be risky for women who are interested in careers as managers. Consultants warn in no uncertain terms against personal emotional involvements with working associates. B. Harragan stated: "What the unwritten and unverbalized canon of male ethics adds up to for women is clear: Any corporate woman employee who engages in intercourse with a fellow employee has jeopardized her chances of significant advancement within that particular corporate structure. She is irrevocably labeled "inferior" and must go elsewhere to move upward with a clear path."[14]

A middle-level white woman noted: "The phrase, 'she slept her way to the top,' is male chauvinist slander, whether it's said by a man or a woman. The fact that a woman sleeps with her boss doesn't mean she doesn't have ability, any more than it means he doesn't."

Unfortunately, because of the prevailing double standard, men do not receive such counsel. In the poststudy feedback sessions in 1986 and in 1976–78, black male managers reported a related phenomenon: They are always accused of pursuing white women, even if they are not. They indicate that it is very difficult to form even a close working relationship with white women because white men quickly perceive a sexual connotation in the relationship. A number said that even a casual conversation with a white woman is sometimes looked upon in sexual terms by white males. Finally, several indicated that a few black men, but not white men, have lost their jobs because of affairs with white female coworkers.

Considering the racist attitudes of society about black male sexuality and their "desire" for white women, it is not surprising that the first army officer and the first Harvard professor who had formal sexual harassment charges brought against them and severe disciplinary action taken were black men. The charges were filed by white women.

The potential for office affairs is ever present, and traditionally they have occurred between male power figures—managers and professionals—and powerless women—lower-level supervisors, secretaries, and clerks. Intimate relations will be on the upswing as more and more women fill the managerial ranks at various levels. Psychiatrist R. Seidenberg noted: "As people who have interesting careers have always noted, work is very sexy, and the people with whom one is working are the people who excite. A day spent launching a project or writing a paper or running a seminar is more likely to stimulate—intellectually and sexually—than an evening spent sharing TV or discussing the lawn problems or going over the kids' report cards."[15]

A number of recent studies have argued that intimate relationships on the job have led *not* to a decrease in productivity for those involved but to an increase in productivity.

Corporate policies cannot stop sexual relationships at work nor should they interfere, as long as such relationships are based on free choice and do not adversely affect productivity. Unfortunately, unless both individuals have equal power and status, free choice is hard to determine. What must be changed in the corporate and societal structure is the dual standard that permits men to pursue whomever they want, regardless of the woman's wishes.

Strategies to Deal with Social-Interaction Problems

How do women deal with being excluded from informal work groups? How do they deal with the difficulty of finding mentors and sponsors? How do they deal with men's misinterpretation of their business lunch and dinner invitations? How do they deal with sexual harassment?

How women handle these problems depends on the individuals they deal with, the specific situations at hand, and their personal goals. However, a number of suggestions are applicable to most situations. With regard to exclusion from informal work groups, I would suggest to women that the only time they should concern themselves about this is when that informal work group has the ability to influence their jobs and/or careers. In this case, the most practical and realistic way of gaining entrance is to have the power through information, resources, political connections, and the like to make men want to include women. Trying to be one of the "boys" puts women in a disadvantageous position and at the mercy of the "boys." Women should recognize that the only reason to become part of the informal network is to gain an advantage—not to give the advantage to the informal network.

Women should also recognize that there are numerous informal networks. The best strategy is not to be a part of as many as possible but to be a part of several key informal groups. In addition, the success of women depends to a considerable extent on their ability to form their own informal networks.

As women have more difficult times finding mentors and sponsors, it is incumbent upon them to sponsor and support one another. In addition, they should seek out companies with formal or informal mentor programs that emphasize moving women up the corporate ladder. (See chapter 4 for further advice on this.)

Concerning invitations to lunches and dinners, women should recognize that these situations offer some of the best ways to gain insight into the person they are dealing with. Thus I suggest that women should never stop initiating such work-related activities despite the possible misinterpretations. If they have a bad experience because of some infantile sexist behavior on the part of their male guest, chalk it up to experience and learn from it. The only real protection women have is their ability to know themselves and to be able to read and understand the people they are dealing with. In addition, they must have confidence in themselves when the rumor mill starts spreading vicious gossip about "love affairs" and sleeping their way to the top.

Finally, with regard to sexual harassment, the only real defense is to know that there is no reason why they should put up with this behavior. When it happens, take action—the law is with women.

La Rouche and Ryan write:

> Often women who complain of sexual harassment on the job are accused by their peers of bringing it on themselves. But I don't accept this view. A man's behavior toward a woman is determined by his own history and personality rather than by a woman's style of dress or manners. Her decolletage doesn't control his behavior; he does. Otherwise how can one explain the difference between one man's macho wisecracks and another man's respectful invitations?[16]

Power and Authority Problems

A major problem confronting women in corporate America is related to their power and authority. As discussed in chapter 5, the issue of survival in the corporate fishbowl is in large part an issue of power. There are two main sources of power—institutional (that is, that vested in office) and personal power. I suggested that employees regardless of race or gender can assume more power and authority than their office gives them if they dare to risk it. A white, lower-level male made these stereotypical comments that may apply to some women but do not apply to most who have joined corporate America: "Most women, because of their early socialized training, are setting themselves up as weaker and as poor decision-makers. This is a process that cannot be worked out; rather, a new generation must carry the good qualities with them from childhood." The real issue for women is that the power and authority inherent in the office for men does not necessarily apply to women. It is very difficult for men with their sexist attitudes not to strip the position of some crucial power and authority when a woman takes over.

Thus it is not surprising that in 1986 only 25 percent of the men and 9 percent of the women believe that women have the same power and authority as men. An index was formed from responses to the following survey questions:

To what extent do you agree or disagree that:

In general, employees accept a woman's authority as much as they accept a man's in a similar situation?

Many men in work groups listen less to work related opinions of women than they do to those of other men?

In general, customers accept a woman's authority as much as they accept a man's in a similar situation?

Many women have the same power as men in similar positions?

Many men employees are unable to work comfortably with women; they bypass them and go to their superiors?

It is important to note that the higher women advance in the corporation, the less likely they are to believe that women have the same power and authority as men. Let's look at some of the employees' comments on these issues:

> It is my belief that many of the problems existing between male and female will forever remain. The element of trust evades both genders. Men just can't seem to believe women are equally intelligent and capable in the business world as they perceive themselves to be. I have heard men request to deal with a man rather than a female.
>
> —Hispanic, female, craftsworker

> I feel men are now at the point where they will ask for a woman's opinion, but they do it strictly out of courtesy or because they're obliged to do so. In a recent incident, for example, my boss (a man) asked me (a woman) and another man for advice. He listened to both of us and then said, "Thanks, Fred, that's what I'll do." I felt invisible.
>
> —white, female, middle-level manager

> As a female who works with men, I can tell you that many times you are treated with respect but many times they don't take you serious. Seldom are you equal.
>
> —white, female, craftsworker

> Too often people of color and women have the visible position (title, pay, etc) with few actual meaningful duties, responsibilities, or ways to really impact the business. This is particularly true with women of color. There is a feeling of 1980's tokenism.
>
> —black, female, lower-level manager

> Men do not accept women as their equal. They give me the impression that women are here and men are expected to deal with them, but not as equals. They (men) define a place or position for you and you stay there. They think women are dumb and scatterbrained. They don't listen to women. Most of them don't even understand their own wives; how do you expect them to understand women in the workplace.
>
> —white, female, lower-level manager

I think many women managers are faced with a 'blind spot' effect when attending meetings predominately occupied by male managers. The women are invisible (I use that rather than ignored, only to give men the benefit of the doubt that they wouldn't intentionally be that rude) to the men in the conference, meeting, presentation, or whatever.

—white, female, lower-level manager

At lower and middle level management, I don't see too many problems with men and women working together. I do notice, at some upper level staff meetings, that our upper level will talk differently if only men are present. He acts uncomfortable when his one woman staff manager is there.

—white, male, upper-level manager

Some women managers can't seem to give orders to men. The men just won't take orders from women.

—white, male, craftsworker

I have worked with many extremely capable women who have been promoted to positions of authority only to find they are tolerated but not valued. The more competent the woman, the more difficult it is for her to gain acceptance and recognition.

—Hispanic, female, upper-level manager

The ultimate effect of women not having the same power and authority as men is that their performance will be stifled. In all of my studies, women who perceive that they have less power and authority are more likely than those who perceive they have equal power and authority to feel that their job performance has been negatively affected. For example, 39 percent of those who believe they have less power and authority than the men, compared to 22 percent who say they have the same power and authority, believe their performance has been negatively affected because of how they perceive the company values them.

Obviously the final consequences of such women's failure to perform their jobs as effectively as they can gives corporate men the excuse to justify their discrimination against women.

Another reality for women is that their view of how they are valued and rewarded is directly tied to the issues of power and authority. It seems fair to assume that, if the corporate world valued and rewarded women equally, women would have the same power and authority as men.

I have found that women who do not believe that they are rewarded and valued are more likely (62 percent) than those who believe they are (45 percent) to believe that women do not have any or very little of the same power and authority as men.

Strategies to Gain Power and Authority

What can women do about this situation? First and foremost they must recognize that, because of sexist socialization, many men have all types of problems simply with the fact that women are working. These men will question or ignore women's personal power and authority and withhold institutional power and authority.

If women acknowledge that in most cases the institutional power and authority given to men simply by virtue of their positions will not be given to them, they will then be able to develop strategies to gain that power and authority, both on an institutional and personal basis.

Once on the job, a woman manager must make certain that the boss, subordinates, peers, clients, and others recognize that she is in charge. To do this, women must understand the different players and use different techniques to get the message across. Many self-help books come up with strategies like "You must move strongly." Some social scientists have argued that women should use the techniques they have learned through their own socialization; others say women should adapt the male techniques. I say that the techniques women adopt, whether "male" or "female" or a combination of both, should depend on the situation and the people involved. What is important is that women, regardless of the techniques they use, must come across as confident, competent, and in charge. This will be a very difficult task considering the sexist orientation of most men managers.

A woman must recognize that many will criticize any power and authority technique she uses. Similar techniques used by a man would be considered appropriate and would be praised but, used by a woman, are considered immoral and harshly criticized. The most important question women should ask is "Do the techniques bring me the power and authority to accomplish my job and career goals?" If they do, go for it.

Dual Performance Standards

One of the most serious problems women must face in corporate America is the dual standards that are used to measure women's performance. R. Schuller's conclusions support this proposition. He argued that society has classified jobs as "male" or "female." Management is considered a male job and nursing is considered a female job. Men who are managers and women who are nurses are congruent types. Female managers and male nurses are incongruent types. People who are in traditional (congruent) jobs will usually receive better performance evaluations than those who are in incongruent jobs because society assumes that their abilities and skills are better suited to the jobs. Put another way, sex-role socialization has made society believe that men, not women, have the requisite abilities and skills to do managerial jobs. Thus, if a woman is in a managerial job, her performance will not be considered as effective or as good as a man's because of the sexist assumption that she lacks the necessary skills and abilities. The converse would be true if a man were a nurse.[17]

One of the studies that found sex discrimination in performance appraisals was Kay Deaux and Tim Emswiller's evaluation of male and female ability. They asked male and female college students to evaluate, on the basis of taped interviews, the intelligence and competence of one of four stimulus persons. The sex of the subject, the sex of the stimulus person, and the level of competence of the stimulus person were alternated. Highly competent men were evaluated significantly better than were highly competent women by both genders. In addition, the researchers found that men anticipated doing better than the person they evaluated on either a masculine or a feminine task, but women predicted a higher score for themselves only on the feminine tasks.[18]

Mary Cline et al. also produced some interesting findings. Forty-two male and forty-two female subjects selected from a large city, a small town, and a university campus were asked to evaluate four pen-and-ink sketches and four quotations. Two sketches and two quotations were associated with fictitious women's names while the other two were associated with fictitious men's names. Conclusions showed that, first, men devalued work produced by women relative to work produced by men. Second, women tended to devalue work produced by men relative to work produced by women. Third, the cross-sex devaluation was limited to the quotations and did not influence the evaluation of the sketches. The judges did not generalize prejudices across all types of work produced by the opposite sex. Finally, this patterning of results was found in populations drawn from three very different settings, suggesting that sexism exists in all of society's institutions and geographic sectors.[19]

In brief, these studies suggest that sexism plays a crucial role in performance evaluation. They also concisely point out how sex-role socialization has had a negative effect not only on men's attitudes about women's performances but also on some women's attitudes toward their own and other women's performances.

I would be remiss if I did not state that in 1981 D. J. Wendelken and A. Inn questioned the validity of studies such as those just cited. These researchers, along with D. E. Thompson and T. A. Thompson in 1985, suggested that gender is not as significant as previous research has suggested. However, I strongly disagree with their findings, and so do many corporate employees.[20]

The prevalence of sexist attitudes has meant that women have had to be better managers than men to get ahead. In my 1986 study, 83 percent of the women and 27 percent of the men believed this to be the case in their company. In 1976-78 the figures were 72 percent and 27 percent. Some of the employees' comments will help in understanding this problem.

> I have a woman boss, and I feel she has to work much harder in order to have her ideas accepted, compared to the men in my office. She also takes on more responsibility in our office because the men do not want to accept it.
>
> —white, male, lower-level manager

> I think a lot of women tend to feel and think that they have to be better at their jobs than a man would be. They overdo their role

as a management person, which often times causes a lot of problems in their work relationship with those who work under them.

—black, female, middle-level manager

If white males had been forced to work as hard to get where they are as women do, perhaps the productivity in this country would not have declined over the years.

—black, female, craftsworker

In some cases women may have to work harder than a male counterpart to achieve the same level of recognition. Unfortunate but true.

—white, male, craftsworker

Women in higher management have to work twice as hard. They don't receive the same kind of help as men do. It seems as if they are thrown into positions they have no experience in—in the hopes that they will fail.

—black, female, craftsworker

I have consistently had to compete against white males, whose accomplishments were less than mine, for limited job opportunities. I have also experienced salary inequalities.

—white, female, middle-level manager

There are competent women who outperform their male counterparts in work assignments but remain underutilized and unrewarded.

—black, female, lower-level manager

I believe women in general in non-traditional jobs have to be better than most males in the same job because they are forced to defend themselves all the time . . .

—white, female, craftsworker

Women are led to believe they must be "stars" to get ahead while the majority of upper level white males are "mediocre" at best in their management positions.

—white, female, middle-level manager

The notion of proof of ability has been discussed extensively in the literature. In our society, men are expected, and they themselves expect, to succeed in their chosen occupation, to receive financial rewards and satisfaction from their work, and to receive approval and support for their efforts from their families. When a talented man with demonstrated ability does not succeed, for whatever reason, it is unquestioningly apparent to him and to those who know him that he has been the undeserving victim of injustice or rotten luck.

Women "have to prove by their performance that they do belong. . . . they have to prove success, and on a continuing basis. They have to prove that their careers will not be dual, discontinuous, and consequently marked by a lack of commitment—a burden of proof to which a man is never asked to submit."[21] When, to this sexist attitude, is added an atmosphere in which, as tokens, women must perform every action under the critical scrutiny of the nontokens, it is neither surprising nor paranoid for many women to feel pressured to perform as superwomen.

Solutions to Dual Performance Standards

How can women combat these dual standards? There is no sure solution to this problem. It depends on the circumstances women are in and their goals. I do not agree with La Rouche and Ryan, who urge women not to protest injustices or discrimination against women because most people do not admit to their own sexism and will only become defensive. They urge women to find ways to dramatize their potential—the same potential bosses look for in "management trainees." "Do new things in new ways. Walk around with a management textbook under your arm."[22] This advice is nonsense. How will a sexist boss recognize the efforts women put forth to be perceived as competent? The answer in the vast majority of the cases is that he won't. Only when the corporate culture and strategies are committed to removing sexism and when the bosses know that the corporate leadership wants women treated equitably will changes occur.

One positive strategy for women is to select a company with a track record and commitment to changing the sexist attitudes and behaviors of its work force from the top to the bottom. This can be determined by finding out what types of race/gender-awareness workshops are conducted. How long have they been conducted? Are they a requirement for all people at all levels or are they just a token gesture? Do the top officers, including the president, take time out of their schedules and spend time dealing with these issues of equality? Where are women in the organization in terms of levels and jobs? Does the company have a formal or informal program to provide mentors for women? How is the EEO/AAP department organized? What are its staffing levels? Do internal women's organizations exist with company support? Does the company actively support external women's organizations? Do the company's publications reflect a pluralistic workforce? Answers to these questions will give women and minorities a good indication of their company's commitment to fair and equitable treatment within the context of corporate bureaucracies.

Here are some practical steps that women can take if they choose to hang in there. None of these suggestions are guarantees, however, that women will be partially, let alone fully, recognized by an inherently biased, male-dominated, bureaucratic structure.

1. Until such time as things become fairer across the board, women must make certain that their educational credentials are superior or at least equal to those of the men with whom they want to compete.
2. Because it is so difficult for women to find mentors, they must be much more concerned than their male counterparts about managing their bosses.
3. Women must make certain that they give 125 percent in effort and never let down despite the negative situations they must face.
4. Women must take greater and more frequent risks to be recognized. They must also be very much aware that any failures will be blown out of proportion by the male establishment.
5. Women must take on additional responsibility and tasks, which many men do not have to do to be recognized.
6. Women must constantly be creative and think of new ways of doing things. In the process of being creative women must recognize that they might not get credit for their ideas, but that there is always the chance that they will.

What I am suggesting is that if women decide to try to get ahead in a sexist corporation, they might as well deal with the reality that they must be better than men. Remember, the higher women go, the more visible they become, the more eyes are focused on them, the more "perfect" they must be, and the more superior their performance must be.

Impact of Dual Roles on Women's Careers

One factor that clearly affects a woman's career is how she balances work and family conflict, a conflict that is strongly rooted in the sexism of husbands and bosses who cling, consciously or subconsciously, to the notion that a woman's place is in the home. In my book *Child Care and Corporate Productivity,* I found that only 25 percent of women with children eighteen and under did not have problems balancing work and family conflicts. Let's look at some of the comments:

> Women want to be respected and treated equally on the job but a woman has so many responsibilities (family life, etc.) that add stress on the job that many believe that they really cannot handle the job as well as a man and that is false.
>
> —white, female, craftsworker

> Society's standards impose child care responsibilities on the mother rather than the father, in most cases. Working mothers are then often judged as "not fully committed to the business" because they have the child care duties. However, while a working mother may arrive fifteen minutes late because she takes children to school, her male counterpart has done nothing but read the newspaper in those fifteen minutes.
>
> —white, female, upper-level manager

> Women tend to socialize less after work because they continue to hold the majority of "at-home" responsibilities such as child-care. It is frustrating that the company can't be more understanding about child-care problems (sickness etc.) that often take primarily women away from work. The company should be more flexible and pro-active in offering day-care, flex time, etc., realizing that family life is an equally important, if not more important, part of

employees' lives. Kids count; they are our future. And it is important that we all work together to raise them right.

—white, female, middle-level manager

I think one of the biggest problems women face is raising children. Child rearing still seems to be handled by women single parents with children. These factors leave them with additional factors (such as a child's illness) to cope with.

—white, female, middle-level manager

Most women have a problem before they even start because they are also responsible for a home and the family life either before and after each work day or both. Most men come home relieved of all pressures at work, ready to relax. Most women don't have this luxury. How to do it quickly and smoothly I don't know.

—white, female, craftsworker

Mothers are held back or reprimanded if they must be off with ill children or take them to the doctor for emergencies. Very unfair.

—white, female, craftsworker

It's sad to see how women have become "devalued" by society. Women have contributed a lot to society, but men (and a lot of women) have been brainwashed to believe that women should not contribute, that they should be subservient to men. We're made to feel guilty for leaving the home, for "leaving our children." The fact is, many women are happier as workers and children feel that they benefit from happier mothers. They would also benefit from more participatory fathers.

—white, female, middle-level manager

Most jobs are inherently stressful, especially for the upwardly mobile. When this stress is added to family responsibilities and conflicting messages about proper roles, the total stress level on the job for some employees, particularly female employees, is extremely high.

S. F. Berk wrote in 1985 that women employed full time outside the home spent approximately thirty hours per week on household tasks and that women who were not employed outside the home spent about sixty hours on such tasks. She also noted that 70 percent of the total time spent on household chores was contributed by women, 15 percent by men, and the remainder by other members of the household.[23]

Having effectively two full-time jobs creates stress conflict both at home and on the job. A certain level of on-the-job stress, caused by employment uncertainty, office politics, budget crunches, tight time frames, lack of corporate resources, and, sometimes, long hours, is inherent for most employees. For upwardly mobile employees, factors such as employment insecurity, office politics, and long hours are added to extraordinary work loads, a great deal of pressure, and more than average responsibility. For all employees, on-the-job stress along with family stress can create an overload: too much to do with too little time in which to do it. Ultimately, owing to both physical and mental problems that are its by-products, overload lowers corporate productivity.

J. Grimaldi and B. P. Schnapper made this observation on the eventual negative impact of stress on employees:

> The relationship between stress and illness is well documented. In fact, high blood pressure, ulcers, stomach disorders, and heart disease are familiar examples of stress-related health problems. Low back pain and even colds and flu can result from stress. In fact, some medical experts have estimated that as many as 60 to 80 percent of their patients have stress-related complaints.[24]

In a 1984 child-care study designed to explore the tremendous impact of dual careers on family/work stress and, we can assume, on the careers of women, an index was formed from responses to four individual questions related to stress. The questions that comprise the index were:

> To what extent has balancing family and work responsibilities created stress on the job?

> To what extent has balancing family and work responsibilities created stress at home?

> With regard to your child-care needs, how much of a problem is handling dual roles as parent and employee?

How frequently have you spent unproductive time at work because of child-care related concerns?

Overall, 75 percent of the women, single or married, and 70 percent of the single men experienced problems in at least one of the above areas. About 22 percent of these groups had problems in three or four of the areas.

On the other hand, only about 29 percent of the married men had problems in at least one area, and only 5 percent of the married men experienced difficulties in three or more areas. The measurement of degree of stress was based on the number of questions to which participants responded positively at least to some extent.

The figures dramatically demonstrate the unique, comfortable position in which many married men in management find themselves; but that comfort may be short-lived. As career opportunities for women increase and as the pressures of these careers intensify, wives will become increasingly intolerant of the extreme imbalance in responsibilities at home, and more and more married men will begin to feel the stress and conflict of dual-career lives. As this happens, married men may find themselves no longer immune to dealing with family problems in the work place.

U.S. laws state that women have an equal right to participate in the work force, yet society as a whole still manifests ambivalence about the impact working women have on their families and even about whether women should be working at all, especially on a permanent, full-time basis. Remember, 45 percent of the men and 24 percent of the women believe that working women have led to the breakdown of the American family. Some individuals in this society blame all family problems, including the high divorce rate and juvenile delinquency, on working women.

Conflicting role messages have led to significant conflicts not only in the house but at work largely because the sexist socialization of women and men maintains traditional role patterns in a time when they are outmoded. The result of the sexist role segregation is that women experience a higher incidence of missed days, tardiness, leaving work early, and dealing with family issues during working hours than do married men. Ultimately, women experience more stress, which negatively affects corporate productivity. Many women try to make up for their lowered productivity by taking work home and coming in to work on weekends; but this effort, while laudable, further increases stress and family and work conflicts by consuming valuable, limited time.

Solutions to Women's Dual-Role Problems

The main solution to dual-role problems of women is to get their corporations to address the issue of work and family conflict and child care. This will be no easy task. The main reason corporate America has failed to deal with the family and work conflict and with child care especially is that these are seen as almost exclusively women's issues. Corporate America is still dominated by older men who come from traditional, sexist, family role models and who still believe, consciously or unconsciously, that women should be at home taking care of the children. Women who defy tradition and insist on working, they believe, must simply accept as their own responsibility the problems of balancing dual family and work roles and resolving the issues of child care. These corporate managers have not yet realized that most women are in the work force to stay and that their numbers will continue to increase. As the *Wall Street Journal* observed, "Many male executives persist in believing that working mothers, now a majority of women in the work force, are only working temporarily."[25]

Townsend gave some good advice:

> Your job has grown to include occasional overnight travel. Your husband and kids feel this cuts into their time.

> Your husband is lying about how the kids feel. Ask them. Then ask yourself what makes your heart leap. Then divorce your husband or your job. Take into consideration that good jobs are scarce and men are a dime a dozen.[26]

Thus, women must adopt a two-pronged attack: (1) get their corporations to develop a systematic approach to child-care issues or seek out a company that has; and (2) deal with the issue of having a more equitable sharing of home duties and child rearing by their significant other. The resolution of these two major issues will give women a great deal more time to work on their careers and also improve their chances for advancement.

Conclusions

This chapter clearly demonstrates that women are faced with a whole host of problems that men do not confront in surviving in the corporate fishbowl and making it into middle and upper management. Overwhelming percentages of women and significant percentages of men believe that women are excluded from informal work groups by men, women are sexually harassed on the job, women's power and authority are limited or questioned by men, and women must be better performers. On top of all this women have to deal with being full-time corporate employees and full-time family workers.

I suggest that women stop believing the corporate propaganda that the major influences on their careers are their skills and competencies. Women must recognize and understand that they have some unique problems in addition to all the other corporate games and inequalities men have to deal with. The fallacy of the following comment—its implicit denial and the function that serves in preserving the white male hegemony—should by now be clear:

> As a woman I feel that I have been given many career opportunities because of my qualifications and my performance. I feel respected as an employee and that being a female had very little influence on my opportunities.
>
> —white, female, middle-level manager

She has clearly bought into the corporate "line," and when she fails to continue up the ladder, she will have few options other than blaming herself and denigrating her own ability to explain her failure.

I have suggested that women must develop and use a repertoire of techniques to make it in corporate America. These strategies will depend on their individual goals and on the people and situations they are dealing with.

I do not subscribe to the notion that women should act like

men. Regardless of whether women adopt a conformity role, the male establishment will give only very limited middle- and high-level opportunities to women. The old-boy network is not ready to share any significant amount of its power. Therefore, if women really want more than just a few opportunities, they must change the system, not join it.

A few companies are sincerely trying to advance women into their middle and upper hierarchy. Women should seek them out, looking for the characteristics suggested in this chapter. However, women should remember A. Astrachan's warning from his book *How Men Feel: Their Response to Women's Demands for Equality and Power:* Only about 5 to 10 percent of all men truly support women's full equality. Furthermore, he found that another 25 percent support women's equality only for pragmatic reasons.[27]

9

Extraordinary Problems of Minority Employees and Their Solutions

Minorities confront problems in reaching their corporate dreams that whites—particularly white males—never confront head-on. Minority women must deal with the "double jeopardy" of racism and sexism combined. For them, fulfilling the corporate dream can be overwhelming. The array of minority groups that make up this society face problems that are sometimes similar and at other times quite different.

Discrimination against Different Minorities

Economic issues are probably chief in determining the level of race discrimination within this society. Although political and social competition are important, the competition for a finite portion of desirable land, money, and jobs largely determines the intensity and depth of the threat felt by the dominant white society. Once a minority group begins to take something to which the dominant group feels exclusively entitled, minorities become subject to all the manipulation, exploitation, and harassment—in short, oppression—that the dominant group can muster. The relative population of the minority group, as well as its skin color, also influences white America's attitudes and behaviors. The minority group's response to society, in turn, is thereby influenced.

The discrimination encountered by each minority group in this study is unique, in kind and in degree. Each group has its particular legacy of both positive and negative stereotypes, which come not only from the white majority but also from other minority groups. The degree of hostility with which each group reacts to its treatment by corporate America differs.

The greatest burden of racism appears to have fallen on the black race for a number of reasons: the bitter legacy of slavery, blacks' dark skin color, their larger numbers, and their geographical dispersion. The results of this burden, as shown throughout the data collected in this study, are that black employees are the most sensitive and empathetic to the plight of minority employees, and the most outraged at the racist treatment they observe in American corporations today.

The Hispanic group, the second-largest minority in the United States, is second only to blacks in its negative reactions to the treatment and situation of minorities in corporations. However, within the umbrella term *Hispanic* are five distinct groups: Mexicans, Cubans, Puerto Ricans, Latinos from Central and South America, and other Hispanics primarily from Spain. When their responses are analyzed, we find that Puerto Ricans, many of whom have black origins, respond more similarly to blacks than do the other Hispanic groups. People who classify themselves as having "other Spanish" origins (that is, from Spain or its colonies) are usually white in color and respond similarly to whites. This strongly implies that the skin color of the Hispanic managers greatly influences their responses in this study.

Participants' Perceptions of Racial Discrimination

Participants' comments about the current problematic situation of minority employees in corporate America give a qualitative dimension to the statistics presented later. The following quotations from minorities present what they perceive as the basic facts about their treatment and work environment:

> Many personal experiences have been mostly positive. I am Hispanic, and, therefore, a minority. I am a role model for my "entire" family and the company has set a good example for hope as

far as my family is concerned. They feel the world holds much for them because of many of my successes. I do run across people at times who question my validity as a supervisor and possibly my experience and education. I can only say for myself that these people give me the little extra push deep down inside that helps me to be an "over-achiever" and to give 110 percent along with my personal pride in myself and heritage.

—Hispanic, female, lower-level manager

I work in an office of about 60 people where I'm the only minority. Two also transferred from another office. With about 50 people, I was the only minority and I'm temporary. That doesn't sound very committed to pluralism to me.

—black, female, craftsworker

As a minority (1) in a "token" position to meet AAP/EEO; (2) constantly hear racist comments and jokes; (3) handled with "kid gloves" by both peers and upper level management.

—black, female, lower-level manager

I am totally dissatisfied with my current job. I am constantly harassed due to my being a minority.

—Hispanic, female, craftsworker

I am the *only* minority person in this office and am stunned and ashamed of the racism in this office. I am always told "it's nothing against me" by other reps and my boss—I have ten years with this company and I have experienced a supervisor that puts down minorities in section meetings and allows ethnic statements and jokes told in the meetings. She always states our meetings are "closed meetings."

—Hispanic, female, craftsworker

I work in the Real Estate Department and am often referred to as the cleaning lady which is racially and sexually discriminating and definitely a stereotype.

—black, female, craftsworker

In my department, although this situation has improved, it was hard working with 80 people and being the only black in the office. I wish they would hire more people of color.

—black, female, craftsworker

There are many more women in the workplace than people of color. This company shows racism when producing reports on personnel and trying to make people of color look better than they are by counting a black woman twice and not showing the breakdown. White women get counted only once. Why falsify reports by counting women who are people of color twice?

—black, male, lower-level manager

I have found that whites can't or will not even say good morning to blacks even if they're the only two people in the room.

—black, male, craftsworker

It seems every time an employee is angry with another employee of color (or opposite sex) they resort to name calling regarding their race/sex.

—American Indian, male, craftsworker

For the first time in my career, I have a person of color as a supervisor. Because of the fear the company has put in this person, I'm afraid my potential won't be recognized as it has been in the past.

—black, female, craftsworker

This very survey was opened by some member of my work unit and some derogatory remarks were penciled in. This, in conjunction with a recent derogatory letter I received in the mail, causes me to wonder if there will ever be a better workplace.

—black, male, lower-level manager

It often appears that white males do not want a woman of color supervising a white male. Also, it often appears that having three levels of minorities reporting to each other is forbidden, i.e., district manager, 2nd level, 1st level, craft. It also appears that a minority male is always put to supervise other minority clerks, female supervisor hardly ever over white males.

—black, female, lower-level manager

An example of racism: A pregnant Hispanic female cannot tolerate smoke while pregnant; all peers who smoke are white and watch as the Hispanic worker vomits each time they smoke!

—black, female, craftsworker

In addition to those basic "facts" of corporate life, many minorities made personal comments that depict an unequal and in fact hostile environment:

> Many people, I've noticed, are still uncomfortable working with people of color, especially if they also happen to be very good at what they do.
>
> —Asian, female, lower-level manager

> The company's policies on pluralism should not allow room for people to defeat the purpose of fairness to everyone. For example, people stop looking at candidates of a different race or gender as soon as the "required" pluralistic mix is achieved.
>
> —Asian, female, lower-level manager

> The race issues in the workplace workshop caused me to "flashback" to 1977 when I experienced the racial awareness workshop as a participant. The ignorance remains, even with young employees. Views in stereotypical terms? There is no doubt in my mind. To quote one manager, "nothing has changed."
>
> —Hispanic, female, lower-level manager

> I'm sick of working twice as hard as my white counterparts to get half as far in my career.
>
> —black, female, craftsworker

> I have a college degree and experience in the management of people and resources. I would like to use these skills, as well as other skills I feel could benefit the company, in a more challenging position. I question, however, this company's real commitment to pluralism and wonder if I'll get a chance because of my race.
>
> —black, male, craftsworker

> People of color can do a good job only with full support from higher managers. I am a person of color (Mexican) and I can do a better job for this company. Because of my white middle level manager, I will not get ahead. It is sure funny, I feel I can give this company a great deal, but because of a vain, petty man, I will never get the chance to prove myself.
>
> —Hispanic, male, lower-level manager

Some readers by now might be thinking that these complaints are aberrant and unjustified. As we saw in earlier chapters, a number of comments, especially by our white respondents, tended to blame minorities' problems in the corporations on minorities themselves, if they did not altogether dismiss them. The following comments are symptomatic of such blindness:

> I feel that some comments are taken too literally. I feel that some women and blacks have become too sensitive and that sometimes comments are blown out of proportion. I feel that some use racism and sexism as a crutch.
>
> —white, female, craftsworker

> I think there are too many instances where people of color "milk the system" as the "hammer" to their unfair advantages. This results in low morale, and an "I don't give a shit" attitude, etc.
>
> —white, male, lower-level manager

> I have some close people of color acquaintances that believe in a full day's work for a full day's pay. However, I have observed many instances of game playing (hide and seek). The pendulum was too far to the right, but in our trying to adjust and make it better for women and people of color, the pendulum now swings too far to the left.
>
> —white, female, craftsworker

Despite these comments considerable numbers of whites *do* clearly see minorities facing discrimination. Their comments are revealing.

> People of color at this company continue to experience the effects of tokenism, stereotyping, and/or racism in their relationships with many white employees.
>
> —white, male, upper-level manager

> People of color get shafted every day and in every way.
>
> —white, male, lower-level manager

I feel that less emphasis is being placed on racism than in the past. I feel a sense of regression both internal to the company and external in society as a whole.

—white, female, lower-level manager

I believe in human rights. I can't imagine how one company can have so many from the white middle class.

—white, female, craftsworker

I still think people of color are given an awful hard time.

—white, female, lower-level manager

This company is still full of discriminatory men. A black woman faces more obstacles than a white woman. Black males are accepted easier than black or white woman.

—white, female, lower-level manager

Many problems are shared by women and people of color regarding obstacles to success at this company. White men are most often the obstacle.

—white, female, upper-level manager

We have not put a high priority (demonstrated by our behavior/ actions, not words) on promoting people of color to director level and above assignments. That's not good enough.

—white, female, upper-level manager

All I can say on this matter is too many whites and not enough color. Let's get more in the company and we will be able to exchange our ideas of culture, environment, etc. All in all, we'll all find out in the end that we are all God's children.

—white, female, upper-level manager

In comparing the white males' concerns about "reverse discrimination" in chapter 7 with minorities' concerns about race discrimination in this chapter, some fundamental differences emerge. Minorities' comments are more closely based on hard facts (for example, few or no minorities in their work group, few or no minorities in different managerial levels). White males' perceptions of reverse discrimination are almost exclusively personal and subjective (for example, unqualified minorities bypassing them; a sentiment that minorities are getting all the opportunities—despite the fact that most white males work in groups dominated by white males, especially at the middle and upper management levels).

Following are some hard data about race discrimination that supports the notion that white males still have considerable advantage over minorities.

A Recent History of Race Discrimination in Corporate America

In 1964 Garda W. Bowman, in her study of 2,000 corporate employees who were almost exclusively white, found that 77 percent believed that being black, 71 percent believed that being Chicano (Mexican), and 68 percent believed that being Asian was harmful for advancement in business. In 1972 I found those numbers substantially lower. For example, 68 percent of the blacks compared to 58 percent of the whites believed that being black was harmful to advancement in business.

In research conducted for my book *Racism and Sexism in Corporate Life* (which used 1976–78 data), I revised the question about the impact of race on career to ask specifically whether employees believed their race would be harmful, irrelevant, or helpful to *their own* career advancement. Black males (46 percent) and white males (45 percent) were most likely to believe that their race would be harmful. From 6 percent to 16 percent of other race/gender groups felt this way.

In 1986 there was a dramatic decrease in the number of white males who believed their race to be a handicap. Only 29 percent of white males, in contrast to 64 percent of black males and 39 percent of other minorities, saw race as a problem. These figures correspond with the general increase in racist views expressed by whites and the sense that, under the Reagan administration, things are going backward in terms of equality for minorities.

In comparing data on a number of identical questions asked in 1972, 1976–78, and 1986 (for example, minorities have a more difficult time finding a mentor, minorities are excluded from informal work groups, minorities must be better performers than whites), it becomes clear that most employees, regardless of race, believed that racial discrimination decreased between 1972 and 1976–78 and increased between 1976–78 and 1986. For example, on the question of whether blacks had to be better performers, 88 percent of the black managers and 33 percent of the white managers believed in 1971–72 that the statement was true. These figures dropped in 1976–78 to 82 percent of the black managers and 17 percent of the white managers. By 1986, however, the figures swung higher: 96 percent of the blacks and 33 percent of the whites believed that blacks must be better performers than whites to advance. In 1976–78 about 40 percent of the other minorities concurred, but in 1986, 66 percent did.

Race Discrimination in Corporate America Today

In the 1986 survey more than 60 percent of the employees responded that racism exists, at least to some extent, in their companies. As one might expect, a much higher percentage of blacks (92 percent) than other minorities (77 percent) and whites (63 percent) recognize this. The following comments are illustrative:

> I honestly believe I have been discriminated against by my second level manager. However, the only reason I do not file a discrimination suit is because of my family. He already has destroyed me financially.
>
> —Hispanic, male, lower-level manager

> There is no question in my mind that black men have a very tough problem of discrimination within the company that must be resolved. In general, I believe some black men represent a physical threat to white men.
>
> —white, male, middle-level manager

> Do black men exist? In 13 years with the company, why have I only met four black male employees?
>
> —white, male, lower-level manager

> I feel women have progressed faster than minorities because of subconscious racism. Women are a minority and *white*.
>
> —black, male, middle-level manager

To take a more accurate measure of the extent of employee perceptions of racism in corporate America, I asked the participants in
the 1986 survey a series of questions, which were then formed into
an index. The questions were:

Today to what extent do you believe racism exists in your
company?

How frequently do you hear racist language in your company?

To what extent do you agree or disagree with the following:

Other employees accept the authority of a minority who is a
manager as much as they accept a white person's in a similar
situation.

Many white members of work groups listen less to work-related
opinions of minorities who are managers than they do to those
of white managers.

Many minorities who are managers have a harder time finding
a sponsor or mentor than white managers.

Many minority employees are excluded from informal work
groups by whites.

Minorities who are managers have to be better performers than
white managers to get ahead.

White managers are generally unable to work comfortably with
minorities who are managers; they bypass them and go to their
superiors.

Zero percent blacks compared to 10 percent of other minorities
and 19 percent of the whites believe that there is no race discrimination in their company. Likewise, 75 percent of blacks, 36 percent
of other minorities, and 16 percent of whites believe that a great
deal of race discrimination exists in the company. Table 8 in the
appendix shows that 92 percent of black managers believe that

there is a great deal of racism in the company. White craft women and all white men are least likely to see a great deal of racism in the company.

In general, minorities and white women at higher levels are substantially more likely to see racism than those at lower levels. Of white, female managers, 22 percent at the lower level, 44 percent at the middle level, and 57 percent at the upper level believe that there is a great deal of race discrimination in the company.

Most minorities and women at middle levels and above remain consistently critical of the treatment accorded minorities and women. Contrary to white men's responses, minorities and women do *not* develop a more optimistic evaluation of their careers and work situations as they move up the corporate ladder. One explanation is that managers from the dominant group feel more a part of the group that helped them get there. For women and minorities, group identity diminishes as they progress up the management ladder, because fewer same-sex or same-race superiors, peers, and subordinates are found at the higher levels. As their status becomes more obviously "token," they feel more isolated and thus become more alienated. Finally, as minorities and women move up the pyramid they are usually placed in "no-line," less-powerful departments. Naturally they develop an increasing sense of powerlessness, in contrast to their white male peers, whose situations hint at a string of further advancement possibilities.

As with gender discrimination, education has minimal impact upon white male responses to the racism index. In contrast, the more educated that white women and minorities are, the more likely they are to notice a great deal of race discrimination. Of white women, 11 percent with high school, 30 percent with a college degree, and 44 percent with at least some graduate training believe that there is a great deal of race discrimination.

On the whole, frequency of contact with minorities on the job does not significantly alter the responses of the employees about race discrimination in the company. For white women, but not white men, the more frequently they have social contact with minorities outside of work, the more likely they are to believe that a great deal of racism exists in the company: 37 percent who have very frequent contact versus 18 percent who have none believe that there is a great deal of racism.

What this pattern indicates is that perceptions of racial discrimination on the job in many cases have *nothing* to do with the actual experience of working with minorities but with personal feelings. The fact that social contact outside the work place modifies white women's perceptions of race discrimination and not white men's suggests the tenacity with which white males cling to their subjective perceptions of racism—likely, in large part, because they sense that their privileged position is under attack. It is easier to reconcile the obvious inequities by believing that minorities face many problems as the result of minorities' own deficiencies. Yet we must keep in mind that more than 75 percent of white males see discrimination in their company.

The Problem of Racist Stereotypes

As noted in chapter 6, the dominant white society has developed many stereotypes about minorities. Equal percentages of black men and women (4 percent) hold at least some racist stereotypes and attitudes. Twenty-six percent of white men, 21 percent of other minority men, 7 percent of other minority women, and 19 percent of white women do also.

Racist stereotypes are carried of course into the corporate world. Middle- and upper-level managers who are willing to admit to it can recall that almost every discussion pertaining to the upward mobility of minority-group members has included statements implying some set of presumptive social characteristics, coupled with generalized assumptions about lack of skills or ability. The slightest hint of minority behavior, real or imagined, that seems to support these biases is invariably used as "proof of the pudding." Whole sets of such attributions render minorities and blacks, in particular, less than well suited for influential positions in the minds of traditionalistic white managers.

The following comments pinpoint two problems minorities must face:

Once a new minority employee is hired, she/he does have to prove herself/himself in order not to be viewed in a stereotypical manner. This is not true of a white employee.

—black, female, craftsworker

Whites can't accept minorities because they're not used to them working at the same level they are. Whites are used to minorities being only helpers or on the cleanup group, not working side by side with them.

—black, female, craftsworker

Chapter 6 points out that the toughest stereotypes for minorities (and women) to counteract are all related—directly or indirectly—to their abilities and qualifications. Similarly, legitimate complaints made by minority managers about discrimination are frequently discounted by whites. Sixty-five percent of the whites in the 1986 study believe that a minority could not be demoted without bringing on undeserved charges of discrimination. This leads to other stereotypes, such as "minorities have chips on their shoulders." Let's look at some of the participants' comments:

Blacks always cry discrimination when let go from a job. Nine times out of ten they deserve it. Employers have to be very careful in this area. This is garbage. I don't care what color you are. If your performance is not up to par, hit the road and don't cry it's because I'm black.

—white, male, craftsworker

They don't necessarily work as hard because they know they can't be fired or it's harder to fire them than us whites.

—white, female, craftsworker

It still takes ten times longer (if ever) to take disciplinary action on people of color than whites. Upper management still runs scared.

—white, male, lower-level manager

We have on our crew the worst, most incompetent, and lying employee you could imagine. A man who has been transferred to at least four different job crews and he can't be eliminated simply because he is black and has a black third level for a "mentor." Now you tell me where is the fairness in keeping such a person employed? This is complete prejudice towards all other employees who try to be good employees. The man is worthless.

—white, male, craftsworker

I think it is sad to have a black female employee intimidate the company and all employees due to her color and the fact she continually files EEO complaints.

—white, female, lower-level manager

Because it can become a federal case to take disciplinary action against the performance of a person of color, I think managers may cop out to avoid the hassle, thereby dropping standards and hurting morale, reinforcing the traditional stereotypical mentality.

—white, female, lower-level manager

With EEO being so strong, management is afraid to make waves with an employee who is colored or some other minority. They don't want the employee to claim the supervisor is discriminating against them—which they will always claim if they get into trouble. Most of them are lazy and will try to get away with doing as little as they can. Our department has some that sleep on the job, read books, do needlepoint, and are continually late but they are never reprimanded for it. The white girls in our office are "called on the carpet" for every little thing they may do that isn't above standards, i.e., making an error. I feel the white women are the ones discriminated against in this company.

—white, female, craftsworker

Many minorities come into the company with a chip on their shoulders, and as a result, think that employees around them "owe" them.

—white, female, craftsworker

Most minorities create their own situations as far as biased company opinions; they tend to blame the company where the problem is the individual himself/herself.

—white, female, lower-level manager

T. Kochman made some relevant comments to explain the issues that allegedly follow demotions, the "undeserved charges of discrimination." He outlines general differences in black and white styles of emotional expression, and agrees with R. L. Jones that blacks incorporate their feelings more fully into their decision making, business meetings, and negotiation sessions. Blacks tend to feel freer to react to whites' "efforts to get them to set aside their feelings as unrealistic, illogical, and politically devious." That is, efforts to appease legitimate black anger cut off valid feelings from their causes, thus discrediting the feelings as inappropriate or unwarranted."[1]

Another important stereotype directly related to "qualifications" is the racist concept that many minorities come from cultural backgrounds not conducive to being successful in business. A white, upper-level male wrote:

> I think that minority employees have a greater problem in some cases succeeding in jobs because there are fewer who have had success oriented backgrounds, i.e., succeeded in school, succeeded in engineering, accounting, computer science and other more difficult curricula in college. Their measure of success may tend to be materialistic in more cases than whites, rather than intrinsic.

Like many stereotypes, the previous comment contains a grain of truth for deprived and uneducated minority people. However, these comments belie a major problem. Many whites and minorities make distinctions about poor, uneducated whites versus educated, middle-class whites, but they do not make these same distinctions when it comes to minorities. This dualistic perspective is embodied in the fact that 97 percent of the blacks surveyed and 90 percent of the other minority groups and whites believe that most minorities are as qualified as whites, while at the same time 23 to 43 percent of them believe that most minorities come from different cultural backgrounds that will interfere with their managerial success. Note also that 31 percent of the employees—regardless of race and gender—believe that minorities need special training to be successful managers. Is this a measure of self-doubt? Have some of these minorities internalized racist views about minority cultural deprivation? Are different minority groups referring to other minority groups but not their own? For example, are blacks saying, "we are qualified, but Hispanics, Asians, and Native Americans are not qualified because of cultural differences?" In all probability the answer is yes to all of these questions.

The persistence of racial stereotypes is more likely to be caused by a lack of understanding, insufficient meaningful interaction, or simply racial bias than by vital cultural differences. Minorities, especially blacks as the "most different" minority group, are not given a chance to disprove the white imputation of undesirable characteristics. Many minority managers interact effectively with whites every day, but many white managers are unable or unwilling to acknowledge effective interaction. The white managers are not comfortable in these interactions, but they do not identify their own uncertainties as the cause. A white, middle-level manager admitted: "The white community considers blacks to be different without really knowing them. Their lack of social and business contact with blacks has tended to segregate them (blacks) in their own minds. Therefore, they categorize blacks into one group."

In addition, because of racist stereotypes and attitudes, the same behavior on the part of whites and minorities receives different interpretations depending on which actors or actresses are "on stage." Minorities who are assertive, self-confident, and ambitious are characterized as being too aggressive, arrogant, and wanting too much too fast. A white male with these characteristics is viewed in a very positive light.

The fact that white managers have great difficulty acknowledging their different interpretations of the same behavior by a minority and a white may relate to the social unacceptability of such attitudes in all but reactionary circles today. It has been pointed out over the years that, *in general,* different minority groups have different styles of operating. For example, Native Americans and Asians usually exhibit a less confrontational behavior style than do blacks and Hispanics. Ethnic background also affects whites' operating styles. Italians, in general, are much more verbal and expressive with their hands than Anglo-Saxons. Looking more closely at the general differences in style between some blacks and some whites, Kochman wrote:

> Whites tend to avoid dynamic opposition. This is because they see confrontations as leading to intransigence, a hardening of oppos-

ing viewpoints, with the result that neither opponent will listen to the other's viewpoint, regardless of its merit, let alone concede the possibility of its validity. Thus whites equate confrontation with conflict. Their goal is "open-mindedness": flexibility in approach and the recognition that no one person has all the answers. To realize these aims, whites place their faith in a mode of intellectual engagement that weakens or eliminates those aspects of character or posture that they believe keep people's minds closed and make them otherwise unyielding. . . .

Blacks, in general, do not believe that the presence of affective and dynamic opposition leads to intransigence. Quite the opposite: They often use formal argument as a means of testing their own views. Thus they speak their minds with the expectations that either their views or those of the opposition will be modified as a result of a successful challenge, a point against which one or the other opponent has no effective reply.[2]

In 1981 I argued that, from the point of view of many white men, minorities have different values that are, to say the least, disconcerting. As oppressed people and people from different cultural backgrounds, minorities have developed operating and survival behaviors that conflict at times with the traditional corporate value systems and modes of operation. They are much more likely than white men are to be forthright in their corporate dealings and to be more critical of corporate policies. Many will openly challenge supervisors, a practice that traditional managers see as disloyal. They are more likely to take risks and to seek new directions—both essential survival techniques for oppressed people. By contrast, many white men, as Lou O'Leary, a former vice president of AT&T, and others have noted, are more likely to be indirect, conforming, and set in their ways, and less likely to take risks.

Of course, there are similarities in behavior among all Americans. It has been effectively argued that cultural differences among American blacks, Asians, Hispanics, Native Americans, and whites are not significant in terms of objectives or means of reaching objectives.

To survive, minorities must develop bicultural competency at a very early age. This ability is developed both consciously and unconsciously through all of our society's organizations. C. Valentine explained the survival strength demonstrated by the development of bicultural competency:

> Most minority people are prevented from activating or actualizing their lifelong socialization into white patterns, the same patterns which so many Euro-Americans easily use to achieve affluence and ease. Most minorities are reduced to peripheral manipulations around the edges of a system which might have crushed them entirely long ago if they had not acquired and developed such multiple competencies as they could.[3]

In other words, the cultural argument against equality cannot be justified with logic. It is employed in a racist and a class-biased manner, rather than on an individual case-by-case basis. Although many minorities come from lower-class backgrounds, many variations in life-style and attitude exist within a given class, and much more in an entire race. Further, more and more minorities are coming from middle-class backgrounds. Nevertheless, a minority person who grew up in deprivation should have no more difficulty in becoming an effective manager than a white person who has overcome an underprivileged status. To think otherwise is to succumb to the values of cultural imperialism. Finally, society must recognize that there are significant cultural differences among the various black groups, such as Cape Verdeans, Jamaicans, Southern blacks, and Northern blacks.

In sum, the vast majority of the minority managers are bicultural and can operate effectively in the corporate structure if given the opportunity. Since many minorities choose not to adopt an exclusively white culture, they are labeled as culturally handicapped. Many whites assume that the white culture is the only functional one for the business world and that other cultures are incompatible with white culture. They cannot understand that other cultures have as much meaning and value as theirs. This results in their trying to ignore and/or suppress the minorities' culture. Thus, U.S. corporations find themselves confronted with serious problems related to low productivity and low employee morale. They would well benefit from adopting some of the cultural and value differences that minorities bring into corporations.

Strategies to Counteract Racist Stereotypes

What can minorities do about stereotypes to survive and make it up the corporate ladder? (My advice is primarily centered on a collective strategy because the white-male power structure will allow few minorities in; for the mass of minorities to have an equitable chance, the majority of them must adopt the advice I present.) First, minorities must achieve a sound understanding of racism and how it presently works in this society and in corporate America. Minorities must understand that there are still serious questions in the minds of many whites, especially white males, about minorities' ability to succeed in the corporate sphere. Because of stubborn and overwhelming negative stereotypes, minorities must clarify for themselves their own strengths and weaknesses. Part of the racist game is to blame the victims for their oppressed position. As long as minorities base their estimations of self-worth on white society's opinions of them, they will be on a constant merry-go-round, trying to repair their so-called defects as defined by whites. As soon as one "defect," like needing the right education, is fixed along comes another: "Minorities must improve their attitude." If the "attitude" improves, white society will say, "Minorities need more experience to be really qualified." By the time racist society finishes "rounding out" the minority with the proper qualifications, the minority will be so well rounded that he or she could be a basketball for the NBA.

Wasting energy by buying into racist white stereotypes does not leave minorities time to develop the proper game plan, which could concretely enhance their chances of being successful in corporate America. What is more, they begin to question the successes they do achieve. More than half of the 100,000 or more minorities I have spoken to over the past sixteen years say they would not want to get a job offer solely because of their race. Like anyone else, they want to succeed because of their abilities. But as the previous chapters have shown, *no one* ever gets ahead strictly on ability. And the higher one goes, the less merit and ability and the more subjective criteria are considered. Therefore, if race can be an asset, I say go for it. In-groups do not willingly give opportunities to out-groups, and since few corporations have been forced to meet hiring quotas, it is self-evident that fewer minorities—particularly in comparison to white males—have gotten where they are today because of their race.

Many minority consulting firms lately have been advising minorities to assimilate, to adapt the characteristics of the white male as much as possible to be successful. I vehemently disagree with this approach. Some have come to me in my personnel position at AT&T with proposals to teach minorities not only the "proper" hairstyle but also the right words to say, where to live, how to socialize, and so on. In other words, they guarantee that they can make minorities into white male clones except for their color and perhaps gender. This, they believe, will ensure success. First of all, as I have argued before, a major failure of corporate America is that corporations have been run by people who are too similar in body, mind, and soul. As a result, they generally think alike and come up with similar solutions to problems. Experiments I have done with college students show that heterogeneous groups are much more likely to come up with more creative and different ideas than homogeneous groups. Thus, from the corporate view, manufacturing minority clones of white males is *not* the efficient, productive way to go.

From a minority standpoint, to believe that adopting the white male model to the nth degree is the ticket to success simply indicates a lack of appreciation for the tremendous power of race and gender in our society. Of course, there is a certain amount of conformity which all must maintain in order to be part of corporate life, but to strive to be a white male clone is destructive to the integrity and uniqueness of minority cultures and deracinates the individual minority group members. No matter how much a minority tries to be a white male, the fact is that a white racist will *never* appreciate the similarity of minorities. Nor will they value this effort at assimilation. Rather, they will misread it as an objective affirmation of their superiority to the detriment of pluralism.

How much more valuable it would be for all concerned if minorities would look at themselves in the mirror in the morning with genuine affection and respect for themselves and their own uniqueness. When they come home from work at night, they should be able to feel the same way. Research has shown that many women are developing severe physical and psychological diseases as they try to be like men. The same will happen to minorities who try to be white.

In sum, to combat racist stereotypes, faith in oneself and one's ability is crucial. Fair gave some excellent advice when she wrote that minorities must believe in themselves. They must develop positive approaches to the challenges facing them. They must fight for their rights and put fear and doubt aside. She concluded by saying "expect the best—and get the best."[4]

Now let's turn to some of the specific problems minorities face in corporate America that whites, especially white males, do not have to face.

Dual Performance Standards

One of the frustrations minorities must face is that, despite the stereotypes and propaganda about minority advantage, in general they simply have to be better performers than whites to get ahead.

Throughout my sixteen years of survey research, this question has always produced one of the largest disparities in response patterns. Ninety-six percent of blacks, 66 percent of other minorities, and 33 percent of whites agree that blacks must outperform whites to advance. Broken out by race and gender, more than 40 percent of the white women and 25 percent of the white men concur. Let's look at some of the comments on why people believe this is the case:

> I feel that people of color do have to do an exceptionally good job. If they mess up, that is what is noticed, not any of the good things.
>
> —American Indian, male, craftsworker

> Unfortunately, there is no chance of movement within our city and very little chance for people of color within the company without being an exceptional person. Average people of color don't get promotions or opportunities to help on special projects with their jobs.
>
> —black, female, craftsworker

> A good example was when all Hispanic people got a letter in the mail about a job that was going to be open. Well, a non-Hispanic

person got one by mistake and "feathers started to fly." The biggest question was "why wasn't everyone told about it and then the best qualified picked from everyone instead of just the Hispanic group?" I was really upset when this happened since I am Hispanic because other people felt, once again, that we were getting more than they were.

—Hispanic, female, craftsworker

The "burden of proof" falls heavily on their shoulders when trying to perform their jobs—superstars—that is what is expected.

—white, female, lower-level manager

I feel there is a disparity in the definition of "successful manager" between minorities and whites. White definition: keep your position, lie, cheat, make a lot of money, squeeze your people for all they are worth. Minority definition: build trust, respect, and skills of your people. Build competent teams.

—Hispanic, male, lower-level manager

To start with, most minorities were hired because of Affirmative Action. These minorities had to be special, with good educations and all the rest. As a minority, I have had to prove my capabilities over and over in every shop I have been in, only to be bypassed in every way, promotions, shift bids, etc. I have seen managers lie, change records, to get friends promoted. On the other hand, I have seen managers do everything in their power to get a minority *demoted*.

—Hispanic, male, craftsworker

I feel in the days when affirmative action was in vogue, people of color were taken advantage of because they were led to believe they would advance. As a degreed individual with experience and qualifications, I was led to believe this only to see my white male superiors get the credit for any job that I had done well.

—black, female, lower-level manager

I am a person of color (Hispanic male). We have to be better performers to be considered equal, if ever. Yet one human mistake triggers racial slurs from white peers/work group.

—Hispanic, male, craftsworker

A black, female, middle-level manager hit on the head an important aspect of the "better performer" syndrome: "Black workers are asked for proof of their qualifications and skills. Caucasian workers are viewed in terms of their potential for growth and skills development."

As one might expect, there were many comments from whites who did not believe that minorities had to be better performers. The following representative quotations vary from "rational" theories about minorities lacking in qualifications to irrational myths about darker skin color and slanted eyes:

In some cases, race discrimination reversal is the norm. The darker the skin or slant eyes shape, the higher you go.

—white, female, craftsworker

I feel that there are several examples of people of color being put in positions which they are not truly qualified for only to meet quotas.

—white, female, lower-level manager

The company effort to bend over for the efforts of "formerly oppressed people" has created a void for those with talent and abilities who may be deserving of promotion simply because they do not fit the necessary standards of meeting commitments.

—white, female, craftsworker

I believe that the company is sincere in its desires for pluralism, but I also believe that the company turns its head at the underachievement of most minorities, and/or the blatant sub-standard quality of many minorities' performances. I believe I see this sort of thing happening with craft employees and management doesn't do anything about it until the craft employees mess up real bad.

—white, male, craftsworker

They all think the world is against them. Since they have laws to protect them, they do just about whatever they feel. If I was a black with my own work record, I'd probably be management.

—white, male, craftsworker

Many people of color (in this company, but especially in my department) do not have the intelligence to be effective managers, but are selected only to meet quotas. That is not to say that there are not intelligent people of color outside the department or the company.

—white, female, craftsworker

Some social scientists have found hard data to support the view that certain minorities, especially blacks and Hispanics, have to be better performers than whites to get ahead. For example, Robert M. Jobu found that Japanese-Americans have achieved socioeconomic equality with whites, while Chinese-Americans are nearly equal. However, Mexican-Americans, followed by blacks, are far from economic equality with whites. Jobu found that a one-unit change in education meant a salary increase of $522 for whites, $438 for Japanese, $350 for Chinese, $340 for Mexican-Americans, and $284 for blacks. When he analyzed the effect of age on salary, he found that a one-unit change in age meant $174 more for Chinese, $84 for Japanese, $79 for whites, $76 for Mexican-Americans, and only $33 for blacks. Occupational status and prestige converted into the following dollar-value increases for each step up the occupational-status hierarchy: $1,501 for Chinese, $1,088 for Japanese, $969 for whites, $752 for Mexican-Americans, and $471 for blacks.[5]

Findings in another survey showed that a college degree alone meant an increase of close to $1,000 more for a white manager than for a black manager. Further calculations in the same study showed that a one-unit change in job duration meant an increase per year of $360 for a black and $520 for a white. For each additional year of outside work experience, the white earned $220 more per year than the black.[6]

A study by Clay Hamner et al. found that high-performing whites are favored over high-performing blacks, while low-performing blacks are favored over low-performing whites. Each applicant was rated on a scale of 1 to 15, with 1 being the lowest possible rating. On the overall task-performance scale, low-performing black workers and high-performing black workers were both rated as average workers (7.31 versus 8.89), while low-performing white workers were rated below average (5.63), and high-performing white workers were rated better than average (10.36).[7]

This inability on the part of whites to distinguish performance levels among blacks, as a backdrop to whites' insistence that few, if any, blacks can be above average, has grievous implications. High-performing blacks threaten the image whites hold of racial superiority. These blacks are unconsciously overlooked or deliberately discredited. High-performing whites, who reinforce the ingrained stereotype, are inevitably acknowledged and generously rewarded. The low-performing black gives whites the excuse to paternalistically lower the standards to evaluate minorities. Implicit here is the belief, "Considering his or her race, isn't it marvelous that he or she can turn in even a fair job?" The low-performing white, like the high-performing black, threatens the rationalization of white racism. He or she may subconsciously be seen as a traitor to the system: "Since he or she is white, he or she must be performing poorly out of laziness because we know he or she is capable!" The low-performing white, therefore, is harshly dealt with by the assessors. In short, the findings suggest that low-performing blacks are at an advantage and high-performing blacks at a disadvantage as compared with whites.

Although the studies cited relate to blacks, many of the findings are likely to apply to a lesser extent to certain other minorities, especially those who are of mixed racial heritage, have a close physical resemblance to blacks, and are in jobs that are nontraditional for that particular minority group.

All of the data presented in this section support the notion that minorities indeed have to be better performers than whites to get ahead.

Solutions to Dual Performance Standards

How can minorities deal with this inequity? First of all, they must admit that it exists, get angry if they need to, and then put their anger aside and develop a game plan.

Second, minorities should get credentials from the best schools in the country, and concentrate on developing those on-the-job skills that are in limited supply in their work group, so that others will be *compelled* to call upon them to ensure their own success.

Third, minorities must understand that, in order to be better performers, they must be secure enough to take many creative risks. They must seek outside of their work group exposure and alliances that could positively affect how they are evaluated. Fourth, minorities should try to get line jobs with numerically measured results.

Finally, minorities must assume primary responsibility for ensuring that they receive fair, equitable, performance and potential evaluations by making sure that their bosses—at a minimum—review their performance quarterly and their potential yearly. If minorities feel that they are being treated inequitably and dual standards are used, they should pursue it up the hierarchy. If the issue is not resolved, they should file an EEO suit against the company.

Many minorities will say, "But if I file a suit, won't that hurt my career?" I would say yes in most cases; however, unless more minorities file legitimate suits against companies, why will companies change their discriminatory behaviors? I have seen many minorities who have not pursued their rights have their careers terminated anyway in reorganization efforts.

The choice for minorities is to sit there and take it or to fight for equity. If they pursue the former path, nothing will change, except they could lose their jobs if they are right about the company's discriminatory activity against them. If they choose the latter, they might still lose their jobs; however, they also might have a chance to have their grievances redressed. In addition, if companies have sufficient suits filed against them, eventually someone in that hierarchy will begin to take notice and take positive steps toward ending the dual standards.

Power and Authority Problems

Minorities must recognize that, because they lack certain institutional power and authority that white males wield by virtue of their positions, they must be better performers than whites. This takes on added significance when one recognizes that the essence of corporate life is power and authority.

We asked the study participants to respond to four questions related to power and authority. They were:

To what extent do you agree or disagree that:

In general, other employees accept a minority's authority as much as they accept a white's in a similar situation?

Many white members of work groups listen less to work related opinions of a minority than they do to those of a white?

In general, customers accept the authority of a minority as much as they accept that of a white in a similar position?

Many white employees are generally unable to work comfortably with minorities: they bypass them and go to their superiors?

When responses were formed into an index, 38 percent of blacks, 9 percent of whites, and 16 percent of other minorities responded that minorities do not have any of the same power and authority as whites. On the opposite end of the scale, 52 percent of whites, 10 percent of blacks, and 29 percent of other minorities responded that minorities have the same power and authority as whites.

A few quotations from the study participants add substance to the statistics.

In my office in the suburbs, there are only two people of color. The rest are white. I am black. I have had problems racially with employees because our office deals with contractors, vendors, etc. These people usually are white. Most of them have very serious problems dealing with blacks.

—black, male, craftsworker

I feel that people of color occasionally do not get the respect they deserve when in supervisory positions.

—white, female, craftsworker

Whites hate having any minority, especially a black person telling them what to do or having them in a position of authority.

—black, female, craftsworker

I have had several white male peers bypass me on several occasions because they have problems dealing with a black.

—black, female, middle-level manager

I don't feel that there are enough people of color as managers; therefore, many people are resentful of being managed by people of color. I can say this because I worked in such a situation where whites resented having a black supervisor.

—black, female, lower-level manager

Strategies to Increase Power and Authority

To deal with the power issue, minorities must recognize that while the power and authority inherent in the office normally devolves to white males, it does not normally devolve to minorities. However, minorities can assume much more power and authority than the corporate world or their position inherently gives them if they only dare to do so. One way to increase your power and authority is to assume that you have it and act accordingly. It is better to beg for forgiveness than to ask for permission.

From the first day in a new position, minorities must act decisively and with confidence. Any evidence of weakness, indecisiveness, and failure to take charge will only convince the racist subordinate that the minority is an easy target, whose power and authority can be challenged at every turn.

Because they understand how their actions might be misinterpreted, many minorities are at times reluctant to go after or exercise the power and authority to which they are entitled. If whites are not listening to their opinions, however, ultimately minorities must be forceful and deal with the whites in a straightforward manner.

Before taking any action, minorities must decide how important it is to their getting the job done. Notice that I did not say how important it is to their *ego* but to their *job*. If other employees, especially those who work for minorities, do not accept their authority as much as they accept the authority of a white's in a similar position, a quiet private discussion often does the trick. For those who will not listen to reason, minorities should try sending them some clear messages as to who is the boss through pay raises, job assignments, budgets, promotions, and so on. If that doesn't work, get rid of them. Minorities cannot afford to have subordinates who are insubordinate.

A word of caution: Minorities must guard against overreacting to employees' bypassing them for reasons of expediency. Surviving in the corporate fishbowl requires bypassing the chain of command for reasons such as speed and efficiency. Secure bosses who know their subordinates can determine when such bypassing is appropriate. Only if such actions are clearly based on racism or other nonlegitimate reasons should it become an issue.

Finally, minorities (and women) must recognize that retaining power and authority is an ongoing process. As minorities move through their careers, they will always encounter some whites who for racist reasons do not want minorities to have power and authority. Some will go to great lengths to render minorities powerless. To protect themselves, minorities can never become complacent with their current measure of power and authority.

Exclusion from Informal Work Groups

A great deal of power in the corporate structure rests in informal networks. Systematic exclusion from powerful, political, and well-connected informal groups can seriously block access to the power and authority that one needs to perform to one's maximum abilities and enhance one's career. Just as women feel excluded by men, many minorities, especially blacks, believe they are excluded from informal work groups by whites. A significant percentage of whites concur. In 1986, 82 percent of the blacks, 51 percent of the other minorities, and 41 percent of the whites believe that many minorities are often excluded from informal work networks by whites. The following comments by the participants illustrate the problem:

Jokes, racist remarks, laughing, exclusion.

—black, female, craftsworker

I have found that I am not part of my boss' informal network like my white peers are.

—black, male, middle-level manager

I feel that the informal work networks of white men intentionally make things harder for people of color. What is more, they still have a stereotypical view of people of color.

—black, male, lower-level manager

My peers only include me when they want to talk about sex.

—Hispanic, female, lower-level manager

The difference is still seen on the job. You are excluded. You can try to fit in, but you soon realize your peers and superiors view you differently because you don't think like they do or don't always agree with them.

—black, female, craftsworker

Strategies for Inclusion in Informal Work Groups

What can minorities do about being excluded from informal work groups? To survive and make it in corporate America, they must have some access to these groups. Since it is difficult for racist whites to include minorities, minorities must not waste their energies trying to become part of groups that are more social than political. Remember, real informal networks exist primarily to enhance the power, influence, and careers of their members.

The way to become part of informal work groups is to have something—or appear to have something—that the groups want. Short of this, minorities must find ways to socialize at work and nonwork functions with the intention of making contacts and becoming part of the informal work group. Try to find something in common with the leader(s) of the group and build on it. This task will not be easy. Fair observes that the demonstrative behavior crucial to projecting "belongingness" in organizations is such a subtle skill that it is almost invisible. More specifically, skin color acts almost as an automatic cue to Caucasians, who are made anxious by the mere presence of blacks. "Without confrontation or serious affront, the black worker's presence in the workplace leads to negative action by other members."[8]

Despite Fair's comments, minorities must take the initiative to become members of informal work groups. In addition, they must begin to form their own informal work groups. Unfortunately, most minorities do not do very well at forming their own informal networks, largely because of comments like the following:

> It really upsets me to see minorities grouping together. I feel I am being discriminated against when this happens.
>
> —white, male, lower-level manager

> Preserving their ethnic heritage to the exclusion of whites is counterproductive.
>
> —white, male, lower-level manager

> I feel minorities tend to stick together and exclude whites. This adds to feelings of separation in both groups (i.e., whites and minorities). I also feel minorities tend to blame adverse conditions on their race or racial discrimination.
>
> —American Indian, female, lower-level manager

To refrain from forming informal work groups because of such racist perceptions is to allow racism to deny minorities access to a crucial strategy for survival and success in the corporation. Minorities must recognize that whites do not view their own exclusiveness in the same way that they perceive it in minorities.

Most networks have overlapping memberships. Each group has its "snitches" and "plants," and thus an informal work group must be used cautiously and strategically. As I warned in chapter 5, there are only a handful of people you can really trust.

This last point is critical because minorities tend to be more open, honest, and straightforward than most whites. In addition, when the "old boy network" seems to let them in, they feel their acceptance is total and they let their guard down. This is a false assumption and a fatal mistake.

One way in which minorities can be sure that the informal work group will be more useful than harmful to their careers is if sponsors high in the hierarchy introduce them and mentor them. However, as is the case with women, minorities have a much harder time finding such sponsors than white males. An extremely higher percentage of blacks (92 percent) compared to whites (41 percent) agree with this proposition. Sixty-four percent of the other minorities also agree.

Several comments illustrate this problem:

> The sponsor/mentor relationships are almost non-existent for minorities.
>
> —black, female, lower-level manager

> Sponsors for people of color are almost non-existent even when you have tried to be one of the boys.
>
> —black, male, upper-level manager

> Minorities do not have sponsors because there are no minorities at high levels.
>
> —Hispanic, female, lower-level manager

While there are few minorities in real positions of power to be effective mentors, there are still minorities who can sponsor other minorities; therefore, minorities should not have the false notion, especially at the lower levels, that their mentors have to be white.

A most important strategy that minorities must undertake to enhance their overall situation is to overcome some of the competitive individualism and recognize that all their fates are ultimately wrapped up together. Minorities should do exactly what a lower-level white male complains about: "They create a lot of their own problems, once they are promoted; they try to pull only their brothers up."

As minorities move up the corporate ladder they must make special efforts to bring other minorities along. My criticism of minorities would be that the few who have made it into the middle and upper ranks have not made a concerted effort to assist other minorities. Minorities should remember that if they do not assist each other, they cannot expect others to assist them. My advice to minorities is not that they refuse to bring along whites with them— they must do so to be successful—but that they make a concerted effort to bring along minorities. Only when the middle and upper levels of management have a much larger number of minorities committed to recognizing their obligation to help the corporation change its racist attitudes and behaviors will minorities have a somewhat equal chance of advancing up the corporate hierarchy.

Additional tactics and strategies related to mentors are discussed in detail in chapters 4, 5 and 8. Minorities need to consciously follow the advice in those chapters if they want to give themselves an equitable shot at having sponsors who will in turn help them with the problems of being excluded from informal networks.

Other Survival Tactics for Minorities

The first thing minorities, like women, should do is to make a concerted effort to understand the extent of the commitment of the company they are in, or are about to join, to providing equal opportunities to minorities. (See chapter 8 for specific ways to evaluate this commitment.) Once minorities believe they are in the right or potentially right company, there are further things they can do to enhance their opportunities.

Oral and Written Skills

It is perfectly acceptable to the white corporate structure for a white employee to speak with a strong accent or occasionally to use incorrect grammar: it is considered "cute." However, black English has no place in corporate America, and Hispanic and Asian accents are also a handicap, even though German, Swedish, or other European accents are considered "chic." My only advice is that minorities should try, within reason, to eliminate any accent. Those who have a natural uncorrectable accent can minimize negative reactions by speaking flawless English.

By extension it is obvious that written skills are key to the success of minorities. Minority speech can be criticized very subjectively, but what minorities write is a permanent record of their skills and conceptualization processes. Written material is much harder to judge subjectively than discourse. So minorities would do well to develop and continue to develop their written skills. *One* poorly written document can have a long-term negative impact on a minority's career. A Hispanic, male, craftsworker commented:

> It seems that if a minority does an outstanding job, then fine, she/
> he may or may not be praised for it. If she/he does a lousy job or
> messes up, however, the comments and/or derogatory remarks are

directed towards the ethnic background. And the minority will have that held against him or her forever. I wrote a memo once which had a mistake. I am still paying for it.

In short, minorities must develop excellent written and oral communication skills if they expect to be successful. Minorities must remember we use these two skills most frequently and more people observe them than any other skills we have.

Organizing

Minorities should also do precisely what this white, male, middle-level manager criticizes: "Minorities, especially blacks, always stick together. They have all these groups which are only for blacks. They create their own isolation and problems."

It is much easier for a ruling group to destroy one person than a group of people. Organizing and having lunch and dinner together are important ways for minorities to assist one another. Forming organizations for self-help and to pressure and influence corporate leaders' behavior is essential for changing racism in corporate America. Many minorities avoid such tactics because they fear the reaction of whites. Minorities should remember that, at the highest level of most corporations, there are private dining rooms for upper managers and some for middle-level managers, the vast majority of whom are white males. One hears no criticism of *this* practice as clannish. On the contrary, such arrangements are considered conducive to the development of bonds and the sharing of information.

One of the main issues minorities must confront is that, consciously or unconsciously, white American society has engendered deep hostilities among different minorities, and among white women and white males who might support minorities. The following comments suggest prevalent ill feelings about who is getting the most of the pie:

> It appears to me by the volume I see as far as promotability, your high ranking white execs first accept white women, second women of color, third black men, fourth and last any Hispanic or Indian is non-existent.
>
> —Hispanic, male, craftsworker

If serious consideration is not given to increase the number of "people of color" at second level and above, then "usual observation" of the pluralistic environment will look no different than today, with the exception of hair length and makeup.

—black, female, lower-level manager

White women have made great strides in this company. They are much farther along than black people. I cannot help but feel that they've gotten their positions by riding the EEO movement that blacks pushed for in the 60s and 70s. They seem to be more acceptable than black men and women.

—black, male, lower-level manager

Women have made more progress than people of color. They still don't have the power or influence of the white male, however, I feel more efforts have been made for women than people of color. Sexism is more easily overcome than racism because everyone has a woman in their life whether it be a mother, sister, or wife. The same can't be said of a person of color.

—Hispanic, male, lower-level manager

I am unaware of an action pluralistic efforts have taken to acknowledge the minority minorities such as the native americans.

—American Indian, male, craftsworker

I believe the company has become somewhat comfortable with their black employee numbers. It seems as if there is now an overemphasis on the white female.

—black, male, upper-level manager

As stated before, a black woman faces more discrimination than a white woman because she is black *and* a woman.

—white, female, lower-level manager

Without timetables, nothing ever seems to change. I have great hopes that the company's new commitment to pluralism will benefit Hispanics in the corporation. I personally feel with a focus on Hispanics, for people who have been in the company for some years, there is a hope that I will be recognized and promoted and not passed over. I see the recruiting of Hispanics as positive, but I'm not sure of how much commitment there is to follow through by the corporation.

—Hispanic, male, lower-level manager

White women have advanced far more because of the pluralistic attempts made by the company than women of color. Black women are the lost and forgotten entity. Looked over and maintaining a stagnant position. They possess a valuable pool of resources left untapped.

—black, female, lower-level manager

White is white, be it male or female! Look at the organization chart and see how many black faces do you see! In upper management now check for black male faces! Women, in general, and white women in particular, have been promoted at the expense of the black male! Am I angry? You bet!

—black, male, lower-level manager

The blacks definitely have the advantage to hire and promote because of being black. The Hispanic is lucky to be hired—has to work twice as hard to keep a job and has very few chances for advancement.

—Hispanic, male, craftsworker

I strongly suggest that all of the people just quoted and those who share like beliefs constitute a formidable negative force against the achievement of equality in corporate America. These divisive finger-pointing statements miss the major point: White males are still the privileged group by far. To focus on the few exceptional minorities and women who are successful is to ignore the larger picture. Minorities, women, and their potential white-male allies must overcome these petty and distorted attitudes and join forces to change the unequal situation in corporate America.

Dealing with Paranoia

My final point is that minorities cannot avoid some paranoia about racism and thus about white people who are brought up in this society. It is absolutely crucial, however, for that paranoia to be contained within the bonds of healthy skepticism. Minorities must be suspicious of whites until gaining sufficient evidence that they are "all right," that they have dealt with their racism or are in the process of dealing with it. It is exhausting and counterproductive to interpret every negative action on the part of whites as evidence of white racism. I admit that at times it is hard to tell the difference, since racism is no longer in most cases overt. Minorities should, however, always do some reality checking with themselves and others they respect before pouncing on race as the reason for a negative action. If minorities do not do this, the strength of their strategies to survive and make it in the corporate fishbowl will be exhausted on false issues.

Some black psychiatrists have found some healthy aspects to this "paranoia," but they warn that it is extremely difficult to keep the paranoia positive and not self-destructive. "To maintain a high degree of suspicion toward the motives of every white man, and at the same time never to allow this suspicion to impair the grasp of reality, is walking a very thin tightrope."[9]

In 1981, I wrote:

> A pervasive tendency is to deny the very great impact of race on the corporate life and careers of minority managers. Americans in general, and white men in particular, do not like to think of themselves as unfair. Deep cultural and psychological conflicts occur among Americans because they have ideals of equality, freedom, God-given dignity of the individual, and inalienable rights on the one hand, yet they engage in practices of discrimination, humiliation, insult, and denial of opportunities on the other hand.
>
> Many minorities are paranoid because of their treatment by the dominant society. Retreating into a self-imposed ghetto may be the minorities' only psychological defense against the unbearable pain perpetrated upon them by a racist society.[10]

Situations are bound to come up in which minorities, because of their socialization and experiences, will interpret specific acts as racist when they really are not. At the same time, the newer, subtler forms of racism are more difficult to detect and interpret and are often dismissed as the unfounded complaints of hostile or incompetent minorities. So to view minorities, and especially blacks, as merely paranoid and overly critical is an idea that is fatally flawed.

Conclusions

Despite all the propaganda disseminated by white-male-dominated institutions about the tremendous progress made by minorities in the past decade in corporate America, very few minorities and whites find their companies free of racism. Comments by three white males support this position:

> I still think minorities are stereotyped.
>
> —white, male, lower-level manager

> Continued efforts need to be made to insure that people of color are always given an equal chance for success within the company.
>
> —white, male, craftsworker

> I am a middle-level manager, and pluralism appears to be right-on, however, I think that upper management feels threatened at this point.
>
> —white, male, middle-level manager

Minorities, like women, are faced with a whole host of problems that white males do not have to face. They range from general factors such as combating stereotypes about their abilities to the daily necessity of being better performers than whites in order to get ahead. They must perform with the additional handicaps of not having the same power and authority to get their jobs done, being excluded from informal work groups, and having more difficulty finding mentors.

The essential ingredients of minority success are recognition and understanding of racism, development of a positive self-concept, expert technical skills, and more importantly written and oral skills. Minorities must be creative risk takers, on the leading edge of new concepts, strategies, plans, and technologies.

While this is an individualistically competitive society, minorities must forge alliances among themselves and among their white allies in order to be empowered to change racist attitudes and behaviors in corporations. They must recognize, as women must, that none of them will have equal opportunity until all of them do.

Finally, minorities must realize that sitting around complaining about how bad things are will not change anything. Minorities must adopt a "can-do, we-must-do" positive attitude. I end by citing some sanguine solutions put forth by minorities in my studies:

I have taken the pro-active steps to look outside the company to further my career advancement and professional development. The leadership is moving too slowly for me in recognizing women and black women in particular.

—black, female, lower-level manager

If you are having problems and you are not the problem, you should stay and demand that management resolve positively the problem.

—black, female, craftsworker

I no longer let the stress of mismanagement get to me. I decided I will not have the power to change anything so I find solace in doing the best and honorable job I can each day.

—black, male, craftsworker

10
Bringing It All Together

For anyone who wants to make it and survive in the corporate fishbowl, the most critically important advice I can give is to deal with the realities of bureaucracies and of human nature—what is—not what should be or is reported to be.

Bureaucracy is an attempt to organize our environment, which is forever unpredictable. It is therefore our attempt to structure uncertainty, which is impossible. Bureaucracies are our response to limited resources: They evolved, as a necessity, as our population grew and we consumed more and more of our limited resources. To function they require order, and order in turn demands formal procedures, rules, and regulations—none of which can be executed unless divergence is regulated and controlled. This creates a social dichotomy between those who regulate and those who follow. Stratification automatically identifies and separates the powerful from the powerless, the strong from the weak.

In America, inability to become one of the power holders equals failure. Failure means living in the cellar of the social hierarchy. Our leaders represent the ideal—and we all strive towards this position, toward this "success." Yet if bureaucracy represents our struggle to organize the environment, and the environment is inconsistent and unpredictable, then we are living a rigid contradiction. We are basing a civilization of custom, language, thought, and mental health on an unattainable ideal. Social and psychic balance are not attainable in a context that denies reality. We exist in a self-defeating establishment that is promoted by the fear of failure, because in a society that equates personal identity with bureaucratic power, change or the unraveling of uncertainty represents a potential loss of identity and is therefore opposed.

The limited resources of corporations serve as a power tool for the corporate authorities, who can dangle the promise of those limited rewards in front of employees as an incentive for them to behave in the specified fashion. Thus limited resources are used to control employee behavior and enforce conformity to the norms established by the corporate leaders. As noted in chapter 4, corporate leaders have learned well how to mold people. Studies conducted over the past sixty years unequivocally demonstrated that only certain types of white males have made it to the top of corporate America—chiefly those who are young, lean, six feet tall, and conforming, characteristics that obviously have little bearing on one's ability to run a corporation. One reason that the system becomes less fair as one moves up the corporate hierarchy is because the criteria used to select the corporate leaders become more ambiguous. Objective evaluation of the specific technical and professional skills required for the lower hierarchical positions of personnel specialist, accountant, statistician, human-factors specialist, engineer, or writer is much easier than measuring qualifications at the higher levels in areas such as planning, organizing, and leadership. Since these skills are difficult to define and quantify, it is not surprising that the real factors in management-level promotions are how well one fits the physical image of the promotable manager and how much one thinks like the top managers—in short, how much one conforms to the physical appearance, attitudes, and behaviors of the in-group.

The very existence of a hierarchy says explicitly that there is no equality in corporations. The distinction at each hierarchical level in the "perks" employees receive is a way of attempting to control and predict uncertain human behavior. Space and doors are simple examples of the incentives used to control behavior. In one corporation, all the clerks (nonmanagement people) are situated close together in an open-space area. The lower-level managers share small offices for two with no windows and no door. The middle-level managers have larger private offices with no windows and a door without a lock. The upper-level managers have much larger offices with windows, a door, and a lock (but no key). Only officers are granted the ultimate symbol of status—a key for the lock in the door of their extremely large private offices.

Inequity is practiced not only in terms of material benefits like offices but also in terms of intangibles such as social protocol. Bureaucracies have numerous strict rules, formal and informal, for interactions between the levels. One illustration is that at a formal lunch or dinner, and often at informal ones, the senior employee normally occupies a particular seat, which is traditionally reserved for him or her. The senior person is served first, and regardless of how slow the service is and how cold the food becomes, no one dares pick up a fork before the senior person does. All of these "little" things are designed to underscore lines of authority and status and to fit employees into a corporate mold that can be readily manipulated and predicted by the corporate leadership.

Some may argue that they do not see a tremendous amount of conflict and dissatisfaction in corporate America or, at least, in their company. In fact, the one area in which corporations have been quite efficient is in developing strategies to enforce a culture that hides conflict, allows it to be acted out in very controlled terms, or totally suppresses it. Because conflict is covert in most bureaucracies does not mean that it does not exist. It does not mean that it has no negative consequences for the corporation and for its employees.

Surviving and Making It

Employment in corporate America is a power game, a political game, a manipulation game. It is an environment where, in general, the end justifies the means, and where there is a great deal of talk about honesty, trust, and loyalty, but very little of these exist in practice. The conditions of scarce resources foster extremely competitive attitudes. This is compounded by a society that places more value on the accumulation of material commodities than on the development of human spiritual and creative potential.

To survive this game, employees must admit to the reality of bureaucracies and understand the true character of people—where are they really coming from, what are their true agendas, and so on. To understand others, we must first be honest with ourselves about who we are, what are our real agendas, and what we really want to accomplish.

Those who want to advance up the corporate hierarchy must

recognize that they will have to use all strategies from gentle persuasion to fear to accomplish that goal.

Each time an employee rejects a strategy, he or she gives the competition an edge, because the competition might use any strategy at its disposal. Obviously the extent to which one uses various strategies is a moral question; however, being too moral in an unfair, inequitable, bureaucratic structure is to doom oneself to failure, especially if one is very ambitious.

Advancing and surviving in the corporate fishbowl presents problems to all employees, but each race/gender group faces certain unique problems. White males, for example, must deal with the fact that they no longer hold the monopoly on jobs they have traditionally considered to be their own preserve. They must now compete, at least minimally, with women and minorities, who make up the other 67 percent of the population. If they are average and below average, their odds of achieving their desired goals have been reduced. For the above-average white male, however, opportunities have not decreased because the decision makers are themselves white males, and they still favor employees who fit their image.

Crucial advice for all race/gender groups, including white males, is to insist that they have systematic performance, potential, and career-planning discussions with their superiors. Assuming the initiative for their own careers and getting honest feedback from their bosses puts employees in a good position to decide whether they have a future in their corporation and to make realistic career decisions. White males must stop focusing their energies on decrying reverse discrimination and blaming their lack of advancement on women and minorities. Their real problem is the inherently unfair, inequitable nature of the bureaucracy and the neurosis of the human beings in them. White males are better advised to spend their energies on developing strategies to enhance their chances.

The main problems facing minorities and women are directly related to their race and gender, problems that white males do not encounter. Besides constantly countering stereotypes about their abilities, women and minorities find that they must meet even higher performance standards than do white men. They must do this despite lacking the power and authority that white men have and despite their exclusion from informal work groups where a lot of corporate power exists and important information is passed on.

Despite the pronouncements of great progress during the past twenty years in the area of affirmative action and equal employment opportunity programs, there are some serious doubts about progress in the past decade, particularly under the Reagan administration.

Historical data show that from the mid-1960s through the late 1970s many employees, regardless of race or gender, believed that equal opportunities for women and minorities were increasing. However, the 1980s brought a marked increase in racist and sexist stereotypes and, consequently, in race and gender discrimination, despite a pervasive tendency by many within corporations to deny the very great impacts of race and gender on the corporate life and the careers of women and minority managers. Americans in general, and white men in particular, do not like to think of themselves as unfair.

How do women and minorities deal with racism and sexism? They will benefit from following the advice given to white males, but they must first develop a keen sense of their psychological selves. This sense of self is of even greater importance to women and minorities than to white males because they must deal with and understand their oppression and the psychological consequences of such oppression. They must recognize the realities and consequences of racism and sexism, but they must be careful to distinguish between racist or sexist acts and behavior that is simply the result of bureaucratic unfairness.

Minorities and women, like white males, should not focus their energies on crying about how bad "things" are. They must, instead, take positive steps to manage their careers and their lives. After obtaining the necessary "credentials," the first step is to select a company that has shown a true commitment to providing equal opportunities to minorities and women. Once in the company, they must try constantly to excel, to be the innovators and the risk takers, to be noticed and taken seriously. Obviously there are downside risks to being out front, especially for women and minorities, but the potential advantages far outweigh the risks. For those who step out in front of the crowd, the fishbowl becomes smaller and smaller.

What Corporations Must Do

Corporate leaders must also become more consciously aware and knowledgeable about the true nature of bureaucracies. They must be more forthright about the limited opportunities and resources available for rewards. They must admit that bureaucracies do not perceive all people as equal and that the very reason for their hierarchical structure is to discriminate among people.

They must acknowledge the inherently neurotic nature of human beings and their resultant subjectivity. They must acknowledge that people are not promoted and rewarded solely on the basis of merit and ability.

Having acknowledged these realities, corporate leadership can begin to develop strategies to make their companies fairer and more equitable. They must help their managers recognize their own subjectivity and institute mechanisms to ensure that rewards and promotions are delivered in as fair a manner as possible.

A concerted effort must be made to develop a realistic corporate culture that admits the inherent problems of bureaucracies and the frailties of human nature on the one hand and makes a serious commitment to develop and implement strategies that will provide as fair, equitable, and healthy a work atmosphere as possible.

A training program should be developed to give supervisors effective and "bias-free" tools to better evaluate their subordinates' performance and potential, and to prepare managers to deal with their subordinates' career development and planning needs. Parallel sessions for subordinates should aim to enhance their understanding of the programs and to stress their individual responsibilities in these processes. A crucial element of these programs is training for supervisors in the skills of clear, honest, supportive, and knowledgeable communication.

Many excellent training programs and policies are not properly used because there are no incentives, beyond individual interest and initiative, for the employees to use them. An effective reward system recognizes, with bonuses, special assignments, and promotions, those managers who have a good track record of developing and using all of their work force and those employees who take the initiative to improve their skills and marketability.

Recognizing that there are limited promotional opportunities for the large numbers of people who desire and expect promotions, corporations must begin to develop new reward systems that focus more on team efforts than on individual ones.

In any reward system, the potential benefits must be weighed against the possible harm to those who are not recognized. In my view, one of the most destructive reward systems is the so-called "merit" award that is given each year to a select percentage of people for outstanding performance. Corporations that use this system create, from at least two months before the end of the performance period until the awards are announced, a great deal of tension and politicking as employees vie with each other and try to position themselves to be among the chosen few to receive the award. The announcement of the awards has a very negative impact on the 90 percent of the employees who are left out.

Team awards based on the results of the company as a whole or individual units or departments generate much more harmony and cooperation. Making on-the-spot awards for specific projects, activities, or accomplishments is also a way to help motivate people because the reward is immediate and directly related to specific accomplishments.

In addition to such team awards, I strongly urge companies to develop various pay incentive schemes for those employees who are top talent but must, for corporate reasons, stay in jobs for long periods of time because of their expertise, thus being taken out of the mainstream of promotable candidates.

Corporations must discover other informal, nonmonetary rewards. The ultimate goals of these new rewards is to bring corporate promises more into line with realities.

Even if corporations expand their employee rewards and even if they become more fair and equitable, corporate leaders must recognize that the nature of the bureaucracies and of human beings is such that there will always be conflict and dissatisfaction. They should develop strategies to minimize it. The best way to do this is to involve employees in defining the problem as they perceive it and in coming up with solutions—developing, implementing, monitoring, and revising action plans. This should not be a one-shot deal but an ongoing process, because once the process stops, employees will go back to pointing fingers at everyone else, especially upper managers, for the problems that exist. This problem-solving process, if implemented properly on an ongoing basis and with the support of the leadership, is an excellent way to build teams.

Corporate America would do well to adopt the traits of some black African cultures towards team building.

According to R. L. Jones, upwardly mobile "Euro-Americans"—like the character-type described in Weber's *Protestant Ethic*—fear feeling good because of unrealistic concern that any immediate gratification "would have turned them into stone hedonists who would forget about . . . hard work, time management, and future orientation." Jones argues that, on the contrary, it is quite likely that generalized feelings of well-being "might not only motivate us to work more productively, but . . . increase the possibility of . . . creative humanness."

In his view, black psychology is on the whole more conducive to "emotional enrichment and self-expansion" than to rigid self-limitation and self-control. This tendency stems from the fact that in the Afro-American tradition, feelings are a legitimate source of information and experience. Emotions—positive and negative—are valid: black psychology provides a vital "missing link" to the Euro-American concept; it puts the Cartesian split between mind and body into the proper perspective. Jones suggests that corporations should follow the lead of classroom settings that focus on the "total child," encouraging the full expression of his or her emotionality along with the cognitive and rational skills.

Jones cites other aspects intrinsic to the Afro-American tradition that provide a promising model for Euro-American managers: cooperation, trust, and respect. He offers these qualities as a necessary alternative to the rampant competitive individualism that is ultimately so costly and destructive to people in corporate America. Similarly, the Afro-American tradition encourages shared collective power, in contrast to the Euro-American male values of dominance and hegemony. According to Jones, tribal societies provide a paradigm for equitable distribution of power and control between all

gender/race groups. They are a model of "interdependent growth."
In sum:

> The doctrine of Manifest Destiny as it pertains to the control of
> others by white European American males has no place in the late
> 1970s. People all over the world, Blacks, Asians, Browns, Afri-
> cans, Native Americans, and women are telling white males over
> 40 that they want to define who they are and where they are
> going. In a sense, the former subordinates, not only in American
> society but around the world, want to establish their own identity
> and values. Those who cannot accept this constructively should
> consider the possibility that they could become outmoded and
> may well feel alienated in a few years.[1]

Finally, corporate executives must recognize that, to survive in
this new world economy, they must make all employees, regardless
of race and gender, full participative members of the corporations.
They must recognize that a heterogeneous group will produce better
ideas and strategies than the homogeneous groups. K. Sale makes
this point beautifully. He points out that "diversity is the rule of
human life." He maintains that the human organism has evolved so
far because of its ability "to diversify, not specialize: to climb and
swim, hunt and nurture, work alone and in packs." Likewise, social
organizations thrive as healthy organisms when they are widely dif-
ferentiated, capable of a full repertoire of responses. On the other
hand, "they become brittle and unadaptable and prey to any changing conditions when they are uniform and specialized." In short,
individuals and groups achieve full richness of potential when "able
to take on many jobs, learn many skills, live many roles."[2]

Equal Opportunity Emphasis

To ensure the full use of this hetereogeneous work force so that
companies can be competitive and profitable, several strategies are
in order. The following recommendations focus on an overall strategy to try to deal with employees' racist and sexist stereotypes and
behavior. No one method will solve these problems because, in large
part, they are so inbred and reinforced from so many different

sources that an all-out, multifaceted approach must be implemented. Such an approach should encompass (1) comprehensive training for employees at all levels, including top management, and (2) integration of affirmative action/equal opportunity awareness and activities throughout the company's existing functions, in all departments and at all levels.

With specific regard to the issues of equal opportunity (EO), a company can:

Establish goals and timetables for all departments and levels of the corporation, with respect to hiring and promotion of minorities and women.

Conduct multicultural events and strongly encourage employees to attend.

Take concrete, well-publicized action to demonstrate the company's commitment to equal employment opportunities such as on-the-spot awards for individuals who have contributed in a significant manner to the company's efforts.

Develop and implement race-and-gender-awareness workshops as an ongoing part of the company's training and development programs, and expand these programs as the company continues its efforts to eliminate racism and sexism.

Require employees to attend workshops that deal with both racism and sexism because they are interrelated. Previous studies have shown that attending workshops on both issues has a greater positive impact on the employees than attending sessions that deal with only racism or only sexism.

Make certain that all training programs and systems related to managerial/supervisory skills development have modules that deal with some aspect of racism, sexism, and pluralism.

Develop race/gender awareness workshops using trained volunteer facilitators drawn from high-potential middle level and above managers, whose participation should be mandatory.

Require higher-level managers to become mentors/sponsors to high-potential women and minorities. Measure and reward their success in this task.

Develop concrete performance measurement criteria to evaluate all managers' efforts in the equal opportunity area. Establish rewards for those who demonstrate a positive record in these areas and penalties for those who do not.

Demonstrate the company's commitment to EO by promoting individuals who directly or indirectly work in these areas and do an outstanding job.

Make EO-related jobs necessary work assignments for high-potential people and for any person being considered for promotion to middle management and above. These tours should be for at least a year.

Provide those in EO-related jobs extra pay incentives above and beyond normal incentives, when they do an outstanding job.

Require all high-potential managers and those being considered for promotion to middle management and above to belong to and be active participants in community organizations that are concerned with the elimination of racism and sexism, and support their involvement by channeling corporate community-service contributions, financial and in-kind, to the organizations' activities and programs.

Make certain that issues concerning EO and pluralism have time slots on all middle- and upper-management meetings.

Implementation of these recommendations will make EO an integral part of corporate culture and create an atmosphere in which all employees are fully used and developed. The end result will be a more efficient and productive corporation that will be able to compete effectively in the new economic environment.

Companies that deny—as the federal government is doing—the continued presence of racist and sexist attitudes in their work force and fail to take appropriate measures to diffuse them will eventually short-circuit their own productivity and competitiveness. Whatever the cost of the preventive measures described above, it is far less than the cost of ignoring the issues.

In conclusion, the essential point of this book is that in order to survive in corporate America and make it into middle and upper management, employees must recognize and understand the true realities of corporate membership. Only through confronting reality will employees be able to establish realistic expectations and goals and develop strategies that will assist them. And only when corporate leadership confronts reality will employers be able to effectively minimize the inherent problems of bureaucracies and thus more efficiently use and develop their employees.

Appendix

Table 1
Employees' Perceptions of Being Rewarded and Valued
(percent)

	Women							
	None		Limited (1)		Moderate (2)		A Great Deal (3)	
	Craft	Mgmt	Craft	Mgmt	Craft	Mgmt	Craft	Mgmt
Blacks	30	20	35	42	17	20	18	18
Whites	29	19	33	31	22	23	16	27
Others	42	26	31	26	17	19	11	30

	Men							
	None		Limited (1)		Moderate (2)		A Great Deal (3)	
	Craft	Mgmt	Craft	Mgmt	Craft	Mgmt	Craft	Mgmt
Blacks	22	27	43	30	17	23	17	20
Whites	36	17	32	36	19	25	14	23
Others	47	28	25	12	9	40	19	20

Note: The numbers under the column heads—None, Limited, Moderate, and A Great Deal—indicate the number of questions about values and rewards to which employees responded favorably.

Table 2
*College Graduates by Race, Gender, and Age Who Aspire to
Upper-Level Management*
(percent)

| | Minorities | | Blacks | | Whites | |
	Men	Women	Men	Women	Men	Women
Age 30 and under	64	24	76	41	58	47
Age 30 to 40	56	23	75	34	72	55
Age 40 and over	43	10	49	30	60	36

Table 3
Number of Objective Factors Perceived as Advantages for Career Goals
(percent)

| Women | None | | One | | Two | | Three/Four | |
	Craft	Mgmt	Craft	Mgmt	Craft	Mgmt	Craft	Mgmt
Blacks	23	16	20	20	46	54	11	11
Whites	26	12	18	14	44	55	12	19
Others	23	11	29	15	40	55	8	17

| Men | None | | One | | Two | | Three/Four | |
	Craft	Mgmt	Craft	Mgmt	Craft	Mgmt	Craft	Mgmt
Blacks	35	18	13	5	35	48	17	30
Whites	27	10	16	9	43	57	14	24
Others	28	16	9	8	53	48	9	28

Table 4
Irrelevancy of Race, Gender, and Age for Career Goals
(percent)

| | Women | | | | | | | |
| | None | | One | | Two | | Three | |
	Craft	Mgmt	Craft	Mgmt	Craft	Mgmt	Craft	Mgmt
Blacks	12	27	33	55	27	13	28	5
Whites	7	10	15	28	29	35	49	27
Others	20	22	31	41	25	11	25	26

| | Men | | | | | | | |
| | None | | One | | Two | | Three | |
	Craft	Mgmt	Craft	Mgmt	Craft	Mgmt	Craft	Mgmt
Blacks	0	32	52	45	26	18	22	5
Whites	15	23	30	29	23	23	33	25
Others	16	24	22	12	41	36	22	28

Note: The numbers above the column heads indicate the number of factors—race, gender, age—that the employees found irrelevant.

Table 5
Sexist Stereotypes and Attitudes of Corporate Employees
(percent)

	Women							
	None		A Few (1 to 4)		Some (5 to 9)		A Great Deal (10 to 13)	
	Craft	Mgmt	Craft	Mgmt	Craft	Mgmt	Craft	Mgmt
Blacks	10	24	80	75	11	2	0	0
Whites	8	24	71	72	20	3	1	0
Others	11	22	78	70	11	4	0	4
	Men							
	None		A Few (1 to 4)		Some (5 to 9)		A Great Deal (10 to 13)	
	Craft	Mgmt	Craft	Mgmt	Craft	Mgmt	Craft	Mgmt
Blacks	4	11	61	75	26	14	9	0
Whites	2	6	42	67	41	25	15	3
Others	0	8	63	56	25	24	13	12

Note: The numbers under the column heads—None, A Few, Some, and A Great Deal—indicate the number of questions to which employees responded in a sexist manner.

Table 6
Racist Stereotypes and Attitudes of Corporate Employees
(percent)

	Women							
	None		A Few (1 to 5)		Some (6 to 9)		A Great Deal (10 to 14)	
	Craft	Mgmt	Craft	Mgmt	Craft	Mgmt	Craft	Mgmt
Blacks	12	33	83	64	4	4	0	0
Whites	8	21	66	70	22	9	4	1
Others	3	26	29	70	8	0	0	4

	Men							
	None		A Few (1 to 5)		Some (6 to 9)		A Great Deal (10 to 14)	
	Craft	Mgmt	Craft	Mgmt	Craft	Mgmt	Craft	Mgmt
Blacks	9	32	83	66	9	2	0	0
Whites	5	11	57	70	29	15	9	3
Others	0	4	75	80	25	12	0	4

Note: The numbers under the column heads—None, A Few, Some, and A Great Deal—indicate the number of questions to which employees responded in a racist manner.

Table 7
The Extent of Gender Discrimination in Corporations
(percent)

	Women							
	None		Limited (1 to 3)		Moderate (4 to 7)		A Great Deal (8 to 10)	
	Craft	Mgmt	Craft	Mgmt	Craft	Mgmt	Craft	Mgmt
Blacks	0	0	9	2	40	16	51	82
Whites	1	0	26	12	34	29	39	59
Others	0	4	26	7	28	30	46	59

	Men							
	None		Limited (1 to 3)		Moderate (4 to 7)		A Great Deal (8 to 10)	
	Craft	Mgmt	Craft	Mgmt	Craft	Mgmt	Craft	Mgmt
Blacks	0	0	43	9	43	34	13	57
Whites	5	8	50	56	33	24	12	12
Others	6	4	31	32	34	44	28	20

Note: The numbers under the column heads—None, Limited, Moderate, and A Great Deal—indicate the number of questions to which employees responded in a manner indicating that various kinds of gender discrimination were taking place.

Table 8
The Extent of Race Discrimination in Corporations
(percent)

Women

	None		Limited (1 to 3)		Moderate (4 to 5)		A Great Deal (6 to 8)	
	Craft	Mgmt	Craft	Mgmt	Craft	Mgmt	Craft	Mgmt
Blacks	0	0	16	2	19	7	65	91
Whites	20	7	55	35	15	23	10	35
Others	10	4	26	26	29	22	34	48

Men

	None		Limited (1 to 3)		Moderate (4 to 5)		A Great Deal (6 to 8)	
	Craft	Mgmt	Craft	Mgmt	Craft	Mgmt	Craft	Mgmt
Blacks	0	0	13	0	26	7	61	93
Whites	23	22	49	52	17	14	12	11
Others	13	12	22	44	25	20	41	24

Note: The numbers under the column heads—None, Limited, Moderate, and A Great Deal—indicate the number of questions about values and rewards to which employees responded favorably.

Notes

Chapter 1

1. J. P. Fernandez, *Racism and Sexism in Corporate Life: Changing Values in American Business* (Lexington, Mass.: Lexington Books, 1981), 7.
2. K. Welds, "It's a Question of Stereotypes vs. Reality, Limits vs. Potential," *Personnel Journal* (June 1979), 380–83.
3. G. Prezzolini, *Machiavelli* (New York: Farrar, Strauss and Giroux, 1967), 227.

Chapter 2

1. M. Weber, *The Theory of Social and Economic Organization* (New York: Oxford University Press, 1947), 340.
2. K. Mannheim, *Ideology and Utopia* (New York: Harcourt, Brace, 1936), 105–6.
3. K. E. Ferguson, *The Feminist Case Against Bureaucracy* (Philadelphia: Temple University Press, 1984), 6–8.
4. R. M. Kanter, *The Change Masters* (New York: Simon and Schuster, 1983), 248.
5. R. K. Merton, "Bureaucratic Structure and Personality," *Social Forces* 17 (1940): 564.
6. M. H. McCormack, *What They Don't Teach You at Harvard Business School* (New York: Bantam, 1984), 182.
7. Merton, "Bureaucratic Structure," 562.
8. Ferguson, *Feminist Case*, 10–11.
9. H. Levinson, *Psychological Man* (Cambridge, Mass.: Levinson Institute, 1976), 140.
10. P. Selznick, "A Theory of Organizational Commitments," in *Reader in Bureaucracy*, ed. R. K. Merton, A. P. Gray, B. Hockey, H. C. Selvin (New York: Free Press, 1952), 194–95.
11. Levinson, *Psychological Man*, 142–43.
12. Prezzolini, *Machiavelli*, 1.

13. R. W. White, *Lives in Progress* (New York: Holt, Rinehart, and Winston, 1952), 9.
14. T. F. Pettigrew, "The Mental Health Impact," in *Impacts of Racism on White Americans,* ed. B. P. Bowser and R. G. Hunt (Beverly Hills: Sage Publications, 1981), 108.
15. Levinson, *Psychological Man,* 7.
16. White, *Lives in Progress,* 13.
17. K. Keniston, "Alienation and the Decline of Utopia," *American Scholar* 29 (Spring 1960): 172.
18. White, *Lives in Progress,* 14.
19. Levinson, *Psychological Man,* 37.
20. G. W. Mills and H. Gerth, *From Max Weber: Essays in Sociology* (New York: Oxford University Press, 1946).
21. J. P. Wright, *On a Clear Day You Can See General Motors* (Grosse Pointe, Mich.: Wright Enterprises, 1979), 19, 51–52.

Chapter 3

1. Prezzolini, *Machiavelli,* 142.
2. A. H. Maslow, *Motivation and Personality* (New York: Harper and Row, 1954), 69.
3. M. Maccoby, Unpublished manuscript. Used by permission of author.
4. M. H. Fair, *Tools For Survival: A Positive Action Plan for Minorities and Women* (Denver Harris Discovery Learning Academy, 1982), 32.
5. Maccoby, Unpublished manuscript, 1201.
6. A. Gilbert, *Machiavelli: The Chief Works and Others* (Durham, N. C.: Duke University Press, 1965), 1:272.
7. Ibid., 3:1201.
8. Prezzolini, *Machiavelli,* 19.
9. R. Blauner, *Alienation and Freedom* (Chicago: University of Chicago Press, 1964), 15–34.
10. R. D. Caplan and J. R. French, Jr., "Organizational Stress and Industrial Strain," in *The Failure of Success,* ed. A. Marrow (New York: American Management Association, 1972), 49–50.
11. D. Yankelovich, "Work, Values, and the New Breed," in *Work in America: The Decade Ahead,* ed. C. Kerr and J. M. Rosow (New York: Van Nostrand Reinhold, 1979), 3–26.
12. Iacocca, *Iacocca: An Autobiography* (New York: Bantam 1984), 38, 40, 99, 114–15, 117–18, 120, 124, 130.
13. Wright, *On A Clear Day,* 2, 5, 8, 9, 11, 14, 86, 111.
14. Interview conducted by author, June 1986.
15. Interview conducted by author, June 1986.
16. Interview conducted by author, June 1986.
17. Interview conducted by author, June 1986.

18. Kanter, *Change Masters,* 153.
19. Levinson, *Psychological Man,* 54.
20. Ibid., 56.
21. Prezzolini, *Machiavelli,* 19–20.
22. Fair, *Tools For Survival,* 66.
23. Wright, *On A Clear Day,* 52.
24. Iacocca, *Iacocca,* 230.
25. Gilbert, *Machiavelli,* 1:272.

Chapter 4

1. R. Turner, "Modes of Social Ascent through Education," *American Sociological Review* 25:855–867.
2. Ibid.
3. Merton, "Bureaucratic Structure," 562.
4. Levinson, *Psychological Man,* 31.
5. R. Presthus, *Organizational Society* (New York: A. A. Knopf, 1978), 171–172.
6. Ferguson, *Feminist Case,* 106.
7. R. M. Kanter, "How the Top is Different," in *Life in Organizations: Workplaces as People Experience Them,* ed. R. M. Kanter and B. A. Stein (New York: Basic Books, 1979), 25–26.
8. A. Downs, *Inside Bureaucracy* (Boston: Little, Brown, 1967), 230.
9. J. La Rouche and R. Ryan, *Janice La Rouche's Strategies for Women at Work* (New York: Avon, 1984), 223.
10. F. D. Sturdivant and R. D. Adler, "Executive Origins: Still a Gray Flannel World?" *Harvard Business Review* (November/December 1976), 125–132.
11. Ibid., 125–132.
12. E. Aronson, "The Psychology of Insufficient Justification: An Analysis of Some Conflicting Data," in *Cognitive Consistency,* ed. S. Feldman (New York: Academic Press, 1966).
13. W. Moore, *The Conduct of the Corporation* (New York: Random House, 1962), 114.
14. T. A. Beehr, T. D. Taber, and J. T. Walsh, "Perceived Mobility Channels: Criteria for Interorganizational Mobility," *Organizational Behavior and Human Performance* (1980), 26, 250–264.
15. G. Gemmill and D. DeSalvia, "The Promotion Beliefs of Managers as a Factor in Career Progress: An Exploratory Study," *Sloan Management Review* 18, no. 2 (1977), 75–81.
16. P. Pedigo and H. Meyer, *Management Promotion Decisions: The Influence of Affirmative Action Restrictions.* (Paper presented at the Academy of Management annual meeting, Atlanta, August 1979.)
17. E. Hammer, unpublished manuscript, used by permission of the author.
18. Levinson, *Psychological Man,* 94.

19. R. America and B. Anderson, *Moving Ahead: Black Managers in American Business* (New York: McGraw-Hill, 1978), 55–56.
20. M. London and S. A. Stumpf, *Managing Careers* (Reading, Mass.: Addison-Wesley, 1982), 276.
21. Wright, *On a Clear Day*, 7.
22. Merton, "Bureaucratic Structure," 564.
23. A. Wheelis, *The Quest For Identity* (New York: W. W. Norton, 1958), 18–19.
24. M. J. Gannon, *Organizational Behavior* (Boston: Little, Brown, 1979) 107, 108, 109.
25. R. M. Unger, *Knowledge and Politics* (New York: Free Press, 1975), 62.
26. Ferguson, *Feminist Case*, 92.
27. G. Ritzer, *Working: Conflict and Change* (Englewood Cliffs, N.J.: Prentice-Hall, 1977), 114.

Chapter 5

1. T. Caplow, *Managing an Organization* (New York: Holt, Rinehart and Winston, 1983), 81.
2. E. Goffman, *Encounters* (Indianapolis: Bobbs-Merrill, 1961), 114.
3. S. Bok, *Lying* (New York: Vintage, 1978), xvi.
4. Maccoby, Unpublished manuscript.
5. E. Erikson, *Childhood and Society* (New York: W. W. Norton, 1963), 322–23.
6. J. P. Kotter, *Power in Management* (New York: Amacom, 1979), 25.
7. M. A. Allison and E. Allison, *Managing Up, Managing Down* (New York: Simon and Schuster, 1984), 36.
8. Ibid., 199–207.
9. A. N. Schoonmaker, *Executive Career Strategy* (New York American Management Association, 1971), 31.
10. Ibid., 147.
11. Allison and Allison, *Managing Up*, 64.
12. M. E. Dimock, *The Executive in Action* (New York: Harper and Brothers, 1945), 66.
13. Prezzolini, *Machiavelli*, 45.
14. D. McClelland, *The Achieving Society* (New York: Free Press, 1961).
15. Allison and Allison, *Managing Up*, 58.
16. Prezzolini, *Machiavelli*, 76.
17. Kotter, *Power in Management*, 48.
18. Maccoby, Unpublished manuscript.
19. N. V. Iuppa, *Management by Guilt: and Other Uncensored Tactics* (Belmont, Calif.: Pitman, 1985).
20. Ibid., 23.
21. A. Zaleznik and M. R. F. Kets de Vries, *Power and the Corporate Mind* (Boston: Houghton Mifflin, 1975), 3.

22. D. C. McClelland, "The Two Faces of Power," *Journal of International Affairs* 24, no. 1 (1970): 44.
23. C. Reich, *The Greening of America* (New York: Random House, 1970).
24. Prezzolini, *Machiavelli*, 40.
25. Iuppa, *Management by Guilt*, 86.
26. M. Loden, *Feminine Leadership: Or How to Succeed in Business without Being One of the Boys* (New York: Times Books, 1985), 85–87.
27. Kotter, *Power in Management*, 56–58.
28. Ibid., 36.
29. M. E. Dimock, "Expanding Jurisdictions: A Case Study in Bureaucratic Conflict," in *Reader in Bureaucracy*, ed. R. K. Merton, A. P. Gray, B. Hockey, H. G. Selvin. (New York: Free Press, 1952).
30. Gilbert, *Machiavelli*, 1: 57–58.
31. La Rouche and Ryan, *Strategies For Women*, 5.
32. McCormack, *What They Don't Teach You*, 48.
33. Iacocca, *Iacocca*, 35.
34. R. Townsend, *Up the Organization* (Greenwich, Conn: Fawcett Crest, 1970), 210.
35. Kanter, *Change Masters*, 63.
36. Prezzolini, *Machiavelli*, 108.
37. London and Stumpf, *Managing Careers*, 43–44.
38. Ibid., 31–32, 63–64.
39. Schoonmaker, *Executive Career Strategy*, 46.
40. Iuppa, *Management By Guilt*, xi.

Chapter 6

1. Genesis 9:25.
2. B. N. Schwartz and R. Disch, *White Racism* (New York: Dell, 1970), 6.
3. W. D. Jordan, *White over Black: American Attitudes toward the Negro, 1550–1812* (Baltimore: Penguin Books, 1969).
4. T. E. Deal and A. A. Kennedy, *Corporate Cultures: The Rites and Rituals of Corporate Life* (Reading, Mass.: Addison-Wesley, 1982), 164.
5. J. Kovel, *White Racism: A Psychohistory* (New York: Vintage, 1970), 82–85.
6. P. L. Berg, "Racism and the Puritan Mind," *Phylon* 36 (March 1975): 1–7.
7. K. M. Stampp, *The Peculiar Institution: Slavery in the Ante Bellum South* (New York: Vintage, 1956), 11.
8. H. Schuman, C. Steeh, and L. Bobo, *Racial Attitudes in America: Trends and Interpretations* (Cambridge, Mass.: Harvard University Press, 1985), 2.
9. M. Steinfield, *Cracks in the Melting Pot: Racism and Discrimination in American History* (Beverly Hills: Glencoe, 1970), 199.
10. Ibid., 200.
11. A. L. Higginbotham, *In the Marker of Color* (New York: Oxford University Press, 1978), 7.
12. Steinfield, *Cracks in the Melting Pot*, 130.

13. D. K. Fellows, *A Mosaic of America's Ethnic Minorities* (New York: John Wiley and Sons, 1972), 137.
14. W. Schockley.
15. A. Thomas and S. Sillen, *Racism and Psychiatry* (New York: Brunner/Mazel, 1972), xii.
16. M. Harris, *Cannibals and Kings: The Origins of Cultures* (New York: Random House, 1977), 57.
17. Ibid.
18. A. P. Nilsen et al., *Sexism and Language* (Urbana, Ill.: National Council of Teachers of English, 1972), 79.
19. Ibid., 82–83.
20. Ibid., 89.
21. Ibid., 90–91.
22. Ibid., 146–49.
23. D. Spender, *Man Made Language* (London: Rutledge and Kegan Paul, 1980), 14, 106.
24. Nilsen, *Sexism and Language,* 104.
25. J. A. Feinblatt and R. Gold, "Sex Roles and the Psychiatric Referral Process," *Sex Roles* 2, no. 2 (1976): 109–22.
26. R. Benedict, *Patterns of Culture* (Boston: Houghton Mifflin, 1934).
27. J. Singh and A. Yancey, "Racial Attitudes in White, First Grade Children," *Journal of Educational Research* 67 (1974): 370–72.
28. M. E. Goodman, *Race Awareness in Young Children* (New York: Collier, 1964), 36–46.
29. C. V. Willie et al., *Racism and Mental Health* (Pittsburgh: University of Pittsburgh Press, 1973).
30. A. Love, "Blacks Who Put a New Face Forward," *Philadelphia Inquirer* (June 15, 1986), D–1.
31. Ibid.
32. Ibid., D–8.
33. H. B. Lewis, *Psychic War in Men and Women* (New York: New York University Press, 1976), 85.
34. Nilsen, *Sexism and Language,* 30–31.
35. Ibid.
36. Ibid.
37. J. H. Katz, *White Awareness: A Handbook for Anti-Racism Training* (Norman: University of Oklahoma Press, 1978), 11–12.
38. Ibid., 15.
39. J. Harrison, "Warning: The Male Sex Role May Be Dangerous to Your Health," *Journal of Social Issues,* 34, no. 1 (1978): 68–69.
40. Ibid., 65.
41. Ibid., 81.
42. L. Bloom, *The Social Psychology of Race Relations* (Cambridge, Mass.: Schenkman, 1972), 47.

43. See, for example, J. Grambs, ed., *Black Self Concept—Implications for Education and Social Science* (New York: McGraw-Hill, 1972); J. Killens, "The Black Psyche," in *Being Black,* ed. R. Gutherie (San Francisco: Canfield Press, 1970); X. Luther, "Awareness: The Key to Black Mental Health," *Journal of Black Psychology* 1 (1974):30–37; A. Thomas and S. Sillen, *Racism and Psychiatry* (New York: Brunner/Mazel, 1972); J. White, "Toward a Black Psychology," *Ebony* (September 1970), 44, 45, 48–50, 52; C. Willie, B. Kramer, and B. Brown, eds., *Racism and Mental Health* (Pittsburgh: University of Pittsburgh Press, 1973); and S. Yette, *The Choice, The Issues of Black Survival in America* (New York: Berkeley Medallion, 1971).
44. V. E. Schein, "The Relationship between Sex Role Stereotypes and Requisite Management Characteristics among Female Managers," *Journal of Applied Psychology* 57 (1973), 95–100.
45. Nilsen, *Sexism and Language,* 143.
46. Lewis, *Psychic War,* 123–24.
47. J. W. V. Zinden, *American Minority Relations: The Sociology of Race and Ethnic Groups* (New York: John Wiley and Sons, 1963) 52.
48. J. Caditz, *White Liberals in Transition* (New York: Spectrum, 1976), 113.
49. E. Magnuson, "A Melding of Cultures," *Time* (July 8, 1985), 36.
50. D. V. Wilkinson and R. L. Taylor, *The Black Male in America: Perspectives on His Status in Contemporary Society* (Chicago: Nelson-Hall, 1977), 228.
51. J. Crosby, S. Bromely, and L. Saye, "Recent Unobtrusive Studies of Black and White Discrimination and Prejudice: A Literature Review," *Psychological Bulletin* 87 (1980), 546–563.
52. G. Myrdal, *An American Dilemma: The Negro Problem and Modern Democracy* (New York: Random House, 1962), 1xix.
53. G. E. Simpson and J. M. Yinger, *Racial and Cultural Minorities: An Analysis of Prejudice and Discrimination* (New York: Harper and Row, 1965).

Chapter 7

1. R. W. Terry, "The Negative Impact on White Values," in *Impacts of Racism on White Americans,* ed. B. P. Bowser and R. G. Hunt (Beverly Hills: Sage Publications, 1981), 143.
2. Jones, "The Concept of Racism and its Changing Reality," 43.
3. Ibid.
4. Ibid., 32.
5. B. Bowser and R. Hunt, eds., *Impacts of Racism on White Americans* (Beverly Hills: Sage Publications, 1981), 7.
6. Fernandez, *Racism and Sexism in Corporate Life,* 7.
7. Terry, "The Negative Impact on White Values," 121–22.

Chapter 8

1. "Move Over, Male Managers," *Fair Employment Practices* 3, No. 495 B.N.A. (May 3, 1984).
2. S. Fraker, "Why Women Aren't Getting to the Top," *Fortune* (April 14, 1984), 40.
3. J. Alter and D. Weathers, "TV Women: Give Us Some Air," *Newsweek* (July 22, 1985), 70.
4. Ibid.
5. R. M. Kanter and B. A. Stein, "The Gender Pioneers: Women in an Industrial Sales Force," in *Life in Organizations,* ed. R. M. Kanter and B. A. Stein (New York: Basic Books, 1979), 138.
6. Loden, *Feminine Leadership,* 18.
7. La Rouche and Ryan, *Strategies For Women,* 174.
8. Loden, *Feminine Leadership,* 68.
9. Ibid., 61.
10. Kanter and Stein, "The Gender Pioneers," 153.
11. R. M. Kanter, *Men and Women of the Corporation* (New York: Basic Books, 1977), 233–37.
12. Ibid.
13. La Rouche and Ryan, *Strategies For Women,* 74.
14. B. L. Harragan, *Games Mother Never Taught You* (New York: Warner, 1977), 368–69.
15. R. Seidenberg, *Corporate Wives—Corporate Casualities?* (New York: Amacom, 1973), 129.
16. La Rouche and Ryan, *Strategies For Women,* 75.
17. R. Schuller, "Male and Female Routes to Managerial Success," *Personnel Administrator* (February 1979): 35–38.
18. K. Deaux and T. Emswiller, "Explanations of Successful Performance and Sex-Linked Tasks: What Is Skill of the Male Is Luck of the Female," *Journal of Personality and Social Psychology,* 29 (1974), 80–85.
19. M. E. Cline et al., "Evaluations of the Work of Men and Women as a Function of the Sex of the Judges and Type of Work," *Journal of Applied Social Psychology* 71 (1977), 89–93.
20. D. J. Wendelken and A. Inn, "Nonperformance Influences on Performance Evaluations: A Laboratory Performance?" *Journal of Applied Psychology* 2 (1981), 149–158. D. E. Thompson and T. A. Thompson, "Task-Based Performance Appraisal for Blue-Collar Jobs: Evaluation of Race and Sex Effects," *Journal of Applied Psychology* 4 (1985), 747–753.
21. La Rouche and Ryan, *Strategies for Women,* 74.
22. Ibid., 140.
23. S. F. Berk, *The Gender Factory: The Appointments of Work in American Households* (New York: Plenum, 1985), 7–8.
24. J. Grimaldi and B. P. Schnapper, "Managing Stress: Reducing the Costs and Increasing the Benefits," *Management Review* (August 1984): 24.

25. C. Hymemitz, "Women on Fast Track Try to Keep Their Careers and Children Separate," *Wall Street Journal* (September 19, 1984), 35.
26. Townsend, *Up the Organization,* 216.
27. A. Astrachan, *How Men Feel: Their Response to Women's Demands for Equality and Power* (New York: Anchor Press/Doubleday, 1986).

Chapter 9

1. T. Kochman, *Black and White Styles in Conflict* (Chicago: University of Chicago Press, 1981), 18–21, 38.
2. Ibid., 19–20.
3. C. A. Valentine, *Black Studies and Anthropology: Scholarly and Political Interests in Afro-American Culture* (Reading, Mass.: Addison-Wesley, 1972), 33.
4. Fair, *Tools for Survival,* 5.
5. R. M. Jobu, "Earnings Differences of White and Ethnic Minorities: The Case of Asians, Americans, the Blacks and Chicanos," *Sociology and Social Research* 66, no. 1 (October 1976): 24–38.
6. J. P. Fernandez, *Black Managers in White Corporations* (New York: John Wiley and Sons, 1975), 91–92.
7. C. Hamner et al., "Race and Sex as Determinants of Ratings by Potential Employers in a Simulated Work Sampling Task," *Journal of Applied Psychology* 59: no. 6 (1974), 705–11.
8. Fair, *Tools for Survival,* 70.
9. W. H. Grier and P. M. Cobbs, *Black Rage* (New York: Basic Books, 1968), 161.
10. Fernandez, *Racism and Sexism in Corporate Life,* 64.

Chapter 10

1. R. L. Jones, *Black Psychology* (New York: Harper and Row, 1980).
2. K. Sale, *Human Scale* (New York: Coward, McCann and Geoghegan, 1980), 403.

Bibliography

Allison, M. A., and E. Allison. *Managing Up, Managing Down*. New York: Simon & Schuster, 1984.

Almquist, E. *Minorities, Gender and Work*. Lexington, Mass.: Lexington Books, 1979.

America, R. F., and B. E. Anderson. *Moving Ahead: Black Managers in American Business*. New York: McGraw-Hill, 1978.

Aquarius, C. "Corporate Tactics—Games People Play." *MBA* (October 1971): 51–52.

Aronson, E. "The Psychology of Insufficient Justification: An Analysis of Some Conflicting Data." In *Cognitive Consistency*, edited by S. Feldman. New York: Academic Press, 1966.

Astin, H. S., and A. E. Bayer. "Discrimination in Academe." *Educational Record* 53, no. 2 (Spring 1972): 101–18.

Bar-Tal, D., and L. Saxe. "Physical Attractiveness and Its Relationship to Sex-Role Stereotyping." *Sex Roles* 2, no. 2 (1976): 123–133.

Beehr, T. A., T. D. Taber, and J. T. Walsh. "Perceived Mobility Channels: Criteria for Interorganizational Mobility." *Organizational Behavior and Human Performance* (1980).

Belznick, P. "A Theory of Organizational Commitments." In *Reader in Bureaucracy*, edited by R. K. Merton, A. P. Gray, B. Hockey, H. C. Selvin. New York: Free Press, 1952.

Bendix, R. *Work and Authority*. New York: John Wiley & Sons, 1956.

Benedict, R. *Patterns of Culture*. Boston: Houghton Mifflin, 1934.

Berg, P. L. "Racism and the Puritan Mind." *Phylon* 36 (March 1975):1–7.

Berk, S. F. *The Gender Factory: The Appointments of Work in American Households*. New York: Plenum, 1985.

Blauner, R. *Alienation and Freedom*. Chicago: University of Chicago Press, 1964.

Blauner, R. *Racial Oppression in America*. New York: Harper & Row, 1972.

Bloom, L. *The Social Psychology of Race Relations*. Cambridge, Mass.: Schenkman, 1972.

Blotnick, S. *The Corporate Steeplechase: Predictable Crises in a Business Career*. New York: Facts on File, 1984.

Bok, S. *Lying*. New York: Vintage, 1978.

Burger, C. *Survival in the Executive Jungle*. New York: Macmillan, 1964.

Caditz, J. *White Liberals in Transition*. New York: Spectrum, 1976.

Campbell, A. *White Attitudes towards Black People*. Ann Arbor: University of Michigan, Institute for Social Research, 1971.

Caplan, R. D., and J. R. P. French, Jr. "Organizational Stress and Industrial Strain." In *The Failure of Success*, edited by A. Marrow. New York: American Management Association, 1972.

Caplow, T. *Managing an Organization*. New York: Holt, Rinehart & Winston, 1983.

Cline, M. E., et al. "Evaluations of the Work of Men and Women as a Function of the Sex of the Judges and Type of Work." *Journal of Applied Social Psychology* 71 (1977):89–93.

Cooper, M. R., et al. "Changing Employee Values: Deepening Discontent?" *Harvard Business Review* (January/February 1979):117–125.

Cussler, M. *The Woman Executive*. New York: Harcourt Brace, 1958.

Deal, T. E., and A. A. Kennedy. *Corporate Cultures: The Rites and Rituals of Corporate Life*. Reading, Mass.: Addison-Wesley, 1982.

Deaux, K., and Emswiller, T. "Explanations of Successful Performance and Sex-Linked Tasks: What Is Skill of the Male Is Luck for the Female." *Journal of Personality and Social Psychology* 29, no. 1(1974):80–85.

De Bono, E. *Tactics: The Art and Science of Success*. Boston: Little, Brown, 1984.

Dimock, M. E. *The Executive in Action*. New York: Harper & Brothers, 1945.

———. "Expanding Jurisdictions: A Case Study in Bureaucractic Conflict." In *Reader in Bureaucracy*, edited by R. K. Merton, A. P. Gray, B. Hockey, H. G. Selvin. New York: Free Press, 1952.

Downs, A. *Inside Bureaucracy*. Boston: Little, Brown, 1967.

Erikson, E. *Childhood and Society*. New York: W. W. Norton, 1963.

Fair, M. H. *Tools for Survival: A Positive Action Plan for Minorities and Women*. Denver: Harris Discovery Learning Academy, 1982.

Feinblatt, J. A., and A. R. Gold. "Sex Roles and the Psychiatric Referral Process." *Sex Roles* 2, no. 2 (1976):109–22.

Fellows, D. K. *A Mosaic of America's Ethnic Minorities*. New York: John Wiley & Sons, 1972.

Ferguson, K. E. *The Feminist Case Against Bureaucracy*. Philadelphia: Temple University Press, 1984.

Fernandez, J. P. *Black Managers In White Corporations*. New York: John Wiley & Sons, 1975.

Fernandez, J. P. *Racism and Sexism in Corporate Life: Changing Values in American Business*. Lexington, Mass.: Lexington Books, 1981.

Fraker, S. "Why Women Aren't Getting to the Top." *Fortune* (April 14, 1984).

Gemmill, G., and D. DeSalvia. "The Promotion Beliefs of Managers as a Factor in Career Progress: An Exploratory Study." *Sloan Management Review* 18, no. 2 (1977):75–81.

Gilbert, A. *Machiavelli: The Chief Works and Others*. Durham, N.C.: Duke University Press, 1965.

Goffman, E. *Encounters.* Indianapolis: Bobbs Merrill, 1961.

Goodman, M. E. *Race Awareness in Young Children.* New York: Collier, 1964.

Grier, W. H., and P. M. Cobbs. *Black Rage.* New York: Basic Books, 1968.

Grimaldi, J., and B. P. Schnapper. "Managing Stress: Reducing the Costs and Increasing the Benefits." *Management Review* (August 1984):24.

Hamner, W. C., et al. "Race and Sex as Determinants of Ratings by Potential Employers in a Simulated Work Sampling Task." *Journal of Applied Psychology* 59, no. 6 (1974):705–11.

Harragan, B. L. *Games Mother Never Taught You: Corporate Gamesmanship for Women.* New York: Warner, 1977.

Harris, M. *Cannibals and Kings: The Origins of Cultures.* New York: Random House, 1977.

Harrison, J. "Warning. The Male Sex Role May be Dangerous to Your Health." *Journal of Social Issues* 34, no. 1(1978):68–69.

Higginbotham, A. L. *In the Marker of Color.* New York: Oxford University Press, 1978.

Hymenitz, C. "Women on Fast Track Try to Keep Their Careers and Children Separate." *Wall Street Journal* (Sept. 19, 1984), 35.

Iacocca, L., and W. Novack. *Iacocca: An Autobiography.* New York: Bantam, 1984.

Iuppa, N. V. *Management by Guilt: and Other Uncensored Tactics.* Belmont, Calif.: Pitman, 1985.

Jansen, R. B. *ABC's of Bureaucracy.* Chicago: Nelson Hall, 1975.

Jobu, R. M. "Earnings Differences of White and Ethnic Minorities: The Case of Asians, Americans, the Blacks and Chicanos." *Sociology and Social Research* 66, no. 1 (October 1976):24–38.

Jones, J. "The Concept of Racism and Its Changing Reality." In *Impacts of Racism on White Americans,* edited by B. P. Bowser and R. G. Hunt. Beverly Hills: Sage Publications, 1981.

Jordan, W. D. *White over Black: American Attitudes toward the Negro, 1550– 1812.* Baltimore: Penguin, 1969.

Kanter, R. M. *The Change Masters.* New York: Simon & Schuster, 1983.

———. *Men and Women of the Corporation.* New York: Basic Books, 1977.

Katz, J. H. *White Awareness: A Handbook for Anti-Racism Training.* Norman: Oklahoma University Press, 1978.

Keniston, K. "Alienation and the Decline of Utopia." *Amerrican Scholar* 29(Spring 1960).

Kochman, T. *Black and White Styles in Conflict.* Chicago: University of Chicago Press, 1981.

Kotter, J. P. *Power in Management.* New York: Amacom, 1979.

Kovel, J. *White Racism: A Psychohistory.* New York: Vintage, 1970.

La Rouche, J., and R. Ryan. *Janice La Rouche's Strategies for Women at Work.* New York: Avon, 1984.

Levinson, H. *Psychological Man.* Cambridge, Mass.: Levinson Institute, 1976.

Lewis, H. B. *Psychic War in Men and Women.* New York: New York University Press, 1976.

Loden, M. *Feminine Leadership: Or How To Succeed in Business without Being One of the Boys.* New York: Times Books, 1985.

London, M., and S. A. Stumpf. *Managing Careers.* Reading, Mass.: Addison-Wesley, 1982.

Love, A. "Blacks Who Put a New Face Forward." *Philadelphia Inquirer* (June 15, 1986).

Magnuson, E. "A Melding of Cultures." *Time* (July 8, 1985).

Mannheim, K. *Ideology and Utopia.* New York: Harcourt, Brace, 1936.

Maslow, A. H. *Motivation and Personality.* New York: Harper & Row, 1954.

McClelland, D. *The Achieving Society.* New York: Free Press, 1961.

McClelland, D. C. "The Two Faces of Power." *Journal of International Affairs* 24, no. 1 (1970).

McCormack, M. H. *What They Don't Teach You at Harvard Business School.* New York: Bantam, 1984.

Merton, R. K. "Bureaucratic Structure and Personality." *Social Forces* 17(1940):560–68.

Mills, G. W., and H. Gerth. *From Max Weber: Essays in Sociology.* New York: Oxford University Press, 1946.

Myrdal, G. *An American Dilemma: The Negro Problem and Modern Democracy.* New York, Random House, 1962.

Nilsen, A. P., et al. *Sexism and Language.* Urbana, Ill.: National Council of Teachers of English, 1972.

Pedigo, P., and H. Meyer. "Management Promotion Decisions: The Influence of Affirmative Action." Paper presented at the Academy of Management annual meeting, Atlanta, August 1979.

Pettigrew, T. F. "The Mental Health Impact." In *Impacts of Racism on White Americans,* edited by B. P. Bowser and R. G. Hunt. Beverly Hills: Sage Publications, 1981.

Prezzolini, G. *Machiavelli.* New York: Farrar, Straus & Giroux, 1967.

Reich, C. *The Greening of America.* New York: Random House, 1970.

Ritzer, G. *Working: Conflict and Change.* Englewood Cliffs, N.J.: Prentice Hall, 1977.

Sale, K. *Human Scale.* New York: Coward, McCann & Geoghegan, 1980.

Schein, V. E. "The Relationship between Sex Role Stereotypes and Requisite Management Characteristics." *Journal of Applied Psychology* 57 (1973):95–100.

Schoenberg, R. J. *The Art of Being a Boss.* New York: J. B. Lippincott, 1978.

Schoonmaker, A. N. *Executive Career Strategy.* New York: American Management Association, 1971.

Schuller, Randall, "Male and Female Routes to Managerial Success." *Personnel Administrator* (February 1979): 35–38.

Schuman, H., C. Steeh, and L. Bobo. *Racial Attitudes in America: Trends and Interpretations.* Cambridge, Mass.: Harvard University Press, 1985.

Schwartz, B. N., and R. Disch. *White Racism.* New York: Dell, 1970.

Seidenberg, R. *Corporate Wives—Corporate Casualties?* New York: Amacom, 1973.

Simpson, G. E., and J. M. Yinger. *Racial and Cultural Minorities: An Analysis of Prejudice and Discrimination.* New York: Harper & Row, 1965.

Singh, J., and Yancey, A. "Racial Attitudes in White, First Grade Children." *Journal of Educational Research* 67 (1974):370–72.

Sniderman, P. M., and M. G. Hagen. *Race and Inequality: A Study in American Values.* Chatham, N.J.: Chatham House, 1985.

Spender, D. *Man Made Language.* London: Routledge and Kegan Paul, 1980.

Stampp, K. M. *The Peculiar Institution: Slavery in the Ante Bellum South.* New York: Vintage, 1956.

Steinfield, M. *Cracks in the Melting Pot: Racism and Discrimination in American History.* Beverly Hills: Glencoe, 1970.

Sturdivant, F. D., and R. D. Adler. "Executive Origins: Still a Gray Flannel World?" *Harvard Business Review* (November/December 1976):125–132.

Thomas, A., and S. Sillen. *Racism and Psychiatry.* New York: Brunner/Mazel, 1972.

Tiffin, J., and E. J. McCormick. *Industrial Psychology.* Englewood Cliffs, N.J.: Prentice-Hall, 1965.

Townsend, R. *Up the Organization.* Greenwich, Conn.: Fawcett Crest Book, 1970.

Unger, R. M. *Knowledge and Politics.* New York: Free Press, 1975.

Valentine, C. A. *Black Studies and Anthropology: Scholarly and Political Interests in Afro-American Culture.* Reading, Mass.: Addison-Wesley, 1972.

Weber, M. *The Theory of Social and Economic Organization.* New York: Oxford University Press, 1947.

Welds, K. "It's a Question of Stereotypes vs. Reality, Limits vs. Potential." *Personnel Journal* (June 1979):380–83.

Wheelis, A. *The Quest for Identity.* New York: W. W. Norton, 1958.

White, R. W. *Lives in Progress.* New York: Holt, Rinehart & Winston, 1952.

Wilkinson, D. Y., and R. L. Taylor. *The Black Male in America: Perspectives on His Status in Contemporary Society.* Chicago: Nelson-Hall, 1977.

Willie, C. V., B. Kramer, and B. Brown, eds. *Racism and Mental Health.* Pittsburgh: University of Pittsburgh Press, 1973.

Wilson, W. J. *The Declining Significance of Race, Blacks and Changing American Institutions.* Chicago: University of Chicago Press, 1978.

Wright, J. P. *On a Clear Day You Can See General Motors.* Grosse Pointe, Mich.: Wright Enterprises, 1979.

Yankelovich, D. "Work, Values, and the New Breed." In *Work in America: The Decade Ahead,* edited by C. Kerr and J. M. Rosow. New York: Van Nostrand, 1979.

Zanden, J. W. V. *American Minority Relations: The Sociology of Race and Ethnic Groups.* New York: Press Company, 1963.

Index

ABC News, 186
Absenteeism, 10
Academia: and racism, 125; and reverse discrimination, 171, 177; and sexism, 129
Adler, R. D., 63
Advancement, theories of, 57–59; see also Promotion
Affirmative action, 146, 271; and white males, 167–184
African societies, 274–275
Age, 46; and promotion, 71–73; and racism, 158
Alcoholism, 81, 139
Alienation, 35–36
Allison, E., 89, 91, 94, 96
Allison, M. A., 89, 91, 94, 96
Alter, J., 186
America, R., 77–78
American Dilemma, An (Myrdal), 163
Anderson, B., 77–78
Anglo-Saxons, 242
Appraisal of superiors, 50–54; see also Performance evaluation; Rewards and recognition
Asians, 124–125, 151, 234; and confrontational behavior, 242; economic discrimination against, 250; see also Minorities
Astrachan, A., 225
AT&T, 21–22, 102–103, 246
Attitude toward work, 106–108

Baby boomers, 8, 74–75
Background and business success, 157–160
Bacon, Francis, 13
Barnard, Chester, 61, 145
Beehr, T. A., 69
Benedict, Ruth, 27, 129
Berk, S. F., 220–221
Blacks: confrontational behavior, 242, 243; economic discrimination against, 250; and education, 250; history of persecution, 121–126; and informal work groups, 255; and interracial marriage, 133–134; laziness, stereotype of, 154–155, 159; males, 70, 134; mental health, 139; and mentors, 76, 257–258; and minorities, 158–159, 228, 241–242; perception of racism, 236–237; performance expectations, 235, 249, 250–251; plastic surgery, 122, 135; and promotion, 47, 70, 77, 234–235; psychology of, 274–275; quitting, 52; and rewards and recognition, 51, 52; sexual harassment charges against, 207; stereotypes, 152–163; and stress of racism, 139; women, 52; see also Minorities; Racism
Blauner, R., 35–36
Bob Jones University, 121
Bok, Sissela, 85–86

Boredom and work, 36
Bosses, 86; and direction, 107;
    feedback on performance from,
    108–109; and promotion, 75–76,
    79; and secretaries, 101–102;
    understanding, 89–90
Bowman, Garda W., 234
Bowser, B., 180
Bradley, Joseph, 127
Bribery and manipulation, 98
Brown v. *Board of Education,* 124
Bureaucracies, 7–8, 10, 15–30, 267;
    and equity, 19, 268–269; and
    hierarchies, 22, 54–55, 268; and
    neurosis, 24–28, 32, 267, 270,
    272; and promotion, 18, 57–59,
    79–80, 269–270; and rules, 20–21
Burger, Warren, 127

California Constitution, 124
Canaan, 121
Cape Verdeans, 244
Caplan, R., 36
Caplow, Theodore, 83
Career planning, 44, 108–113, 270
Carswell, B. Clement, 175–176
CBS News, 186
Change, exploitation of, 110–111
Chicanos. *See* Mexican-Americans
Child care, 219–222
*Child Care and Corporate
    Productivity* (Fernandez), 7, 219
Chinese, stereotypes, 150, 151
Chinese-Americans, 124, 150
Civil Rights Commission, 6
Civil Rights Act of 1964, 127–128,
    169
Cline, Mary, 214–215
Communications problems, 44, 45
Competition, 8–9; and minorities,
    227; and peer cooperation, 91;
    and promotion, 73–75, 83–84;
    and white males, 11–12, 169–173,
    175–177, 270; and women, 73–74
Confidants, 92
Conformity, 93–94; and promotion,
    58–63, 79–81; and women, 197–
    200, 225

Contest mobility norm, 57–58
Cooperation, lack of, 17
Coping strategies, 28
Corporations, 2–3, 272, 275; and
    equal opportunity, 275–278
Craft employees: and racism, 158;
    and rewards and recognition, 51;
    and sexism, 146
Crosby, J., 153
Cubans, 228

Deaux, Kay, 214
Decisionmaking, 23, 36, 107–108
Decisiveness, 107–108
DeLorean, John, 29–30, 43, 55, 79
Depression, 10
DeSalvia, D., 69
De Vries, M. Kets, 99
Dimmock, M. E., 95, 101
Disch, R., 122
Division of labor, 22
Downs, A., 62
Downsizing, 80, 102–103
Dred Scott v. *Sanford,* 123–124
Drug abuse, 10, 81

Education: and blacks, 250; and
    minorities, 70, 74, 250, 251–252;
    and promotion, 70; and racism,
    146, 158, 237; and salaries, 250;
    and women, 218
Ego-needs, 33, 34; and promotion, 59
Emswiller, Tim, 214
Equal Employment Opportunity
    Commission, 2, 252
Equal opportunity and corporations,
    203, 275–278; and Reagan
    administration, 180, 221
Equal Rights Amendment, 128
Equity and managing, 106
Erikson, Erik, 86
Ethelbert's Dooms, 126–127
Eugenics, 125
Excellence, employer's view of
    company's, 23
Experience and promotion, 70
Exposure, gaining, 110

Fair, M., 33, 55, 247, 256–287
Fairness of treatment, 16–17, 19, 47–48
Family and working women, 141–142, 147, 219–224
Favoritism and promotion, 66, 69
Ferguson, K. E., 19–20, 22–23, 55, 81
Florida, sexism, 127
Fraker, S., 186
Freedom of thought, 37
French, J., 36
Freud, Sigmund, 76
Fringe benefits, 37
Fuchs, Victor, 185–186
Fulfillment, sense of, 35
Function of the Executive, The (Barnard), 145

Galton, Francis, 125
Games playing, 95–96; and manipulation, 97–98; and politics, 96–97
Gannon, M. J., 80
Gemmill, G., 69
Gender socialization, 135–136, 140–150
General Motors, 29–30
Gershuny, Lee H., 128, 144–145
Goffman, E., 85
Gossip, 87–88
Graham, Katherine, 186
Greening of America, The (Reich), 99
Grimaldi, J., 221
Guilt and manipulation, 98

Ham, 121
Hammer, Clay, 250
Harragan, B., 207
Harris, M., 126
Harris poll, 124
Harrison, J., 139
Hartford, 151
Higginbotham, A. L., 124
Hispanics, 135, 151–152; and discrimination, perception of, 228–231; performance expectations, 250

Homogeneity of employees, 61–62
Honesty, 85–86, 103–104, 113
How Men Feel (Astrachan), 225
Huckleberry Finn (Twain), 124
Hunt, R., 180

Iacocca, Lee, 43, 55–56, 104
Idaho, sexism, 128
Illinois, sexism, 127
Image: and promotion, 61, 63, 174–175; and white males, 174–175; and women, 137, 197
Individual development opportunities, 44
Informal rewards, 5, 51–54; *see also* Rewards and recognition
Informal work groups, 194; and blacks, 255; and minorities, 234, 255–259, 264, 271; and women, 209, 224
Inn, A., 215
Insensitivity of corporation, 16–17
Insufficient justification, theory of, 64
Interracial marriage, 116–117, 132–134, 164; laws against, 125
Italians, 242
Iuppa, N. V., 98–99, 100, 113–114

Jackson, Michael, 135
Jamaicans, 244
Janes, R. L., 241
Japanese, stereotypes of, 150
Japanese-Americans, 124, 151, 250
Jefferson, Thomas, 123
Job satisfaction, 44
Job security, 45–46; and motivation, 37
Jobu, Robert M., 250
Johnson Immigration Act of 1924, 124
Jones, J., 176
Jones, R. L., 274–275
Jordan, W., 122

Kanter, R., 20, 50, 61–62, 187, 202
Katz, J., 138
Kenniston, Kenneth, 27
Kochman, T., 240–241, 242–243

Koreans, 151
Kotter, J. P., 97–98, 100, 101
Kovel, J., 122

LaBelle, Pattie, 135
LaBrier, Douglas, 114
La Rouche, I., 103, 206, 209, 217
La Rouche, J., 196–197
Layoffs. *See* Downsizing
Laziness, stereotypes of: and blacks,
    154–155, 159; and women, 143–
    144
Length of service and firings, 5
Levinson, Harry, 24, 26, 28, 50, 59,
    77
Life expectancy and sex stereotypes,
    138–139
Loden, M. L., 100, 187–188, 198,
    199
London, M., 78, 111–112
Love, need for, 59
Lower-level employees, 44; and
    promotion, 71; rewards and
    recognition, 51–52
Loyalty, 102–103
Lying, 85–86

McClelland, David, 95, 99
Maccoby, Michael, 33, 57, 86, 98
McCormack, M. H., 20, 103
Machiavelli, Niccolo, 10, 13, 31–32,
    33–34, 56, 58, 88, 95, 96, 99–
    100, 102, 111
Managing Careers (London and
    Stumpf), 112
Manifest Destiny, 275
Manipulation, 97–99
Maslow, A. H., 32–33, 34
Mannheim, Karl, 19
Mead, Margaret, 27
Media: and racism, 161–162; and
    reverse discrimination, 171, 177;
    women in, 186
Mental health, 26–28, 138; and
    blacks, 139; and women, 139; *see
    also* Neurosis

Mentors, 48; and blacks, 76, 257–
    258; and minorities, 77, 234, 257–
    259, 264; and promotion, 69, 76–
    77, 79; and white males, 77; and
    women, 77, 203, 209, 218
Merit awards, 273
Meritocracy, myth of, 8–9, 11, 31,
    84; and white males, 173
Merton, R., 20, 58, 79–80
Mexicans, illegal aliens, 125
Mexican-Americans, 151, 152, 228;
    economic discrimination, 250; *see
    also* Minorities, 250
Meyer, H., 69
Miami, 151
Minorities, 227–265, 270–272; and
    blacks, 158–159, 228, 241–242;
    clannishness, 155–156; and
    competition, 227; cultural
    differences, 241–242; and
    education, 70, 74, 250, 251–252;
    ego-needs, 33; and informal work
    groups, 234, 255–259, 264, 271;
    intelligence, 158–159; and
    mentors, 77, 234, 257–259, 264;
    and other minorities, prejudice
    against, 241–242; oral and written
    skills, 259–260, 264; organizing,
    260–262; and paranoia, 262–263;
    perceptions of discrimination,
    236–238; performance
    expectations, 234–235, 247–252,
    270–271; and power and
    authority, 253–255, 264, 270; and
    promotion, 65–69, 70, 71–72, 76–
    77, 78, 171–174, 234–235; and
    quotas, 6, 178, 196; risk taking,
    243, 252; salaries, 250; and
    sexism, 146; social contact with,
    237–238, 242; socialization
    differences, 182; stereotypes, 150–
    165; whites' preceptions of, 232–
    234; and white males, 263–264;
    and women, discrimination
    against, 195; *see also* Blacks;
    Racism; Reverse discrimination
Mistakes, accepting, 104

Modern Madness: The Emotional Fallout of Success (LaBrier), 114
Motivational theory, 32–37, 45
Myrdal, Gunnar, 163

Native Americans, 152, 242; history of racism, 122–123
NBC News, 186
Needs hierarchy, 32–33
Networks, 77, 83; *see also* Old boy network
Neurosis, 10, 12, 92; and bureaucracies, 24–28, 32, 267, 270, 272; and racism, 138–139; and role conflict, 85–86
New skills, learning, 37
Nixon, Richard M., 175
Noah, 121

Old boy network: and minorities, 257; and promotion, 66, 131, 189–190; and women, 189–190, 193, 225
O'Leary, Lou, 243
Oral and written skills, 259–260, 264

Paranoia, 262–263
Patience, 112–113
Pedigo, P., 69
Peers, understanding, 90–91
Performance evaluation, 44, 46–47, 270; and promotion, 69–71; and training programs, 272–273
Performance expectations: and blacks, 235, 249, 250–251; and Hispanics, 250; and minorities, 234–235, 247–252, 270–271; and women, 202, 214–219, 270–271
Peter Principle, 59–60
Petrillo, John, 104
Pettigrew, T. I., 216–217
Phipps, Susie, 152
Plessy v. *Ferguson*, 124
Pluralism, 1, 61; and promotion, 61, 65–69, 168

Politics, 3–5, 17, 48; and corporate games, 96–97; and promotion, 3–4, 66, 78–79
Power, 88–89, 99–102; and minorities, 253–255, 264, 270; and women, 210–214
Powerlessness, sense of, 35–36
Presthus, F. R., 61
Prezzolini, G., 25, 26
Productivity, 10, 23, 52
Promotion: and age, 71–73; and blacks, 47, 70, 77, 234–235; and bosses, 75–76, 79; and bureaucratic theory, 18, 57–59, 79–80, 269–270; and business growth, 73, 75; and competition, 73–75, 83–84; and conformity, 58–63, 79–81; and education, 70; and ego-needs, 59; and experience, 70; and favoritism, 66, 69; and image, 61, 63, 174–175; and mentors, 69, 76–77, 79; and minorities, 65–69, 70, 71–72, 76–77, 173–174, 234–235; and motivation, 37; and old boy network, 66, 131, 189–190; and pluralism, 61, 65–69, 168; and politics, 66, 78–79; and sycophantism, 63–65; and white males, 63, 77, 167–184; and women, 6, 46–47, 65–69, 71–72, 77, 78, 176–177, 187–190, 196–197
Protestant Ethic (Weber), 274
Psychoanalytic theory, 25; *see also* Neurosis
Puritans, 122–123

Quitting, 49, 52; costs to company, 195–196; and women, 191–192, 195–196
Quotas, 6, 178, 196

Racism: and academia, 125; and age, 158; and Bible, 121–122; and blacks, perception of, 236–237;

Racism (*continued*)
  corporate efforts against, 274–
  278; and craft employees, 155;
  defined, 120–121; development,
  131–137; and education, 146,
  158, 237; and ego-needs, 33;
  forms, 130–131; history of, 121–
  126; impact, 137–139;
  institutionalization, 130–131; and
  media, 161–162; mental damage,
  138; and social contact, 158; and
  socialization, 115–126, 131–135;
  and stereotypes, 150–162, 238–
  247, 270, 271; stress of, 139; and
  white males, 138, 157–158, 182,
  237–238; and women, 157, 158,
  237; *see also* Blacks; Minorities
Racism and Sexism in Corporate Life
  (Fernandez), 58, 180, 234
Reagan, Ronald: and equal
  employment opportunity, 180,
  271; and racism, 125, 152, 234
Reed v. Reed, 128
Rehnquist, William L., 121, 124
Reich, Charles, 99
Respect from management, 44
Reverse discrimination: and
  academia, 171, 177; and media,
  171, 177; and white males, 9,
  167–184, 233–234, 270
Rewards and recognition, 37, 49–54,
  272–273; and blacks, 51, 52; and
  craft employees, 51; and lower-
  level employees, 51–52; scarcity
  of, 64; and women, 213
Risk taking, 3, 44, 110–111; and
  minorities, 243, 252; and women,
  218
Ritzer, G., 81
Role responsibilities, clarity of, 35
Rules and regulations, 20–21
Ryan, R., 103, 196–197, 206, 217

Salary, 4; and minorities, 250; and
  motivation, 37
Sale, K., 275
Sanders, Marlene, 186

Schizophrenia and racism, 138
Schnapper, B. P., 221
Schockley, William, 125
Schoonmaker, A. N., 91–92, 93
Schuller, R., 214
Schwartz, B., 122
Secretaries, 101–102, 105
Seduction and manipulation, 98
Seidenberg, R., 207–208
Self-assessment, 111–112
Self-confidence, 88
Self-knowledge, 91–95
Self-perception theory, 64
Self-promotion, 109–110
Selznick, P., 24
Sexism: and academia, 129; and
  Bible, 126, 127; and contact with
  women, 146; corporate efforts
  against, 275–278; and craft
  employees, 51; defined, 120–121;
  development, 131–137; and
  education, 146; employees' view
  of, 115–120; forms, 130–131,
  history, 126–129; impact, 137–
  139; institutional, 130–131; and
  language, 128–129, 202; and
  media, 162; and minorities, 146;
  and social interaction, 200–213;
  and socialization, 115, 135–137;
  and stereotypes, 140–150; and
  white males, 146, 182; *see also*
  Women
Sexism and Language (Gershaun),
  128
Sexual harassment, 194, 203–208,
  224
Sillen, S., 125
Simpson, G. E., 165
Single men, dual roles of, 222
Socialization, 11, 12, 115–165;
  gender, 135–136, 140–150; and
  mental health, 27–28; and racism,
  115–126, 131–135; and sexism,
  115, 135–137; and women, 182
South Africa, 125
South Carolina code, 123
Spanish, 228
Sponsors. *See* Mentors

Stress, 10; and promotion, 81; and racism, 139; and women, 139, 246–247
Stumpf, S., 78, 111–112
Sturdivant, F. D., 63
Subordinates, understanding, 90
Suicide, 81, 139
Supervision, problems of, 17
Sycophantism, 63–65

Talents, misuse of, 48–49, 67
Taney, Chief Justice B., 123–124
Team-building, 105, 106, 273–274
Team players, 62
Teamwork, lack of, 23
Technical competence, 21
Terry, K. W., 170, 183–184
Thomas, A., 125
Thompson, D. E., 215
Thompson, T. A., 215
Townsend, R., 108, 223
Training programs, 272
Tribal societies, 274–275
Trips, business, 87
Turner, R., 57–58
Turnover, 10
Trust, 34, 44–45, 85–86; and corporate games, 104–105, 106, 113
Twain, Mark, 124

Understanding people, 84–89
Unger, R., 81
U.S. Commission on Mental Health, 138
U.S. Constitution, 123–124
U.S. Supreme Court, 121, 123–124; and sexism, 127
Upper-level employees: abilities needed, 61; job satisfaction, 44; promotion, 71; and racism, 158; and rewards and recognition, 51–52; and women, 188, 195

Valentine, C., 243–244
Valuation of employees by management, 5, 49–54
Value systems, 12

Vietnamese, 151
Von Hoffman, Nicholas, 56

Wall Street Journal, 223
Warren, Earl, 127
Washington Post, 186
Weather, D., 186
Weber, Max, 10, 15, 17–23, 29, 45, 54–55, 274
Weld, Kathryn, 9–10
Wendelken, D. J., 215
What They Don't Teach You at Harvard Business School (McCormack), 20
Wheelis, A., 80
White, R. W., 25, 27–28
White males: and affirmative action, 167–184; and competition, 11–12, 169–173, 175–177, 270; and image, 174–175; and mentor, 77; and meritocracy myth, 173; and minorities, 263–264; performance, 181–182; and promotion, 63, 77, 167–183; and racism, 138, 157–158, 182, 237–238; and racism, perception of, 238; and reverse discrimination, 9, 167–184, 233–234, 270; and sexism, 146, 182
Women, 185–225, 270–272; black, 52; and competition, 73–74; and conformity, 197–200, 225; and corporations, 185–187; criteria in judging, 188–189; discrimination against, 187–196; dual roles, 219–224; economic situation, 186–187; and education, 70; emotionality, 187; and family, effects of work on, 141–142, 147, 219–224; and image, 137, 197; and informal work groups, 200–202, 209, 224; intimate relationships, 33; and laziness, stereotype of, 143–144; managerial ability, 142–143; and media, 186; and men's clubs, exclusion from, 148, 202; mentors, 77, 203, 209, 218; and old boy network, 189–190, 193, 225; performance standards, 202, 214–

Women (*continued*)
219, 270–271; and power and
authority, 210–214; and
promotion, 6, 46–47, 65–69, 71–
72, 77, 78, 176–177, 187–190,
196–197; qualifications, 147–150;
and quitting, 191–192, 195–196;
and racism, 157, 158, 237; and
risk taking, 218; and rewards and
recognition, 213; selecting
company, 217–218; seriousness

about career, 141; sexual
harassment, 194, 207–208, 224;
and sexuality, use of, 142; social
interaction problems, 200–213;
socialization, 182; *see also* Sexism
Working conditions, 44

Yankelovich, D., 36
Yinger, J. M., 165

Zaleznik, A., 99

Dedication

This book is dedicated to the employees of the American Telephone and Telegraph—Communications Headquarters Personnel Services Division. They made my attempts to survive in the corporate fishbowl a pleasurable learning experience.

Ashima Basu
Lori Green
Estelle Gill
Melanie Alonzo
Vicky Banach
Barbara Behrens
Susan Belanger
Marcella Bilicska
Ida Burrell
Mary Callery
Beth Colnett
Teresa Conte
Melanie DiPerna
Veronica Donlin
Abby Flick
Geraldine Fudge
Evelyn Hamrah
Jack Hofmann
Richard Iwan
Shirley Johnson
Wendy Johnson
Angela Jones

Jane Kiely
Susan Krosnowski
Rita Lachow
Eileen Morris
Kimberly Partoll
Charles Pfister
Marianne Pollock
Barbara Relkin
Elsie Rist
Gerard Rocco
Janet Rodriguez
Mark Rogalo
Janet Romilio
Margaret Serafin
Diane Smith
Elnoria Sterling
Diana Takacs
Alice Vahey
Joey White
Chester Wolczynski
Jill Taylor Conner
Elizabeth Armstrong

Emily Bassman
Pamela Beech
Kenneth Bores
Beth Braverman
Eileen Brennan
Patricia Buerkle
Teri Catalano
Elisa Cordone
Lorraine Dachiel
Rose DuBose
Donna Eckler
Dorothy Farley
Paula Glickman
Katherine Ann Grigg
Maria Hartman
Christa Hebbeler
Kathleen Hughes
Barbara Kelly
B. A. Korostik-Petrillo
Addison Lewis
Carol Lindner
John LoBianco

Maureen Mesce
Martha Nevius
Terry Orchard
Sheryl Partick
Wayne Peeler
Constance Phillips
Barbara Polston
Corinne Potts
Kathleen Roberts
John Rowan
Diane Ruhoy
Renee Scrimmager
Andrew Silber
Louis Smith
Elsie Sommer
Jane Soos
Lydia Soto
Roy Stewart
Cecilia Tampone
Blease Turner
Diana Tyson
Julia Varacalli
Marion Walton
Patricia Zawistowski
Rudolf Raines
Stella Accoo

Maricel Aleu
Evangelina Ayala
Joan Baglyos
Richard Berkowitz
Warren Binkley
Frank Bloomfield
B. A. Breakenridge
Shirley Brooks
Jimmie Burd
Nadine Bush
Eleanor Caporaso
Elroy Cartwright
Karen Colten
Janice Cooley
Virginia Costantini
Marilyn DeNapoli
Anna Eckenrode
Mauro Fanelli
Mona Jean Fasano
Miriam Fleming
Dorothy Franco
Virginia Frino
Brian Gerko
Touran Goins
Sandra Harding

Janice Haus
Hope Jones
Margaret Krayevski
Charles Kreilick
George Lewis
Kimberly Lucas
Lori Macsata
Jean Maurer
Michael Mercurio
Phyllis Miller
Frances Morey
Lisa Murin
Vernasia Norment
Jean Pohorely
Eleanor Pollard
Dorothy Preston
Sandra Ringler
Bohdan Rochman
June Silva
Mary Simila
Grace Stritch
Rae Tilzer
Daisy Torres
Lucille Troth
Jennifer Winters

About the Author

John P. Fernandez is division manager of Personnel Services, AT&T Communications Headquarters Region. In addition, he is president of Advance Research Management Consultants, and he teaches part-time at the University of Pennsylvania. He was previously a manager of education and development at AT&T and an assistant professor of sociology at Yale University. Dr. Fernandez has also served as operations manager for a large, multidepartment division of Bell of Pennsylvania. He received his A.B. magna cum laude from Harvard University and his Ph.D. from the University of California, Berkeley. He has written three previous books, *Black Managers in White Corporations* (1975), *Racism and Sexism in Corporate Life: Changing Values in American Business* (Lexington Books, 1981), and *Child Care and Corporate Productivity: Resolving Family/ Work Conflicts* (Lexington Books, 1985).